THE SHINING SANDS

STANHOPE FORBES

The Beach, St Ives.

oil on canvas, 1800 x 2900mm.

CITY OF BRISTOL MUSEUM AND ART GALLERY.

THE SHINING SANDS

ARTISTS IN NEWLYN AND ST IVES

1880–1930

TOM CROSS

WESTCOUNTRY BOOKS
THE LUTTERWORTH PRESS

First published in 1994 by Westcountry Books
in association with The Lutterworth Press.

CIP Catalogue Record for this book is available from the British Library

WESTCOUNTRY BOOKS
Halsgrove House
Lower Moor Way
Tiverton, Devon EX16 6SS
Tel: 0884 243242
Fax: 243325

ISBN 1 89838 608 0 (flexi edition)
1 89838 606 4 (cased edition)

THE LUTTERWORTH PRESS
PO Box 60, Cambridge CB1 2NT

ISBN 0 71882 925 5 (cased edition)
0 71882 926 3 (flexi edition)

Designed for Westcountry Books by Topics Visual Information
Reprographics by Peninsular Repro Services, Exeter
Printed and bound in Singapore by Singapore National Printers Ltd

CONTENTS

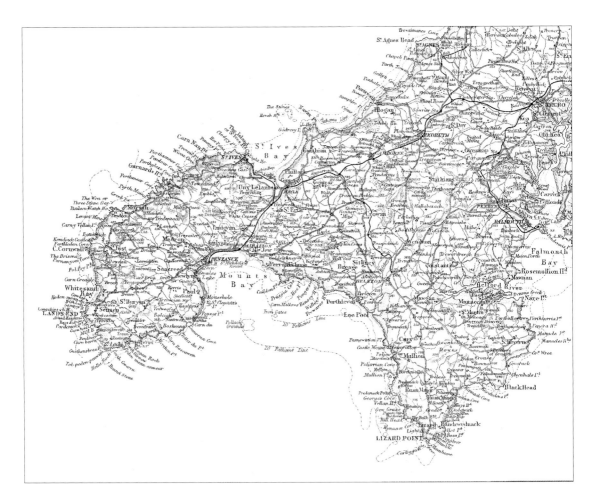

WEST CORNWALL
from a map dated c.1910

ACKNOWLEDGEMENTS

In preparing this book I am indebted to a number of people who supported it in its earlier stages, including Alison Hodge and the late William Desmond. I would also like to give special thanks to a number of individuals whose advice and comment have been invaluable. These include Francis Greenacre, John Halkes, Hazel Berriman and Jonathan Holmes.

A large number of galleries, collectors and photographers have allowed work in their possession to be reproduced in this book. Each is separately acknowledged in the captions to the images and I would like to further express thanks to them here. Among those who have provided considerable help are Monica Anthony, Maureen Attrill, Peter Barnes, Robin Bateman, Flora Berryman, Pep and John Bramfield, Prunella Cinford, Robina Craze, Kate Dinn, Peter Garnier, Christopher Insoll, Neville Jason, Roger Langley, Andrew Lanyon, David Messum, Maryella Piggot, Phoebe Procter, Mary Schofield, Alan and Diana Shears, Tessa Sidey, Leonora Simpson, Dr Roger Slack, John Smith, Mr Symons, The Lord Tollemache, John Tonkin, Archie Trevellian and Polly Walker.

I would like to express my gratitude most particularly to my wife Patricia for the preparation of the manuscript and for her continued support, without which this book would certainly not have been written.

Tom Cross
Cornwall 1994

REFERENCES

Publication references are included within the text. The books and catalogues listed below are recommended for further reading. The letters of Stanhope Forbes, now in the Tate Gallery Archives, are generally referred to in the text as 'letters' followed by the date. The letters of Frank Bourdillon are similarly referenced. The Tuke Registers, referred to in the text as 'Registers' are from *The Registers of Henry Scott Tuke*, published by the Royal Cornwall Polytechnic Society, Falmouth.

Baron, Wendy. *Sickert*. Phaidon, 1973.

Berlin, Sven. *Alfred Wallis, Primitive*. Redcliffe Press, 1992.

Berriman, Hazel. 'Arts and Crafts in Newlyn, 1890-1930'. Catalogue. Newlyn Orion Gallery, 1986.

Birch, Mrs Lionel. *Stanhope A. Forbes and Elizabeth Forbes*. London, 1906.

Cross, Tom. *Painting the Warmth of the Sun*. Westcountry Books and TheLutterworth Press 1995.

Dunbar, Janet. *Laura Knight*. William Collins, 1975.

Emmons, Robert. *The Life and Opinions of Walter Richard Sickert*. Faber & Faber.

Fox, Caroline. *Dame Laura Knight*. Phaidon, 1988.

Fox, Caroline. *Stanhope Forbes and the Newlyn School*. David & Charles, 1993.

Goodman, Jean. *What a Go! The Life of Alfred Munnings*. Collins, 1988.

Jacobs, Michael. *The Good and Simple Life, Art Colonies in Europe and America*. Phaidon, 1985.

Knight, Laura. *The Magic of Line*. William Kimber, 1965.

Knight, Laura. *Oil Paint and Grease Paint*. Ivor Nicholson & Watson, 1936.

McConkey, Kenneth. *British Impressionism*. Phaidon, 1989.

Mullins, Edwin. *Alfred Wallis, Cornish Primitive Painter*. Macdonald, 1967.

Munnings, A.J. *An Artist's Life*. Museum Press, 1950.

Noall, Cyril. *The Art Colony at St Ives*. The Cyril Noall Bequest, Royal Institution of Cornwall.

Sainsbury, Maria Tuke. *Henry Scott Tuke RA, RWS. A Memoir*. Secker, London 1933.

Sutton, Denys. *James McNeill Whistler*. Phaidon, 1966.

Tate Gallery, London. 'St Ives 1938-64. Twenty-five Years of Painting, Sculpture and Pottery'. Catalogue to the exhibition 1985.

Tate Gallery, London. 'Cedric Morris'. Catalogue to the exhibition of 1984.

Tate Gallery, London. 'Ben Nicholson'. Catalogue to the exhibition of 1994.

Val Baker, Denys. *Britain's Art Colony by the Sea*. George Ronald, 1959.

Val Baker, Denys. *Paintings from Cornwall*. Cornish Library, Penzance, 1950.

Waters, Grant M. *Dictionary of British Artists Working 1900-1950*. 2 Vols. Eastbourne 1975.

Whybrow, Marion. *St Ives, Portrait of an Art Colony, 1883-1993*. Antique Collectors Club, 1994.

INTRODUCTION

To early travellers, Cornwall appeared remote and desolate. Cut off from the rest of England by the River Tamar, and bordered by the sea, the county was almost an island, closer in many ways to Wales, Ireland and Brittany than to other parts of England. Rugged moorland, scarred in mid Cornwall by the china clay industry, and further west by copper and tin mining, was softened on the south coast by wooded valleys and a verdant landscape. Isolation had bred a hardy, self-reliant people of independent spirit – farmers, fishermen and miners – who had more in common with their Celtic brethren across the seas than with the Anglo-Saxons beyond the Tamar.

Landscape artists of the eighteenth and early nineteenth centuries travelled far in search of their romantic ideal, but Cornwall had provided few subjects. The problems of travel over its rutted roads had made exploration difficult, and the signs of civilisation – great houses, abbeys and churches – were noticeably lacking. The one native genius of Cornwall John Opie (1761–1807), called 'The Boy Wonder', 'who paints as the bird sings' had left Cornwall at the age of twenty and soon became a fashionable portraitist in London.

JOSEPH FARINGTON

Carclaze Tin Mine, Cornwall, 1823.

Engraving by S. Middiman from Britton and Brayley *Guide to the County of Cornwall.*

ROYAL INSTITUTION OF CORNWALL.

The first major pictorial record of the coastal scenery was made by Joseph Farington (1747–1821), a student of Richard Wilson, who visited Cornwall in 1809 in preparation for his publication Britannica Depicta. His view of St Ives is the earliest known, in which the present form of the town, harbour and the 'Island' are clearly seen. Four years later William Daniell (1769–1837) set sail from Land's End to record the coastline of Great Britain from the sea. His series of aquatints, published as A Voyage Around Great Britain was the most ambitious of the many topographical publications of the nineteenth century. Thomas Rowlandson (1757–1827) also made a coastal tour of Cornwall and was a frequent visitor to Hengar near Bodmin, where he sketched the high tors and wooded valleys around the River Camel. His drawings of the church of St Breward served as the setting for 'Dr Syntax Preaching' in the first volume of William Combe's Tour of Dr Syntax published in 1812.

The magic and mystery of Cornwall was most effectively captured by the masterly genius of Joseph Mallord Turner (1775–1851) who made two extended visits to Cornwall in 1811 and 1813. Although eclipsed by his later European tours, which produced his greatest achievements, the Cornish sketchbooks and the few pictures that came from them captured the imagination of many later artists. On his first visit, made in preparation for his great early work Picturesque Views of the Southern Coast of England, Turner produced more than two hundred sketches, an impressionistic record of conditions of weather, incidents on his journey, the landscape and the coast in changing mood. Indifferent to comfort, he travelled slowly and alone as far as St Ives, on foot or

JOSEPH MALLORD
WILLIAM TURNER

St Michael's Mount,
c. 1836.

watercolour with some body colour, 320 x 440mm.

UNIVERSITY OF LIVERPOOL.

by horseback and occasionally by sea. His panoramic sketch of the town from a high point on the Stennack is now in the British Museum. He returned through Tintagel, whose ruined castle he transformed into a lofty fortress set in the clouds, with burrowing miners working at its base. An even greater grandeur was bestowed upon the already majestic St Michael's Mount, which became a mountain rising from the sea, its medieval masonry transformed into a gleaming classical acropolis. Turner's second visit was brief and made only to the most easterly parts of Cornwall along the River Tamar. His painting 'Crossing the Brook' exhibited at the Royal Academy in 1815 transformed the village of Calstock into an Italianate perspective, the river, bridge and bathing figures in the foreground shining in golden light.

Other artists visited Cornwall in the first half of the nineteenth century, but the county remained remote and isolated from the rest of Britain until the coming of the railway, when Brunel's last great masterpiece, the bridge over the Tamar at Saltash, was opened in 1859. Then, for the first time in its history, Cornwall was in direct communication with the rest of England. Two years later the Queens Hotel was opened in Penzance and in 1878, following the connection of St Ives by branch line, the Great Western Railway's hotel, the Tregenna Castle, was opened above the town.

By the 1880s there was a well developed tourist industry in west Cornwall and artists began to come regularly to the fishing villages of Newlyn and St Ives. They belonged to a new generation who had studied in Europe, in the teaching studios of Paris and Antwerp, where they were trained in the observation and representation of nature. In the summer months, when the ateliers closed, they had joined the artist's colonies of Barbizon and Brittany, and returning to England they sought to continue this shared way of life, painting outdoors by

J. HENRY MARTIN

A December Morning, Mount's Bay, c.1875.

oil on canvas, 540 x 1000mm.

PENZANCE AND DISTRICT MUSEUM AND ART GALLERY.

the sea. They went to the remote villages of Staithes in Yorkshire and Cocksburnpath in Scotland, but more came to Newlyn and St Ives in Cornwall.

Newlyn on the south coast, was the first to attract major attention. At first the artists came on sketching trips, as they had visited the little ports in Brittany, finding their subjects in the life and work of the fishing community and the rural landscape of west Cornwall. Soon they began to settle there, and each year throughout the 1880s and 1890s an important group of paintings exhibited at the Royal Academy came from Newlyn. The twenty-five or thirty painters who formed the Newlyn School added significantly to the quality of British painting. They achieved early popular success, for although 'modern' their work was honest and was not considered extreme. Their paintings were tonal and silvery, combining accuracy of detail with the story painting that had been dear to British art since the Pre-Raphaelites. Authenticity was important, and local people were often used as models, set against the background of their homes and streets. Outdoor or *plein-air* painting was a characteristic of Newlyn artists, and it was not unusual to see painters working in the streets or on the beaches, their easels weighed down with stones against the wind.

The earliest resident artist of Newlyn was J. Henry Martin, who had made paintings of Mount's Bay and the Newlyn area around 1873 and may have been there much earlier. Thomas Gotch and Henry Tuke came on a visit in 1879, Walter Langley in 1880, Edwin Harris in 1881. Langley settled in Newlyn early in 1882, followed by Edwin Harris, Ralph Todd and Leghe Suthers who all took up more or less permanent residence in 1883. Stanhope Forbes, who was to be the most prominent and the longest established, came in 1884 as did Frank Bramley and Chevallier Tayler. A further group came in the following year, including Fred Hall, Percy Craft (who also worked in St Ives), Elizabeth Armstrong (who married Stanhope Forbes), and William Fortescue. Norman Garstin, arrived in 1886, and like Forbes and Langley remained in the area for the rest of his life. Frank Wright Bourdillon came in 1887.

Just ten miles away, across the West Penwith peninsula, St Ives on the north coast attracted it's own colony of artists. From the first St Ives was remarkably international. In the winter of 1883–4 the American, James McNeill Whistler made an extended visit to the town with his young assistants Walter Sickert and the Australian, Mortimer Menpes. They were followed by successive groups of Americans, Scandinavians and Australians who joined the resident English artists. Whistler's series of sketches of sea and sky from the beach – quick impressionistic colour – influenced the St Ives artists. For them, the study of the figure became less important than capturing that strange beauty of the coast, made magic by the ever-changing light and weather and the many moods of the sea. In 1888 an Artists' Club was established as a meeting place for a group of sea painters that included Julius Olsson, Adrian Stokes, Arnesby Brown and Algernon Talmage, all prominent Royal Academicians.

By the turn of the century Newlyn had changed. The harbour had been enlarged, and the fishing trade greatly expanded. Public taste in art was finding new directions and many of the artists left Newlyn. In the early years of the twentieth century, the nearby wooded Lamorna valley became the home of a group of painters whose work explored the more acceptable conventions of Impressionism and Post-Impressionism. John 'Lamorna' Birch, and Harold and Laura Knight were particularly associated with Lamorna; Alfred Munnings and Augustus John made extended visits. The working port of Falmouth also had a special attraction for a few. By the 1920s St Ives was a centre for the scattered groups in Newlyn and Lamorna. Far removed from radical developments in Europe, it remained strongly traditional and rejected modernism. It was not until the 1950s that St Ives recovered its reputation as an artistic centre that brought it to the forefront of international avant-garde art.

This book is concerned with artistic developments in the late nineteenth and early twentieth centuries – the years when the triumphs of Realism melted into the more seductive charms of Impressionist colour that have come to be associated with this far-off corner of England.

THE PURSUIT OF REALISM

The reign of Queen Victoria saw great changes in the social structure of the British Isles. A new professional and bureaucratic class emerged, engaged in great business and commercial enterprises. Possessed of the means to encourage the arts and the leisure to enjoy them, it became a responsive audience for popular work. The triumphant middle class was prepared to see the arts prosper, as long as they were not avant-garde, or associated with those radical or revolutionary views that had so bedevilled many parts of Europe. The artist was accepted as a gentleman, with a zeal for work and pursuing a career of his choosing. It was respectable for women to engage in artistic activity, although professional status was not encouraged, and was achieved by few.

The Great Exhibition of 1851 celebrated the triumph of the machine, but absolute faith in the virtues of manufacturing industry was already faltering. As the dehumanising effect of the factories became apparent, more than half of the population lived in towns, and rural life appeared increasingly attractive. The countryside was valued as never before in art and literature: a dream landscape removed in time and space, peopled by a folk society, closely bound by tradition and shared hardship. This dream became symbolised in paintings that reflected the ordered life that industrial progress was seen to be destroying. Here was the true satisfaction sought by Ruskin: 'To watch the corn grow, and the blossoms set; to draw hard breath over ploughshare or spade.' (John Ruskin *Works* 17, 56.).

A Parisian Teaching
Studio in the 1880s.

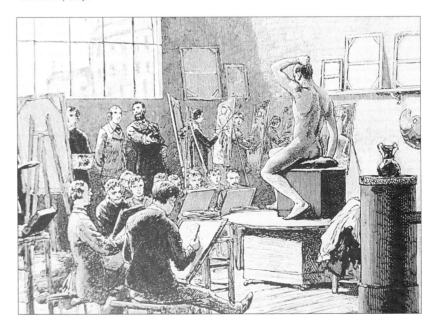

Social change had created a new type of art student – educated and alert young men and women curious to explore the full dimensions of European art. They were generally the sons and daughters of professional or business men, not wealthy, but fortunate enough to have a small parental allowance which, supplemented by the occasional sale of paintings, allowed many of them an extended period of training and travel abroad. These artists were among the first products of a newly developing system of art education in England. As they gained in experience they were drawn towards the European capitals to complete their training, particularly to Paris, which was 'the centre of the world, ... the art school of the world ... and the art market of the world.' (*Magazine of Art* 1881). Although they remained largely within English speaking circles in Europe, they formed an important part of the international art community in the teaching studios of Paris and Antwerp and in the artists colonies in Brittany, Normandy and other rural areas. They became thoroughly internationalised and retained this informed attitude for much of their later lives.

England was lamentably behind the rest of Europe in establishing a sound training for artists and designers. In the 1820s, that eccentric artist genius and enemy of the Royal Academy, Benjamin Robert Haydon (1786–1846), had, by successive petitions to Government, created pressure for a new system of art education fitted to the role that England was beginning to occupy in the world. But as late as 1830 there were no art schools outside London, although many existed on the Continent. In 1836 a Select Committee recommended the creation of art schools throughout the country, and in the following year a 'School of Design' was opened in Somerset House, in premises recently vacated by the Royal Academy. It was intended to serve the needs of industry and the training emphasised basic elements of ornamental design, through copying approved examples. Early teaching deliberately suppressed originality and prohibited the study of the human form, for the Schools did not wish to be accused of wasting public money on a training for which there was no economic need. Later the School of Design was moved to South Kensington where it became known as the Schools of South Kensington, and subsequently divided to become the Royal College of Art and the Victoria and Albert Museum.

In the first half of the nineteenth century, the Royal Academy was the only institution to offer an organised system of art education. In the 1850s and 1860s its Schools were in serious decline, but in 1867 the Academy moved from the old Somerset House to new spacious premises at Burlington House, Piccadilly. The Schools were re-housed and the teachers were drawn from members of the Academy. In the 1870s they included such distinguished figures as Sir Edward Millais, Sir Frederick Leighton and Sir Lawrence Alma-Tadema. However the teaching remained archaic and the training was long – four or five years was considered normal, and was mostly spent making copies of ornamental designs called 'drawing models' and the production of highly detailed and finished drawings of antique casts, requiring weeks or months of preparation. It was only towards the end of their training that students were allowed to work from the living model. Academicians acted as 'visitors' to the life schools for a month at a time, and there was no consistency of teaching.

A number of Newlyn artists successfully threaded their way through this limited training. Stanhope Forbes, who was to become the leading figure in the Newlyn School, was a student at the Royal Academy Schools from 1876 to 1880. Born in Dublin in 1857, he came from a well connected and cosmopolitan family. His father, William Forbes, was manager of the Midland Great Western

Railway of Ireland, his mother was French, born Juliette de Guise, and always a close influence upon her son. Later the family lived in Brussels where William Forbes managed the Great Luxembourg Railway. At the time of the Franco-Prussian war the family were in France, and during this troubled period Stanhope Forbes, encouraged by his mother, began to draw while recovering from illness.

Stanhope Forbes was educated at Dulwich College where he was fortunate in meeting a distinguished teacher of drawing, John Sparks, later head of the South Kensington Schools, who taught him the value of working from observation. Sparks moved to Lambeth School of Art and Forbes followed him there to begin his artistic training proper, and then to the Royal Academy Schools, where he developed an outstanding ability as a portrait painter. In the holidays he was offered portrait commissions in Ireland by Dr Andrew Melville, a friend of his father and a Professor at Queens College, Dublin, but concerned that this might be seen as a search for money, he wrote to his mother asking her not to let his fellow students know that he had become a provincial portrait painter in his holidays. The portrait commissions continued in London, and the first paintings that Forbes showed at the Royal Academy, painted whilst still a student, were all portraits of family friends.

Walter Langley, whose delicate, sensitive portrayal of the working people of Newlyn was to make him one of the most respected painters there, gained a scholarship to the South Kensington Schools to study design for industry. Langley came from a poor background in Birmingham, where he was apprenticed to a lithographer. After eighteen months in South Kensington producing meticulous drawings for gold and silver tableware, he accepted a partnership in the lithographic firm that had apprenticed him. He had ambitions as an artist however, and began to paint more and more seriously.

For a short time Elizabeth Armstrong also studied at the South Kensington Schools, where she was one of the youngest students. Born in Ottawa, she was the only daughter of a Canadian government official who died while she was young; her mother encouraged her early interest in art. They came to England to stay with an uncle in Chelsea, next door to the Pre-Raphaelite painter Dante Gabriel Rossetti. Elizabeth later married Stanhope Forbes, and together they were the most constant and longest residents of the artists in Newlyn.

The creative urge of these students remained unsatisfied by the training that they had received in England. This feeling was well expressed by Norman Garstin:

> *There had grown up in England among the art students an uneasy feeling that all was not well, that things artistic were better ordered in France and Belgium and forthwith there passed across the narrow sea many bands of young men determined to see for themselves what was being done in the Academy at Antwerp, or the Beaux Arts in Paris, in fact in all the numerous 'ateliers' that were so freely opened to them abroad. Millet and Monet with their palettes of revolt, and Bastien Lepage with less revolt, but with a very clear open-air eye. The direct inspiration of nature was the creed of the day, and a feeling of reaction from academic traditions, and studio work as opposed to work on the spot, actuated most of the students. In the main, these young men were filled with this idea of a fresh unarranged nature to be studied in her fields, and by her streams, and on the margin of her great seas – in these things they were to find the motives for their art, and not in the tedious story telling they had left at*

home... (Norman Garstin. Introduction to the exhibition of 'Artists and St Ives and Newlyn', Whitechapel Art Gallery, London, 1902.).

The end of the Franco-Prussian war in 1871, ushered in a new period of internationalism in European art. Communications improved by sea and rail, making possible greater movement between English artists and their European counterparts, and a new spirit of curiosity affected the visual arts. Paris, long seen as the artistic capital of the world, remained the principal centre. News of the great artistic debates in France – the advance of Realism, and the more recent and bitterly contested triumphs of Impressionism – had filtered through uncertainly to London, where attention was still focused upon the work of the Pre-Raphaelites, supported by the opinions of Ruskin.

The fifth, sixth and seventh Impressionist Exhibitions took place in 1880, 1881, 1882, but it was not the advanced doctrines of Impressionism that affected the English students in Europe. In the teaching studios they were introduced to earlier 'Realist' attitudes of Courbet and Millet, and received a training based on close observation of nature and the judgement of tonal values, from teachers who were of a generation before the Impressionists.

France had a fully elaborated system of art training centred upon the École des Beaux Arts in Paris, the direct descendant of that august body, the Académie Royale, established by the Kings of France. This school was the first step on the official ladder that led to the Salon, public recognition, state purchase and financial success. In 1863, under its new Director, Robert Fleury, the École had been reorganised with a new system of courses with free tuition for those who passed the entrance examination. To cater for the large numbers of students flocking to Paris a number of additional private ateliers (painting schools) were set up in the 1860s and 1870s, run by such well established Salon painters as Gérôme, Leon Bonnat, Thomas Couture and Alexandre Cabanel.

Gérôme was the chief classical painter in France and taught a number of the Impressionists. His studio was the most vigorous, and it attracted many English and American students, one of whom described the system of drawing, based on the use of the 'stump' – a pointed roll of paper used to rub charcoal so as to obtain delicate transitions of tone:

In the drawing they use the stump, shading just enough to express the dabs and half tints and always they made them take the whole of the paper, the head within a quarter of an inch of the top, and the feet the same at the bottom if standing. They find where the middle would come, and then how many heads high the model is, looking for the guide lines. Perspective, anatomy, history of art, are each twice a week. Gérôme is very severe with the drawing, and in representing the model as near as possible, which I think is the school for a student. He is liberal and says nothing to the manner, what he wants is to have the student's study serious.......in using the stump, he will not let the beginner put in anything but the principal dabs, and not until he has advanced will he let him put in the demi-tint. With regard to the new students in colour, give him no theories, he has nature before him, let him represent it... (Dorothy Weir Young *The Life and Letters of J. Alden Weir*, New Haven, 1960.).

The study of nature was all important, 'it is the best master; observe it', this the 'ateliers' agreed upon. There evolved a system of instruction based on the careful observation of tone and texture seen in a raking studio light. The science of perspective was taught with great elaboration, as was anatomy. Louis-

Antoine Barye, the anatomist and sculptor of animals, had artists and medical students working side by side on dissected cadavers or making drawings at the zoo to analyse the motions of an animal – a horse trotting or galloping – long before the camera was able to capture such motion.

The Académie Julian, started in 1873 by Rudolphe Julian, offered instruction by teachers of established reputation to both men and women, and became a favourite with foreign students. In contrast the Académie Suisse was started by a retired model who gave no instruction but offered the freedom to work from the nude, and was open to all who could pay the modest daily charge. These studios gave basic training in drawing and painting and equipped their students to enter the 'concours' examinations for entry to the École des Beaux Arts and, most prestigious of all, the competition for the Prix de Rome, which allowed a few selected students to complete their education at the Villa Medici in Rome, the centre of classical learning and art.

Carolus-Duran's studio was also popular with English speaking students. The master was a dapper and sophisticated Anglophile, a highly successful portraitist, who had recently set up a teaching studio in Paris. He emphasised the virtues of direct painting on to the canvas without preliminary drawing, 'search for the mid tones and work broadly from there'. His most brilliant student at this time was the American John Singer Sargent, who was already beginning to make a considerable reputation in his own right. Henry Detmold who worked in Newlyn had also studied with Carolus-Duran for a time, during a student career that included Dusseldorf, Munich and Brussels as well as Paris. He exhibited at the Paris Salon in 1879 and in 1882 when he also began to exhibit at the Royal Academy.

At Bonnat's studio, where Forbes trained, there was no lengthy study of anatomical form, as emphasised in the British schools. The student was encouraged to lay in the main planes of the figure broadly, looking at it as a whole, painting in planes differentiated by the changing light. Tonal differences or 'values' were emphasised, not too many, but sufficient to indicate the main masses, and to describe the relative shapes and proportions. Little emphasis was given to colour as this detracted from the study of tone. Paint was mixed on a large palette held to catch the north light, and when prepared the different tonal masses were laid on the canvas 'au premier coup'.

In Paris and in Antwerp the teaching studios closed at the end of June when the dusty streets became dazzling white and the cities insufferably hot. Those students who could, moved to the country or to the coast to continue with their work in more tranquil surroundings. The cool light of the northern coast of France attracted painters, particularly the coasts of Brittany and Normandy, sparkling with sun and the light and shade of a cloud-fringed sky. This summer migration led to the formation of artist colonies in France and in other European countries. The first, at Barbizon outside Paris, was associated with the Realism of Millet and a group of landscape painters who worked in and around the village of Barbizon and the forests of Fontainebleau, and nearby at Grez-sur-Loing. Other communities became established in coastal areas, particularly in Brittany at Pont-Aven, Concarneau and Quimperlé. Many of the young foreign artists visited these colonies, attracted to the idea of shared work and experience in a rural setting. Later when they returned to their home countries they set up their own groups in remote centres such as at Newlyn and St Ives in Cornwall, or Cocksburnpath in Scotland.

Pont-Aven had long attracted artists. Americans had come as early as 1866, fascinated by the medieval town whose atmosphere was redolent of a rapidly disappearing romantic age. Room and board were cheap and if necessary could be obtained on credit, and there were good models. A large derelict building at the end of the village, half farmhouse, half chateau served as free studio accommodation for visiting painters. Above all there was the fellowship of artists converted to Realism and a gentle, sheltered climate in which they could work out of doors all through the year.

Pont-Aven lies on the south-west coast of Brittany where the first bridge crosses the River Aven as it flows between large granite boulders from a wild countryside of heath, gorse and rough pasture with strange rounded hills and deep woods. Below the bridge the river widens into a tidal estuary, where fishing boats were moored. The town was the centre for the farming community, a handsome and rugged people who wore a picturesque costume and heavy wooden sabots, that had altered little since medieval times. The Bretons held to their Celtic culture and language, a race apart. They were staunch Catholics and held many festivals throughout the year, characterised by the 'pardons' – a mixture of religious meeting and country fair, with church ceremonies followed by singing, wrestling and travelling fairgrounds.

Artist visitors – tourists had not yet arrived – usually stayed in the Hotel des Voyageurs, managed from 1870 by Mademoiselle Julia Guillou, formerly a maid there, who probably received financial help from some of the American artists who visited regularly. A small dining room panelled in oak was the chief talking shop for the artists. Pension Gloanec, near the bridge, provided rooms for artists at half the cost of the 'Voyageurs', or boarded them out in the town and

Pont-Aven.
'The Port' c.1910.

fed them at the long tables in the dining room lined from floor to ceiling with artists' sketches and studies. It was a sign of acknowledgement to be invited to paint one of the panels in the dining room.

The young artists who came to Pont-Aven in the 1870s and early 1880s found an established artists' colony. One of the first English painters to come was Adrian Stokes, who was there in 1876 and who later made his home in St Ives. Five years later the Newlyn artist Edwin Harris recorded his impressions of Pont-Aven:

> In those days there was hardly a village in Brittany which was not occupied by one or two painters. But at Pont-Aven they simply swarmed – English, French, Americans, and representatives of almost all nationalities. This little village, shut in on all sides by the wooded hills, was then and probably still is, a most unhealthy spot in which to make a lengthy habitation. It can boast none of the picturesque wooden architecture, which is so attractive in so many of the Breton towns, but the costume of the natives, who are popularly supposed to gain their living by washing one another's clothes, in the intervals of posing as models, is probably the most picturesque in the whole of Finistere ... Crowding its small hotel, and few inns, and overflowing into the one or two narrow streets, some seventy or eighty painters, mostly quite young, were spending a happy life of hard work, intermingled with joyous recreation. Within the walls of the Hotel des Voyageurs, familiarly known as 'Julia's', after the landlady, a buxom dame whose reputation extended to every place where art jargon flourished in France, were to be found representatives of all the 'Schools' and movements of the day. (Edwin Harris 'Edgbastonia' Vol XIX July 1899 No.218 p.124).

By the mid 1880s about a hundred artists were in summer residence, American, English and French. The English group included Stanhope Forbes, Adrian Stokes, Frank Bramley, Mortimer Menpes and among the French 'the great Bastien Lepage', with his inseparable comrade, Charles Bode, the wood engraver. Paul Gauguin made his first appearance in the town in the summer of 1886 and his work developed a highly charged spiritual message which he discovered in this remote part of Brittany. He returned frequently to Pont-Aven over the next twenty years, until the exotic paradise of Tahiti finally drew him away.

The American Arthur Hoeker described the change of tempo in Pont-Aven as it turned from the pleasures of summer to the more workaday existence of the autumn:

> As the summer slipped away and the days became shorter, the sunlight of August and September faded into the grey of autumn, that Brittany grey, the like of which is nowhere else in the world – a soft, pearly, luminous colour, giving qualities of opalescent light to the landscape and enveloping everything in a tender tone of sentiment and poetry, a joy to look at and an inspiration to the painter. Then the artists began to evolve their Salon pictures, and in flannel blouses and straw-lined sabots, for the roads became muddy and damp, and the ordinary shoe of civilisation was of no avail, they could be seen at big canvasses, utilising all the daylight and plodding away. Easels were set up in the fields, on the roadways, and in cottage and garden, while old and young men, women and children were pressed into service as models. So usual a sight was the painter at work, that his arch enemy, the small boy no longer thought

Artists in front of the
Pension Gloanec,
Pont-Aven, *c*.1880.

Photographed by
Nancy Corson and reproduced
in *Americans in Brittany
and Normandy 1860–1910*.
PHOENIX ART MUSEUM, 1982.

*The figure seated to the left of the
table is probably Alexander
Harrison, a visitor to St Ives in
the 1880s. Others include the
Mayor of Pont Aven, in the
bowler hat, and the staff of the
Pension in traditional Breton
costume.*

*to stop and watch him; or if he did, his was no more than a mild passing
interest.* (Arthur Hoeker 'A Summer in Brittany', *The Monthly Illustrator*
Vol.IV No.2 1896).

The doctrine of 'Realism' that had fired Forbes and his companions had
been promoted inside and outside the ateliers of Paris. Its chief protagonist was
neither from the Impressionist elite nor from the earlier generation of Courbet
and Millet. It was the young and highly talented painter Jules Bastien-Lepage
(1848-1884) who caught the attention of the younger artists.

Bastien-Lepage was a considerable virtuoso in paint, and his manner readily
understandable, for he painted directly from nature what he saw and knew. His
work was considered modern but not avant-garde, forward-looking but not
radical. The overall greyness of his large figure studies, was a product of the
overcast days of his native village, Damvillers, near Verdun in northern France.
The themes of his paintings reflect the dignity of labour, the rights of the lowly
individual and the rise of the peasant working classes, sentiments in line with
enlightened social opinion in England. His paintings of peasants at work in the
fields lacked the brooding grandeur of Millet, but he described in sympathetic
detail the life of simple working folk, reduced by labour and weather to the
condition of the animals they tended. Because he chose to work out of doors, he
was regarded as a *plein-air* painter, although many of his canvasses were
finished in the studio.

BASTIEN-LEPAGE

Poor Fauvette, 1881.

oil on canvas, 1600 x 1240mm.

CITY OF GLASGOW MUSEUM AND
ART GALLERY

*The title means 'little wild girl';
painted in Damvillers, Lepage's
home in north-eastern France,
the picture was exhibited at the
Paris Salon and in Britain and
was described as 'probably better
known in Britain than any other
that Lepage painted'.*
(*Art Journal* 1896 p.200).

Bastien-Lepage was held in great respect by artists and critics in England. His paintings won praise for their high finish and he was favourably compared to the Pre-Raphaelites, especially the young Millais and Holman-Hunt. He had great success at the Salon of 1878 and 1879 with his paintings 'Les Foins' and 'Jeanne d'Arc' both of which attracted particular attention from foreign artists in Paris. His work was also unusually well displayed in London where good examples were shown from 1880 onwards. At the Grosvenor Gallery that year he exhibited a number of his major masterpieces including 'Les Foins', 'La Communicante', 'L'Annunciation' and 'Mon Grandpère'. His work again met with acclaim at a major exhibition in the United Arts Gallery in 1882. Bastien-Lepage visited London several times between 1879 and 1882, and became known personally to a number of the Newlyn painters, for whom he was a decisive influence. Henry Tuke visited his studio in Paris in 1882, with work that he had done in England and was encouraged by his comments:

> *I took a lot of sketches... he looked at each one, and gave it me hot over most,
> which made me all the gladder when he said of my Bournemouth calm sea*

with pier 'trés fin' and of the others 'beaucoup de sentiment de couleur'. (Maria Tuke Sainsbury, *Henry Scott Tuke, A Memoir.* Marlin Secker, 1933).

Bastien-Lepage died of cancer at the age of thirty-six in 1884. A large retrospective of his work in Paris left a great impression on the international art community.

Foremost amongst the Newlyn artists who carried on Bastien-Lepage's ideals of *plein-air* painting was Stanhope Forbes. Having spent much of his early life in France and Belgium, it was natural that after his early training in London he should continue in Paris. In 1880 he went to Bonnat's studio on the edge of the city at Clichy. Also in Paris at that time, attending the Académie des Beaux Arts, was Henry La Thangue (1859-1929).

STANHOPE FORBES

A Street in Brittany, 1881.

oil on canvas, 1600 x 1010mm.

WALKER ART GALLERY, LIVERPOOL.

Painted in Cancale, a small fishing village in Brittany, the painting was exhibited at the autumn exhibition at the Walker Art Gallery in 1882. Forbes acknowledged that the purchase of the painting by Liverpool was a turning point in his career'. (*Strand Magazine* 1901).

NORMAN GARSTIN

Among the Pots.

oil on canvas, 1255 x 1010mm.

CITY OF PLYMOUTH MUSEUM AND
ART GALLERY.

*A Belgian market, painted whilst
Garstin was a student at
Antwerp. He later joined the
studio of Carolus-Duran in
Paris, and he visited Brittany in
about 1882.*

The two had been close friends since their
schooldays at Dulwich College, and had worked
together at Lambeth and the Royal Academy
Schools. Forbes admired La Thangue's dexterity
with paint and emulated his industry, but
observed 'I share his ideas and admire his work
just sufficiently not to fall into imitation'.
(31.7.81.). After a year in Paris and an increasing
commitment to *plein-air* painting, Forbes and La
Thangue went together to Cancale in Brittany, a
centre for oyster fishing, with the shared aim of
working directly before nature.

Forbes produced several paintings as a
result of this visit, including one which showed
unusual talent. 'A Street in Brittany' (1881), was
a portrait of a Breton girl who stands on the
steps of her house in a back road of the small
town. He worked hard at the painting which he
referred to as 'The Street'. 'Always the same
beautiful girl, she grows more perfect every
day, and seems to be as charming as she looks',
but he learnt later that she was dismissed for
stealing at his hotel.

Forbes described the difficulties of working
out of doors, problems with the models, the
sun, the clouds, the ever changing light, the
wind that blew down his easel, the dust that got
in his eyes and in the paint, and the crowd of persistent children. He stayed at
Cancale all that summer returning to Paris in October. Clearly he was now
becoming a professional painter, with work shown at the Royal Academy each
year, and regular sales.

Bonnat's teaching studio now had little to offer Forbes. He was critical of the
other students: 'A Japanese, a Russian, two Danes and a few hundred
Americans fresh from Booooooston' (undated letter), and he was less than
enthusiastic about the teaching. In October 1881 he wrote to his mother that he
was waiting for frames 'to take up to the patron's atelier on Sunday, although I
don't quite know what he can tell me that I don't know already.' It was hardly
surprising that in the following October he again reported to his mother
'Bonnat's exists no longer'.

Forbes probably spent most of the early part of 1882 in London, returning to
Brittany for the summer to the little town of Quimperlé, just beyond Pont-Aven
on the southern coast. It had a good hotel, the Metayer, and excellent fishing,
which Forbes preferred to the endless games of billiards he played in
Concarneau on days when he could not paint. During the summer he made the
acquaintance of other artists working in these centres, including Leghe Suthers,
Ralph Todd and William Blandford Fletcher, all of whom were later to come to
Newlyn. Elizabeth Armstrong was only a few miles away in Pont-Aven, but they
did not meet for a further three years.

After several more visits to London and Paris, Forbes returned to Quimperlé
for the following summer, again visiting Concarneau, which he enjoyed, but
decided that it was too large to do good work in. He returned to the comforts of

the Hotel Metayer and his painting of 'The Church of St David in Quimperlé' and another, 'The Convent', were exhibited at the Royal Academy in 1883. In October Forbes went to Pont-Aven and noted that Adrian Stokes had arrived to paint there for the winter. But clearly he did not feel at home and was unable to share in the conviviality and good fellowship that so captiviated many of the Americans. 'I saw innumerable artistic friends and their works ... the work is not remarkable, even now there are countless daubers and the place inferior in every way to Quimperlé...' (22.10.1883.). He was also repelled by the rough manners of the peasants and criticised their credulity, laziness and lack of education. He described the Breton as 'a very dirty uninteresting drunken sort of creature', and regretted that 'if a woman had an attractive figure it was not apparent because she was always wearing heavy clothing...'.

The two large figure compositions that Forbes exhibited at the Royal Academy in 1884, were the product of this last year in Brittany, 'Preparations for the Market: Quimperlé' and 'Fair Measures: A Shop in Quimperlé'. There is an evident wish to incorporate the figures into their working surroundings, and to paint the reality of everyday events, but they lacked the freshness that had characterised his earlier paintings done in France. Perhaps it was the weight of good examples all about him that made him feel the need to get away from France and make personal discoveries from nature in his home country.

These years of journeying in the coastal towns of Brittany, and the friendships that had been made, were to be of the greatest importance in setting the tone of the group that later came together in Newlyn. It was a period of self-discovery and of constant exchange of ideas with young artists from many countries. Fired with the new doctrine of 'Realism', and keen to match this against their own talents, they believed above all in the value of working out-of-doors. In Stanhope Forbes' words:

Painters began to see that it needed more than an occasional visit to the country to get at the heart of its mysteries; that he who wished to solve them must live amongst the scenes he sought to render, and become thoroughly familiarised with every aspect of nature.

Forbes had made a personal decision that he would follow throughout his life and others also followed, '... to set up easels in country districts, where we could pose our models and attack our work, in sunshine or in shadow, under the open sky'. ('Cornwall from a Painter's Point of View', Stanhope Forbes. Published in the *Annual Report of the Royal Cornwall Polytechnic Society*, 1900.).

ARTISTS FROM THE MIDLANDS

'It was Birmingham that first discovered Newlyn.' So wrote the correspondent to the *Magazine of Art* in 1898, who signed himself 'one of the original Newlynites'. He listed the artists who came to Newlyn in the order of their arrival: 'Before the place was known – that is to say before it was flooded with painters, and before the speculative builder stepped in and erected glass studios and all manner of buildings'. First were Edwin Harris and Walter Langley (it was probably one of these who wrote the letter); then Ralph Todd, Leghe Suthers, Fred Hall, Frank Bramley, Tom Gotch, Percy Craft and Stanhope Forbes. They were followed by Henry Detmold and Chevallier Tayler; then came Elizabeth Armstrong (later Mrs Stanhope Forbes) and Frank Bourdillon, and in the last group William Fortescue and Norman Garstin. The writer states firmly that 'those who came later belong to a different period'.

With the coming of the railway, Cornwall had begun to attract visiting artists on sketching expeditions, and in the 1870s and 1880s each annual exhibition of

Newlyn in the 1880s.
photo by Gibson.
ROYAL INSTITUTION OF CORNWALL.

HENRY POPE

Newlyn, c.1870.

etching

CITY OF BIRMINGHAM
MUSEUM AND ART GALLERY.

the Royal Academy included a number of Cornish subjects, usually coastal views of Land's End or the Lizard. The picturesque rock formations of Kynance Cove were a particular favourite. But Newlyn itself had attracted little attention. As part of the panorama of Mount's Bay it was second to the romantic splendour of St Michael's Mount and the displays of pageantry that surrounded it. The only artist known to work in Newlyn for an extended period was J. Henry Martin (1835–1908) who was painting there as early as 1873. He made many studies of the town and its inhabitants, painted with directness and wit, including the earliest and one of the most complete views of the town seen from the old breakwater in evening light, the grey roofs tumbling to the water's edge, called 'A December Morning in Mount's Bay'. It is believed that he had trained in Antwerp with Frank Vinck, and his work has a feeling of the Dutch masters. Henry Martin painted in and around Newlyn for a period of about eleven years. At about the time that other artists began to arrive Henry Martin left Newlyn for Plymouth where he worked for a number of years.

The first Birmingham artist to visit Newlyn was probably Henry Martin Pope (1843–1908), son of a cabinet-maker who had been apprenticed to a lithographic printer and later studied painting in Birmingham. (In spite of the similarity of name and date of death, there is no known connection with J. Henry Martin, mentioned above.). He became a landscape painter, teacher and etcher, and with some of the other Newlyn artists was a founder member of the Birmingham Art Circle and the Easel Club. His etching of the slip at Newlyn dating from the 1870s may have influenced other Birmingham painters to visit the town.

Walter Langley and Edward Harris were both from Birmingham and had studied at Birmingham School of Art. Harris stayed there to teach while

Langley went on to the South Kensington Schools. William Wainwright was born in Birmingham, and William Banks Fortescue worked as an engineering designer in the town. Frank Bramley and Fred Hall both trained at Lincoln School of Art, which had a connection with Birmingham through its principal teacher E. R. Taylor, who had previously taught at Birmingham School of Art.

With its rise as a great industrial city, Birmingham had become a centre for highly skilled designers, engravers and jewellers. Public exhibitions of paintings were held as early as 1814, and in 1821 a school and museum of casts and models had been created in Ann Street. Wealthy businessmen formed considerable collections of work by English and European artists, many of which were later given to the public art gallery. A society of artists was formed, and by the mid nineteenth century the annual exhibitions of the Royal Birmingham Society of Artists attracted work from all over the country, including that of many senior academicians. In 1881 six young artists were chosen as the first Associates of the Society. They included Walter Langley, William Breakespeare and William Wainwright. Three years later William Banks Fortescue, Edwin Harris and Frank Richards were also elected. All of these artists were to come to Newlyn. Walter Langley with his friend William Wainwright were founder members of the Birmingham Art Circle, and their exhibitions, held twice a year in the New Street Gallery, became a good market for many artists who took up residence in Newlyn.

Newlyn lies at the western end of Mount's Bay, sheltered from the prevailing westerly winds and winter gales, the first protection for sailing vessels rounding the fearsome rocks at Land's End. In the 1880s the town was in two distinct parts – Newlyn Town ran along the high cliff to the west, a substantial line of grey roofed cottages that fringed the harbour. To the east where the land is low lying and marshy was Street-an-Nowan, where a few old cottages clustered around the mouth of the Coombe river. The beach between the two parts of the town was the main means of communication, with a narrow causeway, covered at high tide, for pedestrians. The two communities the 'Newlyn Towers' and the 'Street-an-Nowaners' were separate and distinct, each with its own family ties and loyalties.

Newlyn was a working town and an unpromising situation for a school of painting. There was not a good house nor a genteel villa in the town, just white-washed fishermen's cottages, irregularly built around open courtyards, reeking with pilchard oil and consisting of mud walls, bare floors and open roofs. Doors were always open and relationships were close, with families extended by elderly relatives and orphaned children. Expectations of prosperity were not high, friendship and mutual support in times of hardship were more valued than privacy. Working space for artists was made by taking away the wall dividing two cottages, setting a pane of glass into the roof and calling the apartment a studio, with access by planks and ladders.

The first painter of the Newlyn school to settle in the town was Walter Langley (1852–1922). The slim bearded face that gazes from his photograph taken about 1881 is reflective, withdrawn and somewhat melancholy. He is lightly built, a somewhat self-consciously artistic figure in his wide-brimmed hat, trimmed beard and moustache, at the start of his painting career. The recognition that had come to Langley had been hard won and preceeded by a long period of early struggle.

After an initial visit to Newlyn in 1880, Langley settled there with his first wife in 1882 and lived in Newlyn for thirteen years, before moving to Penzance where he died in 1922 at the age of seventy. Langley described himself as 'The first figure painter to depict incidents in the life of the fisherfolk'. His work is an earnest endeavour to reach out in sympathy to the misfortune and distress that was so much a part of the life of the working people of Newlyn, and to describe, in scenes of high drama, the sombre and sometimes tragic events that surrounded the life of the seafaring community. If his painting lacks the charm and sparkle of some of his contemporaries, it surely reflects his concern for the persistent hardship faced by the poor.

Many of the artists who came to Newlyn were from prosperous, professional families and had independent means or financial support during the difficult early years. Walter Langley had none of these advantages. He was born in 1852 into a working-class family from Birmingham, the eighth surviving child of a family of eleven children, brought up in a back-to-back courtyard dwelling house, with communal ash pits, privy and water pump. His father William Langley was a tailor and his mother, Mary Ann Langley was illiterate, but a great strength to the family, and a support to her son, as his early letters to her testify. He attended Hurst Street School, Birmingham, before being apprenticed to a lithographic printer in Birmingham at the age of thirteen. He also had a general training in drawing and industrial design at the Birmingham School of Design, where a fellow student, Edward Harper, remembered his liveliness and his industry:

Walter Langley.

The photograph was taken by Robert T. Thrupp, of 66, New Street, Birmingham, who styled himself 'Photographer to the Queen'. It was Thrupp who supported Langley during his earliest years in Newlyn.

> *My first admiration of Langley was not owing to his skill in drawing, but to his agility as a clog dancer, for he sometimes gave us an exposition of that art on the hard resounding pavement while others were demonstrating the elasticity of the human frame on the iron rail. In the rush up the long flight of steps which followed the opening of the door, Langley was always first, and he would hardly look up from his work until we were unceremoniously bundled out the moment the clock struck.* ('The Art of Walter Langley' by Walter Turner, from *W.J.Wainwright RSW, RBSA*. Cornish Bros. Birmingham 1935).

Towards the end of his apprenticeship, Langley's designs for jewellery were exhibited at the Royal Birmingham Society and he gained a scholarship to the South Kensington Schools to study decorative design. Here his skills developed considerably and he formed his ambition as an artist, and began to paint seriously. Cutting short his training in London, he accepted partnership in the firm of lithographic printers he had earlier been apprenticed to, but he continued to paint as much as possible and attended evening classes at the Birmingham Society of Artists and the Midland Art Guild.

Langley became a leader amongst the younger and most promising artists in Birmingham. From 1873 he was a regular exhibitor at the Royal Birmingham Society of Artists, and gained a reputation as a watercolourist of unusual skill. He became a particular friend of William Wainwright, and for a time they shared a studio in Paradise Street, Birmingham. Langley visited Newlyn in 1880 for a holiday, and painted several views of the town. With a background and training in design rather than fine art, Langley was less influenced than some of his contemporaries by French attitudes to painting, and he made only one working visit to Brittany in 1881, at the same time as Harris and Breakespeare, where he painted a number of scenes of Breton life. The early influences upon his work are from the Dutch school – watercolours of domestic scenes which he studied in the museum collections of South Kensington, and such artists as Hubert von Herkomer and Francis Hinkley, both of whom were regular

WALTER LANGLEY

But Men Must Work and Women Must Weep, 1882.

watercolour, 775 x 510mm.

CITY OF BIRMINGHAM MUSEUM AND ART GALLERY.

exhibitors with the Birmingham Society of Artists. Langley was to retain a feeling for the work of the Hague School and visited the Netherlands three times.

While still engaged in the lithographic trade, Langley began to see the possibility of financial independence through painting. He achieved this with a proposal from a Birmingham photographer, Mr Thrupp of New Street, who was also a dealer in artists work, and who offered Langley the substantial sum of £500 for a year's work. It was Thrupp who took the photograph of Langley on p. 29. Langley now had family responsibilities, he had married Clara Perkins, who was to bear him four children Lorraine, Gabriel, Cecil and Eleanor. Nevertheless he decided to give up his commercial work and with Clara and his young family he moved to Newlyn to begin a professional career in art. By January 1882 he had found a house, Pembroke Lodge, on the southern edge of the town, near to the Penlee quarries, and a studio about half a mile away towards Penzance.

When he came to Newlyn, Langley was a mature man of thirty, with an established reputation in Birmingham. Soon after his arrival he produced some of his finest work, effectively capturing moments of personal crisis experienced by the fishermen's families. Shipwrecks were a tragic part of Newlyn life. The large watercolour 'For Men Must Work and Women Must Weep' painted in 1883, describes the emotions of two women who watch the troubled sea from their cottage window as they wait for news of their loved one. The lamenting young wife, totally overcome by grief, her face in her hands, is comforted by an older woman, perhaps the sailor's mother, whose face shows that she still has a half-hope that all might be well. This scene of despair is described with great economy of detail through the careful rendering of textures in the simple cottage interior and the rough dresses of the two women. The few incidentals of life at sea – the tarred hat, fishing line and ropes – identify the seafarer's home, while the drama of the situation is emphasised by the cold light of dawn creeping through the cottage window.

Langley took the title of the painting from Charles Kingsley's highly emotional poem 'The Three Fishers' (see page opposite).

Langley had great sympathy for the working people of Newlyn. The fact that he was from a working-class background made him exceptionally sensitive to the struggle of the seafaring community. He painted their hardship, and despair, and shared their experience of tragedy – always a close companion in a fragile world where families could be devastated by the loss of the bread

WALTER LANGLEY

In a Cornish Fishing Village; The Departure of the Fleet to the North, 1886.

watercolour, 610 x 1220mm.

PENZANCE AND DISTRICT MUSEUM AND ART GALLERY.

earner. 'It may be that it is because I have worked my way up that I am more interested in all who work', he said. He was 'For ever impressed with the signs of the struggle for existence which are so apparent throughout nature, and which entails here and there so much misery and pain.' (*Kings Heath and Moseley Journal*, July 1897, Vol.VI. No.62 p.72.). He also had strong political views, he was Liberal, and when Asquith came to Penzance, Langley was invited to be one of the platform party. He was criticised for his friendship and support of Charles Bradlaugh, a socialist politician and atheist who had refused to take the Parliamentary oath on his election to the House of Commons.

Many young artists who later came to Newlyn studied at the Royal Academy of Antwerp. Frank Bramley, William Wainwright, Edwin Harris, and Fred Hall, were all students there between 1879 and 1883. Close relationships had formed between certain schools in England and on the Continent. Birmingham and Lincoln Schools of Art both had contacts with the Royal Academy of Antwerp, a remarkable school, established by David Teniers in the seventeeth century. From 1878 to 1885 the Professor of Painting, later Director, was Charles Verlat, much admired as a teacher and known as an Anglophile. During his Professorship the Academy became known as 'Verlat's'. His students gained a great deal from his realist approach and his insistence upon technical competence and study of the natural world.

In addition to the usual classes in drawing from the antique and the model, the school included 'an atelier for painting animals in the open air'. Regular and punctual attendance was required and there was a competitive 'concours' examination at the end of each year. Students were introduced to the traditions of northern European painting, particularly Dutch and German, through the museum attached to the school, and they worked alongside talented students from other European countries. In addition to the quality of teaching, no fees were charged at the Academy and the town was cheap to live in.

Because of their previous training three of the Birmingham students – Bramley, Wainwright and Harris – were thought of as specially advanced, and were allowed to join a group of privileged students who had the use of a spacious studio in which full-length life-size studies from the nude could be made without distractions from other students.

Edwin Harris (1855–1906) went to Antwerp in 1880. Although three years younger than Walter Langley, the two were boyhood friends. Much of their early training overlapped, and for a number of years they were part of the same

THE THREE FISHERS

Three Fishers went sailing away to the West,
Away to the West as the sun went down;
Each thought on the woman who loved him the best,
And the children stood watching them out of the town;
For men must work and women must weep,
And there's little to earn, and many to keep.
Though the harbour bar be moaning.

Langley found this poem deeply moving. While reading it he heard the alarm signalling disaster at sea:

He went out into the black night – an awful storm was howling – and he saw the blue rockets being fired from Penzance as a signal to those who were at sea. The scene was in the last degree impressive – a fearful constraint on his cozy fireside – and the idea at once suggested itself.

('Edgbastonia', July 1890 Vol.X. p.101.)

group of young artists in Birmingham. Harris was born and brought up in Ladywood, a suburb of Birmingham, and at fourteen had entered Birmingham School of Art where Langley was a fellow student. After his training he continued there as an assistant master for two further years before going to Antwerp. During his time there Harris began to exhibit small figure studies which received favourable comment at the exhibitions of the Royal Birmingham Society of Artists, and he was later elected to membership of the Society. On his return to Birmingham in 1881 he took a studio in Paradise Street where Langley and Wainwright were working. It is probably at Harris' studio that the first meetings were held that led to the formation of the Birmingham Art Circle.

Harris made two visits to Brittany, in 1881 and 1882, where he painted at Pont-Aven and Dinan with his fellow Birmingham student W. A. Breakespeare. Frank Bramley and Elizabeth Armstrong were at Pont-Aven at the same time, and they all stayed at 'Julia's', and from this visit Harris gave us that graphic description of Pont-Aven quoted earlier [see p.20]. After some weeks at Dinan, Harris and Breakespeare ran out of money, and had no means of returning home. To pay for their keep Harris attempted a portrait of their landlord, with some fear as he had no experience of portraiture. Fortunately the results were good, and other orders were made. The two artists soon turned out sufficient work to cover all their expenses and pay for their journey home.

If one is concerned to discover the first artist to stay for any length of time in Newlyn, then note must be taken of the claim made by Harris's biographer that, 'he spent almost all of 1881 in Newlyn with eight other painters in the house'. Other artists mentioned being 'Mr Fred Brown, before his professional days, Mess. Wainwright, Whitworth, Malcolm Lloyd and others'. The writer goes on to say 'Mr Walter Langley is generally regarded as the "artistic father" of the small Cornish fishing village, but Mr Edwin Harris was before him, and is undoubtedly one of the first pioneers amongst the Newlynites'. (Mr Edwin Harris. 'Edgbastonia' Vol.XIX July 1899 No.218 p.124). The reference to Fred Brown is of importance. There is no other known mention of Brown in Newlyn, and he is not in any way grouped with the Newlyn artists, rather the reverse, for he became one of their chief critics. Although his early work was influenced by Bastien-Lepage, Brown became deeply involved in the events that led to the formation of the New English Art Club and became identified with the 'Impressionist' group, which included Wilson Steer, Sickert and Clausen who took over the group on opposition to the Newlyn painters. The 'professional days' referred to are no doubt Brown's appointment as Professor of the Slade School in 1893, a position which gave him a base for considerable influence upon other artists and generations of students. Harris returned for a short visit in 1882, but he did not settle until 1883, a year after Langley had moved to the town.

There is a quiet domesticity about Harris' work which contrasts with the sombreness seen in Newlyn by Walter Langley. Whereas Langley's work is serious in mood, Harris' is light and gentle and he portrays the hours of happiness in the cottagers' lives. A typical painting is 'The Lesson' (1889) a study in the soft lighting of a cottage interior, with a local model, Kate Jeffery, who also sat for Langley and other artists. Such simple groups of mother and child express the pleasure in family relationships, domestic tasks and games, sharing the sentimentality of Langley with nothing of his pathos and drama. In Newlyn, Harris' work developed from a minute finish to 'the broad horizontal touch' for which Stanhope Forbes set the vogue.

That sense of withdrawal into the private world of the family, which characterises Harris' early work, later became part of his personal tragedy. He had married early and by the time that Stanhope Forbes came to Newlyn, Harris and his young wife were able to provide a civilised and welcome addition to the somewhat limited social life of the town. Forbes recalled: 'We had a very pleasant evening at the Harrises yesterday... I wish I knew more people like these, for it is a change and an agreeable one to get into the society of ladies occasionally and it is perhaps more elevating than the tap room of the Three Stars Inn, where, in the company of a few Penzance tradespeople and farmers, we sit and consume our glass of grog and smoke a cigarette or two of an evening'. Later he wrote, 'I dined with the Harrises and met little Bateman and his wife (he in grand tenure). Wonderful dinner, beginning with ducks and ending with a joint. After dinner music. Little Bateman plays the flute beautifully. When they had departed about 11 o'clock, Langley sat down, played dance music and we had a little dance – quadrilles, waltzes, polka etc. Mrs Harris pronouncing me quite a good dancer'. (Letters of Easter Sunday 1884 and an undated letter, probably July 1885). Forbes was also introduced to Mrs Harris' uncle who was a picture dealer from Birmingham. It would appear that Harris already had an outlet for his work through this useful contact.

In 1884 a son was born to the Harrises, but only three years later their domestic contentment was savagely broken by a severe illness, probably cancer, which led to the early death of Harris' young wife. Her suffering was shared by the artists and their wives as they sought to give whatever care they could to her and support for the distraught Harris.

Over several months Forbes recorded her sad deterioration. In March 1887 he wrote:

Poor little Mrs Harris still lingers on – Tayler has again spent the night at the house. I walked in last night and saw poor Harris for the first time since the bad attack came on. He is of course very knocked down but is wonderfully calm in spite of it. She is not yet 25 poor little thing.

After his wife's death Harris moved to Street-an-Nowan with his son and nurse. In spite of his loss he continued to paint domestic scenes of great charm, based on careful observation. If they were to a formula it was an acceptable one in which a succession of pretty girls, usually with children, are pictured in simple tasks about the cottage. Later Harris turned increasingly to portraiture. He left Newlyn in 1895 and spent most of the rest of his life in Birmingham, where he died in 1906.

For the Newlyn artists the pursuit of Realism meant the scrutiny of nature in order to discover some aspect of truth or moral value. It was not sufficient simply to record the outside world, the artist must also draw from it a sense of purpose, it looked to those moments of heightened understanding which occur at times of personal tragedy, despair or suffering, rather than to everyday reality which could not sufficiently carry the weight of the social message. Such tragic themes as disaster at sea or bereavement were understood as comments upon the fraility of human existence, and descriptions of the nobility of labour and honest poverty indicated God's purpose in ordering the world. Other subjects such as the virtues of family life and the contrasts of youth and age, could offer rewarding moral principles within Christian teaching.

The great monuments to Realism in French painting – Courbet's 'Stone Breakers' and 'Burial at Ornans' and Millet's 'The Sower' – which belong to the

EDWIN HARRIS

The Lesson, 1889.

oil on canvas, 345 x 600mm.

PRIVATE COLLECTION.

1850s, are all statements of political liberalism. British artists had also begun to find subjects in the life of the poor, as described in the work of Dickens, and painted by the Pre-Raphaelite painters. The most important painting of contemporary life in which poverty and labour play a large part is 'Work' by Ford Maddox Brown begun in 1852 and finished in 1863. It depicts a gang of navvies working in a Hampstead street amid passers-by who reflect all levels and conditions of Victorian society – rich and poor, idle and industrious, working and unemployed. Its moral context is emphasised by biblical quotations inscribed on the frame which celebrate the value of work. 'See thou a man diligent in his business, he shall stand before Kings', and 'In the sweat of the face shall thou eat bread'. The painting also contains in good measure those peculiarly English preoccupations with social class, character and story-telling that were such an important part of nineteenth century painting in England.

The Newlyn artists who explored this area of human emotion were preceded by a small number of highly appreciated Victorian artists including Luke Fildes (1843–1927), Hubert von Herkomer (1849–1914) and Frank Holl (1845–1888), whose work had aroused great interest when seen as illustrations in the contemporary news magazines, such as the *Graphic*. One of Fildes best known images was an illustration produced for the first edition of the *Graphic* in

1869. Entitled 'Houseless and Hungry', it shows a scene outside a police station, where paupers queued in the cold to obtain a ticket which would admit them to the casual ward of the workhouse. This illustration had considerable effect upon a number of English artists, and also on the young Van Gogh who thought it superb and who treasured his copy of it. Its characters were described by Charles Dickens as 'Dumb, wet, silent horrors'.

Hubert von Herkomer also explored working-class subjects of old age, poverty and homelessness, and with keen observation presented these as wood block illustrations for the *Graphic* and as large canvasses at the Royal Academy. His work had a direct influence upon a number of the early Newlyn artists, and later, through his teaching, profoundly affected a number of artists who were to come to St Ives.

None was more successful at depicting the grey and grave aspects of life, particularly disaster at sea, than Frank Holl. Born in London, he travelled widely in Europe, but it was in the grey northern light of Belgium and the Netherlands that he found his natural environment. Themes of mourning and disaster recur in his work. One of his greatest paintings 'No Tidings from the Sea', commissioned by Queen Victoria, was completed in 1870. Painted in the fishing village of Cullercoats in Northumberland, it described the terrible plight of an old woman and a young woman with her child who wait, half mad with suspense and misery, for news of a fishing boat that has not returned with the fleet. The same subject was painted on several occasions by Walter Langley and Frank Bramley.

Contemporary with these English painters and illustrators, sharing many of their preoccupations, was a group of painters working in the Netherlands. Known as the Hague School, they came together in the 1870s, finding their subjects in the semi-rural city of the Hague and the life of the nearby fishing villages surrounded by meadows, polders and picturesque waterways. A leading member was Josef Israels (1824–1911) who painted the tragic and poetic qualities of life at Zandfoort, a small fishing village near Haarlem. His paintings were frequently shown in London and Birmingham and had a significant effect upon a number of the Newlyn painters. At the International Exhibition in

LUKE FILDES

Houseless and Hungry.

ILLUSTRATION FROM
THE *GRAPHIC*, 1889.

London in 1862, his monumental painting 'Fisherman Carrying a Drowned Man' (1861) was extensively praised. Israels repeatedly returned to the tragic consequences of death at sea, the plight of the mourning widow and the sad-faced fishermen; the contrasts of youth and age; children at play, solitude and grief – the very subjects chosen by the Newlyn artists. Like Langley he frequently worked in watercolour, often at a large scale and exhibited with the Royal Institute of Painters in Watercolour, which Langley joined in 1882.

Frank Bramley (1857–1915), is arguably the most talented and dedicated of the Newlyn artists, who identified closely with the life of the fishing community. A quiet and retiring man, like Langley, he was inclined to melancholy. He was wholly absorbed in his painting and somewhat solitary, playing only a minor part in the social life of the artists' community.

Bramley's early life had followed a similar pattern to other Newlyn painters from the Midlands. He was born at Sibsey, near Boston in Lincolnshire and trained at Lincoln School of Art. In 1879 or 1880 he went to Verlat's Academy in Antwerp, where he became a close friend of W.J.Wainwright and for a time they shared a house. Fred Hall also from Lincoln, and Edwin Harris were students in Antwerp at this time. Bramley exhibited his paintings, mostly of Flemish subjects, in the annual exhibitions of the Royal Birmingham Society of Artists from 1878 onwards.

In 1882–83 Bramley made an extended visit to Venice, and at first enjoyed the student atmosphere. He wrote to his friend Wainwright:

As to your getting a good studio, there's not such a thing in Venice. They are small, and often a good deal of reflection, in fact just ordinary rooms with large windows – little better than in Antwerp. Models in my opinion are very good. With a little trouble you can get anyone to sit. The colour of the costumes is as good as you could wish. The girls are very pretty, and the men most neatly made. (W. J. Wainwright, RSW, RBSA, by Walter Turner pub. Cornish Bros, Birmingham 1935).

JOSEF ISRAELS

Fisherman Carrying a Drowned Man, 1861.

oil on canvas, 1265 x 2450mm.

THE NATIONAL GALLERY, LONDON.

However he found the Venetian winter very trying and his health began to fail. He later said that Venice almost killed him. In spite of these difficulties two of his Venetian scenes were accepted as his first exhibits at the Royal Academy in 1884.

Bramley came to Newlyn in the winter of 1884–85 at about the same time as Stanhope Forbes, and at the same age – twenty-nine years. Like Forbes his principal subject was the figure, but Bramley was more concerned with mood and character. Trained in the discipline of northern painting in Antwerp, his work tended more to tonality, less to colour, and wherever possible he avoided action, preferring to set his models indoors in the known situation of his studio, carefully translating the soft indoor effects of light and shade.

Bramley shared the cramped accommodation of the fishing community, yet appeared to be unconcerned by the conditions in which he lived and worked. His home and studio was one room in a thatched cottage at the corner of the Rue des Beaux Arts, the roof pierced with a skylight. The floor below was occupied by an elderly crippled woman called Mrs Barrett who ran a dame school for tiny children and who also sold vegetables. She had lost both arms in a railway accident, but kept order among her charges by swinging a stout cane held under her armpit at any miscreant. Stanhope Forbes' father once popped his head in at her door and asked her 'How do you amuse the children?' to which she replied 'I do sing em litle 'Ims'. Frank Bramley, who could hear every sound in the room below, confided to Forbes that the litle 'Ims' usually took the form of violent outbursts of wrath, her favourite expression in admonishing the row of infants who sat on the little bench being 'Sit down you stinking elephants'. (1.6.1886.).

In Newlyn Bramley's painting began to blossom. In 'Primrose Day' painted in the spring of 1885, a sad faced girl sits at a table. The primroses she has gathered are arranged in a jug on the table, others are still in the hat in which she has gathered them. The creamy yellows of the flowers form soft pools of colour among the shadows of the room, but it is the contemplative expression of the child's face that holds the attention, and also the portrait of Disraeli hanging in the background. This small painting combines Bramley's patriotic feelings with his religious beliefs. Primrose Day, 19 April, was traditonally the day when primroses were at their best. It was also the anniversary of the death of Benjamin Disraeli, Earl of Beaconsfield, and founder of the Primrose League, a Conservative party organisation with imperial views which had been formed two years earlier with the objects of 'the maintenance of religion, of the estates of the realm, and of the imperial ascendancy'.

A more ambitious and substantial figure painting 'Domino' (1886), is set in the same cottage interior, where two girls sit around the table engrossed in their game. It is a study in light and dark in which the setting is as important as the figures. The whitewashed wall, the white table-cloth and dress of the older girl and the carelessly thrown piece of linen on the floor make a cascade of high tones against the darker greys of the floor and staircase, and give a beautifully orchestrated diagonal movement that focuses attention upon the faces of the young players. When 'Domino' was exhibited in the Royal Academy in 1886, the first major interior scene from Newlyn, it was realised that Bramley had adapted the new forms of Realism to an indoor setting. One reviewer thought it 'A perfect blend of simple but profound human drama, and of beautifully executed and very carefully observed effects of light and colour and tone'. (*Art Journal* 1889, p 100).

'How they paint their pictures: The Realist School'.

FRED HALL

Caricature of Frank Bramley from the Pall Mall Gazette. 28 June 1894.

The dragged mark of the square brush is noticeable in many of Bramley's paintings – a characteristic for which he was to become well known. Each change of colour was first carefully mixed on the palette and judged in relation to the surrounding tone and colour of the subject. It was then laid on the canvas to facet the change of light on dress, wall or table. This testing manner of painting allowed Bramley to render the 'envelope of light' that surrounded the model by describing each object in its correct spatial position. The technique of 'square-brush' painting used by many of the Newlyn painters, was an innovation, and much criticised when first seen in the Academy. It was described as a French method, which many found unacceptable, and a departure from English conventions whereby paint was brushed along the form rather than across it, producing a bland and often rubbery effect.

A delicate symbolism, revealed by naturalism, is the hallmark of Bramley's best work, and is well illustrated in his next important figure painting which was shown at the first exhibition of the New English Art Club in 1887. He gave it the evocative title 'Weaving a Chain of Grief'. A young woman dressed in black, is clearly in mourning. Her expression and gesture is of the deepest grief and an air of profound melancholy surrounds her. But the same set, in a well lit conservatory where she arranges the flowers and drying leaves of late summer, is full of light and colour, and backed by an atmospheric description of the sea and Newlyn harbour seen through the conservatory windows. The symbolism

FRANK BRAMLEY

Domino, 1886.

oil on canvas, 850 x 1110mm.

CRAWFORD ART GALLERY, CORK.

of the subject – the persistence of life in death – is emphased by the strong contrasts of light and dark, and by the cascades of joyous colour that surround the mourning figure of the girl.

One of the greatest paintings to come from Newlyn and one of the finest emotional statements of Victorian art was 'A Hopeless Dawn' (1888), a scene of tragic loss set in the intimate theatre of Bramley's small room in Newlyn. In this large painting the cold light of dawn softly illuminates two figures which appear to grow from the darkened background, hands and heads in piteous attitudes. The women have kept their vigil through the night waiting for their loved one to return from sea, and we see them at a turning point in their lives. The older woman, mother of the fisherman, sits in the window seat, an open bible in front of her, and comforts the young wife, prostrate upon the rough floor. Through the window the sea is still turbulent and the sky heavily clouded. The only colour in this otherwise grey scene is from a single candle, guttering in its holder, which still throws a warm light on the bowls, jug and a cut loaf on the table, a simple funeral feast prepared but uneatcn. The other candle has already burnt to a point of glowing red, and the lamp placed in the window – a pathetic beacon to the returning boatman – has been extinguished. On the cottage wall a print of Raphael's cartoon 'Christ giving the Keys of the Kingdom of Heaven to St Peter' indicates Bramley's spiritual message, and was further reinforced by a quotation from Ruskin that was exhibited with the picture when it was shown at the Academy:

FRANK BRAMLEY

A Hopeless Dawn, 1888.

oil on canvas, 1215 x 1650mm.

TATE GALLERY
(CHANTRY BEQUEST).

Human effort and sorrow going on perpetually from age to age; waves rolling for ever and winds moaning, and faithful hearts wasting and sickening for ever, and brave lives dashed away about the rattling beach like weeds for ever; and still, at the helm of every lonely boat, through starless night and hopeless dawn, His hand, who spreads the fisher's net over the dust of the Sidonian palaces, and gave unto the fisher's hand the keys of the Kingdom of Heaven. (Catalogue to the Collection of the Tate Gallery).

The models were real fisherfolk, painted in a sustained effort of concentration, and with an understatement which contrasts with the heightened drama of the situation. Before it was submitted to the Royal Academy Stanhope Forbes said of the work:

We saw Frank Bramley's picture which is not only good for him, but I think one of the finest pictures I ever saw. It will well establish his reputation I feel sure. The dramatic interest in it is so great that even the public will admire it and I need not say that it is freely drawn and finely painted. Newlyn will be very strong this year. (February 1st 1888).

Forbes was right. The religious theme of this painting, with its simple yet emotional story, achieved great popular success. It was purchased from the Academy by the Chantry Bequest – the first Newlyn painting to be so honoured – and proved to be one of the most popular of that collection which was to become the nucleus of the Tate Gallery. It characterised the best of Newlyn painting and confirmed the group's reputation in London. It was by far the most successful painting by Bramley, overshadowing his other work and establishing his reputation as a painter of melancholic figure subjects.

Fred Hall (1860–1948) brought humour and incident to Newlyn, without adding to the weight of earnestness that characterised some of the less talented members of the group. His delicate landscape studies and small paintings of figures in cottage settings have a lightness of touch and a sensitivity to the forms of landscape that is closer to the kind of Impressionism practised by painters of the New English Art Club who were not painting in Newlyn. He found a sparkle of colour about him which evaded many of his companions. The painter and writer Frank Richards warmed to his work, and described Newlyn as:

bright, the colour of everything is decidedly fresh, pure and brilliant, according to the day; the sea and sky effects are charming, especially in the summer, when we get a good deal of the Italian blue; and the reason of the general impression that it is a grey or dowdy place is, simply, because the subjects chosen and painted by Newlyners have always been grey ones, with the exception of Mr Fred Hall's work. (Frank Richards, 'Newlyn as a Sketching Ground', *The Studio* Vol.V 1895. p. 174–5).

Fred Hall was born at Stillington, Yorkshire, where his father was a doctor. From 1879 to 1881 he attended Lincoln School of Art where Frank Bramley, three years older, was also a student. Hall and Bramley became close friends, for a time living in the same house where they painted each other's portraits. In 1882 Hall followed Bramley to Verlat's Academy in Antwerp. Bramley had already completed his studies, but Hall may have overlapped the other artists from the Midlands – Wainwright, Breakespeare, Harris and Suthers. He certainly worked in the lifeclass with William Blandford Fletcher. Hall left Antwerp in 1883 and worked for a short time in the small painting colony in Southwold. He first came to Newlyn shortly after Bramley, probably in 1883 or early 1884. Stanhope Forbes, always quick to identify newcomers to the artists' colony, does not mention his presence until late in 1885, but in the previous year Fred Hall exhibited a painting in London called 'An Orchard near Newlyn, Cornwall', so at least one earlier visit is indicated. He probably settled in Newlyn in the winter of 1885–86 and stayed for about eleven years.

Fred Hall pictured the country people of Newlyn at work in the fields or fishing and in repose. One of the best known paintings of his early years is the large figure composition 'Home from the Fields' (1886), in which a small group of working men and women slowly return to their village after a hard day's work. The low viewpoint places the figures against a darkening sky and gives them an heroic air – weary but proud men and women whose life is circumscribed by the constant round of toil. In subject and in treatment this painting looks to Millet's celebrations of the life of the peasant worker, but Hall's treatment is worked with the flatter 'square brush' technique favoured by Bastien-Lepage, and the general arrangement of the figures with their emphasised silhouettes is also reminiscent of Lepage.

In 1887 Fred Hall exhibited for the first time at the Royal Academy. His two paintings 'Old Birds' and 'April' show those qualities of humour that exist in his many illustrations and cartoon drawings. Two genre paintings, both entitled 'The Goose', and exhibited at the Royal Academy in the following year, depict the killing and plucking of a goose that laid a golden egg in a poor cottager's home. As described in the poem by Tennyson, the goose brought prosperity but also caused much mischief. Hall placed this incident in a setting of a Newlyn cottage. These light-hearted paintings struck a popular vein and it may have been their sale that led Stanhope Forbes to write 'Fred Hall is back, his purse full of money. He has been very fortunate lately'. (8.7.1888.). For the Academy in the following year, Hall painted a sequel, again in a half humorous vein. 'I Know an Old Wife' (1889), was set in the same cottage but now the old cottager, who was so much harassed by the goose incident, quietly watches a mouse foraging on the floor of her untidy kitchen.

Fred Hall was quiet and retiring but he by no means lacked wit and his observation was sharp, as demonstrated in the large number of caricatures of his fellow Newlyn artists that he made in the early 1890s. These revealing drawings are warm and sympathetic, but they capture the character of his subjects with precision. Stanhope Forbes is shown as impossibly thin and angular, very much a Victorian country gentleman, clad in a long greatcoat and deerstalker hat; Walter Langley is the untidy Bohemian artist, bearded and sporting a wide brimmed rakish hat. Harris, similarly hatted, has a distinctly aesthetic air, his hand extended limply and a loose jaw that can scarcely hold the heavy pipe; the jaunty rotund Todd appears full of self importance. Chevallier Tayler strides along the promenade looking 'like Jacques Tati walking along the beach in "Monsieur Hulot's Holiday"' (*Artists of the Newlyn School 1880-1900,* Fox and Greenacre, 1979). Hall's own self portrait is rather less revealing – a small portly figure, gazing somewhat vaguely into the distance as he pulls on his pipe.

As his work progressed in the late 1880s Fred Hall developed a lighter touch and a more impressionist treatment in his landscapes and figure studies, many of which were shown at the Royal Academy. He also began to divide his

FRED HALL

Home from the Fields,
1886.

oil on canvas, 1150 x 900mm.
DAVID MESSUM FINE ART.

FRED HALL

The Goose.

'...it cluttered here'

'...she dropped the goose
and caught the pelt'.

These two anecdotal paintings,
set in a Newlyn cottage, were
shown at the Royal Academy in
1888. Their sales were referred
to by Forbes in a letter to his
mother: 'Fred Hall is back, his
purse is full of money'.

time between Newlyn and Porlock in Somerset, where he went on painting trips
with Leghe Suthers. In 1890 Fred Hall had a most successful exhibition at
Dunthorne's Gallery in London, with a series of studies of the members of the
Devon and Somerset Staghounds. These were based on silhouette drawings of
horses and riders, first made directly on to his studio walls and very much in
line with his caricature drawings. They were popular and one reviewer asked:
'Why does Mr Fred Hall give his time to the painting of landscape when he
possesses the genius of a caricaturist of the highest order.' (*The Cornish
Chronicle*, 1891). As a result of this exhibition, and probably at Phil May's
suggestion, Hall later made many comic caricatures which were reproduced in
various magazines, *Black and White* in 1891, *The Sketch* and the *Pall Mall
Budget* in 1893 and 1894. (*The Sketch* 21 March 1894, p.417, 9 May 1894, p.85).

It is humour rather than caricature that inspires such a gentle study of
wellbeing as 'The Result of High Living' (1892), in which an overfed dog is
given a medicinal draft by an equally portly physician. But from time to time

Edwin Harris   *Walter Langley*   *Ralph Todd*

Hall's somewhat quirky turn of mind took him into the world of fantasy and symbolism. His Royal Academy exhibit of 1893, 'Pixy-led' depicts a young girl who stands on sloping ground looking in astonishment at the tiny pixie figures that dance in the grasses below her feet (rep. RA pictures 1893, No.76). This combination of the atmospheric mystery of the English countryside with rural magic was described as a 'very peculiar picture'. (*Western Morning News* 31.3.1893.).

Allegory and religious symbolism informs the large canvas 'The Shepherd' shown at the Academy in 1895. In this country scene, a shepherd and his dog led the flock through a gate into a landscape of idyllic gentleness, lit by a mysterious flickering light. (rep. RA pictures 1895, no.137).

Hall probably left Newlyn in about 1897, and in the following year married Agnes Dod, a young and beautiful girl who inspired many fine portraits. After a year in Liverpool the couple moved to Dorking, and Hall took a studio in West Kensington. In 1911 he moved with his family to a cottage in Donnington Square, Newbury where he lived for the rest of his life.

A companion from a well-known Birmingham family, who also spent time in Newlyn was William John Wainwright (1855–1931). Educated at Sedgeley Park College near Wolverhampton, he showed an aptitude for drawing and at sixteen was apprenticed to the stained glass works of John Hardman, a distinguished

FRED HALL

Caricatures of the Newlyn Artists.

TATE GALLERY, LONDON.

Frank Bramley   *Stanhope Forbes*   *Chevallier Tayler*   *Fred Hall*

craftsman who had collaborated with Pugin on the windows of the rebuilt Houses of Parliament. During the eight years that he was with Hardman's, Wainwright became an important designer for the firm, mainly in ecclesiastical art, and worked on windows for St Paul's Cathedral and St Mary's, Coventry. He also received instruction at Birmingham School of Art.

In 1874 Wainwright entered the Royal Academy of Antwerp, sharing a studio with Frank Bramley. In previous years English students at Verlat's had distinguished themselves at the Academy. William Logsdail and Frank Bramley had both won the 'Concours' competition and Wainwright was equally talented. He became a favourite of the director, Charles Verlat, who was impressed by his work in watercolour, and who encouraged him to compete for the 'Concours' competition with a life sized study called 'Job'. This was awarded first place, but the National Academy would not allow Wainwright to receive their gold medal on the grounds that the competition was limited to oils. This led to an open breach between Verlat and the Academy.

During 1881 Wainwright continued his training in Paris, but on a holiday in England he travelled to Cornwall and spent a few weeks in Newlyn, This was shortly after Langley had come to live in the town. One watercolour of Wainwright's 'On The Beach at Newlyn', exhibited at the Birmingham and Midland Institute in 1890, is known to exist. In Paris Wainwright worked hard, ten hours a day, and began to find a style that he would continue to use. It was probably during this time that he met Thomas and Caroline Gotch and painted the portraits of these two idealistic young people, Thomas in the dress of an artist, hair rumpled with an earnest and distant gaze.

In Antwerp Wainwright had been much affected by the art of the past, and as his style matured a great deal of his work was based on historical themes and studies of personality and gesture in period costume. One of these 'The Singers' (1883), represented youths in medieval costume singing to an unseen audience. The *Spectator's* critic could not conceal his dislike of the painting's foreign influence, but had to admit a grudging respect:

> *The drawing shows very plainly the marks of foreign teaching, and has a good deal of that somewhat unpleasant ability which marks much of the French works, but it is well and strongly drawn, is full of power, and has a definite style and meaning in its painting, in fact it is by a man who knows his business, and is neither namby-pamby nor trivial. Whether it is not insolent is another question.* (*The Spectator* 26 May 1883).

The painting was exhibited at the Royal Society of Painters in Watercolours, and gained Wainwright membership. It was also bought from the exhibition by James Statts Forbes, uncle to Stanhope Forbes, and an important collector of modern works. While still in Paris Wainwright was elected to the Royal Birmingham Society of Artists, and was to be a great supporter of their exhibitions, showing some 232 works during his lifetime.

Wainwright had earlier been converted to the Roman Catholic faith, and this directed him towards historical or devotional themes. Before coming to Cornwall he had corresponded with the Falmouth painter Napier Hemy, much respected for his paintings of the sea, and soon to become a Royal Academician. Hemy, also a Catholic, had expressed the hope that Wainwright would visit him in Falmouth, because 'You are the only Catholic artist I know of in England in whose work I take any interest. But then there is no work at all I think finer and stronger than yours'. (Turner *op. cit.* p.26). However on his return from Paris Wainwright lived for a short time in London, and in May 1884 came to Newlyn to join his friend Frank Bramley. Wainwright fitted easily into the Newlyn group. He lodged for a few months with his other Birmingham friends, the Harrises, and then moved into shared accommodation at Cliff House with eight other artists.

Two major paintings date from Wainwright's stay in Newlyn, the first was a figure painting 'Ferdinand and Miranda' (1884), a subject from Shakespeare, set in an orchard. Miranda, dressed in Elizabethan costume of soft greys, fawn and black, has seen the distant figure of Ferdinand approaching, but he, unaware of her presence, listens to the music of the invisible Ariel. The other, a more typical Newlyn picture, was 'Mackerel in the Bay' (1884), in which a group of three men on a high headland assist the mackerel fishermen by signalling to the boats below that they have sighted the shoal of fish. This theme was taken up by other artists, notably Percy Craft in his painting 'The Huer' shown at the Royal Academy in 1883.

William Wainwright was not included in the list of 'original Newlynites', probably because he had already developed a style of painting based on historical and religious subjects. Like Langley, he remained principally a watercolourist, and perhaps for that reason he exhibited only once at the Royal Academy, at the start of his career. Although much respected for his abilities – Stanhope Forbes thought him 'a better man than Langley even' – Wainwright was not fired by that fascination with all aspects of Newlyn life that so captured the other members of the group, and his work has little in common with them. Stanhope Forbes last refers to his presence in Newlyn in November 1884, and by the following April he had returned to Birmingham where he was to become a prominent member of the Royal Birmingham Society of Artists.

Although Wainwright's painting is not central to the development of art in Newlyn, there is one way in which he made a major contribution. Wainwright was already acquainted with Stanhope Forbes. They could have met in Paris, or through Forbes' uncle, and it is believed that it was partly at Wainwright's suggestion that Forbes first visited Newlyn:

Two Birmingham men, the well known water-colour painter Mr Walter Langley, and Mr Wainwright had settled themselves at the moment in a Cornish fishing-village, and in writing to Mr Stanhope Forbes spoke volumes in its praise. The transition and change from Brittany to the country just across the water implies little to a lover of marine things. So much that is direct, picturesque and primitive belongs in common to both coasts. (Marion Hepworth-Dixon, *Magazine of Art,* 1892).

If this was so then the consequences of this action upon the future of painting in Newlyn far outweighed the importance of the paintings that Wainwright produced during his short stay there.

Leghe Suthers (1856–1924), was a regular visitor to Newlyn over a period of some ten years. He was not a resident, but used Newlyn as a sketching ground and also worked in his native Southport in Lancashire. He was one of the group of English students at Verlat's Academy in Antwerp before visiting Brittany in the summer of 1882, and he came to Newlyn with his friends from Antwerp, Frank Bramley and Fred Hall. In France he had made the acquaintance of

LEGHE SUTHERS

View of Newlyn from the Bottom of Addit Lane.

PENZANCE AND DISTRICT MUSEUM AND ART GALLERY.

WILLIAM WAINRIGHT

Mackerel in the Bay, 1884.

oil on canvas

PRIVATE COLLECTION.

Stanhope Forbes who, arriving in Newlyn wrote: 'the man I returned from Brittany with last year, Suthers has been here all summer.' (January 1884).

Although his work did not become well known, Suthers was one of the Newlyn community and is acknowledged as 'one of the original Newlynites', sharing in their early success. His first year in Newlyn was interrupted by a visit to Venice, following the example of Frank Bramley, an experience he found equally unpleasant. Forbes recalled 'Bramley was nearly killed by it and Suthers gave me a wretched account.' (8.6.87.). Suthers' first painting exhibited at the Royal Academy in 1885 was 'Venetian Red', probably painted in Venice the previous year.

In 1886 Suthers' exhibit at the Royal Academy was 'Dame Trimmer' – a study of a reluctant young boy in a cottage interior whose hair is being trimmed by his grandmother. This is crisp tonal painting executed with the square brush, very much in character with Newlyn work. However there is doubt as to whether this painting was executed in Newlyn. Suthers was known to be away from the town during the early part of 1886, and ships masts can be seen in the cottage window – unlikely in Newlyn where the cottages were set back from the harbour. (See Fox and Greenacre op. cit. p. 127). The use of back lighting and strongly silhouetted figures against the cottage window is a device employed frequently by the artists trained in Antwerp.

In October 1886 Todd and Millard, who shared a studio in Newlyn, invited Suthers to join them in a studio exhibition. The next year Suthers again exhibited at the Academy with a painting entitled 'La Mascotte', which was hung 'on the line' as part of the Newlyn contingent that made Forbes write: 'Newlyn is simply triumphant'. (26 April 1887). Although his own painting 'Their Ever Shifting Home' received scant attention.

Suthers was one of the more minor Newlyn painters; nevertheless it is surprising that for an artist of evident talent and some early success, such a small amount of work is known. In spite of his many absences from the town he continued to be associated with Newlyn although he did not take part in the many social or sporting occasions arranged among the artists. He kept in close touch with his home town of Southport, and regularly took part in Spring Exhibitions there; for his work at the Royal Academy from 1885 to 1891 he gave his Southport address. Thereafter it would appear that Newlyn and later Paul was his base. He last exhibited at the Royal Academy in 1900, a work from Porlock where his close friend Fred Hall had begun to work during the late 1880s. In the last years of his life Suthers spent the greater part of his time in Porlock. He died there, a batchelor in 1924.

LEGHE SUTHERS

Annie Rowney of Newlyn.

oil on canvas, 310 x 225mm.

ROYAL CORNWALL MUSEUM, TRURO.

'A BREATH OF FRESH AIR'

In December 1883 Stanhope Forbes wrote to his mother from France, and enclosed a rough sketch which showed him rowing towards the English shore, with square ended paint brushes as oars, a canvas rigged as an improvised sail, and a palette as his ensign. His sketch was entitled 'Singular attempt to cross the channel by a young artist'. He was coming home. A month later he was in Newlyn. His arrival brought a significant addition to the growing group of artists. He was to become the most influential artist in Newlyn, and the longest established, living there until his death in 1947 at the age of ninety. He married in Newlyn and with his wife Elizabeth, who was also a fine painter, became the recognised leader of the artists' group. He constantly championed the artistic life of the area, and it was his enthusiasm and encouragement that attracted many other artists to the town. A friendly, vigorous man, outgoing and convivial, he had positive views on art and on the value of working directly from nature. He had the qualities of a man of action, with great energy, proselytizing zeal and a sense of mission. His attitude to life lacked cynicism as his paintings lacked symbolism.

Stanhope Forbes came from a practical and cultured family. His father, his eldest brother William and his uncle, James Statts Forbes, (a well known collector of European painting), were all dedicated to creating and running the vast railway networks of the nineteenth century. Stanhope Forbes inherited their practical genius, an impulse towards action rather than reflection, and an ability for organisation. His friend Norman Garstin said:

> *Stanhope Forbes comes of a stock which is essentially of the nineteenth century, full of its movement and its restless activity... he is penetrated with the actuality of life, he sees no visions, and he dreams no dreams; but, on the other hand, he sees with extraordinary clearness and simplicity, and renders with extraordinary clearness what he sees.* ('The Work of Stanhope A. Forbes ARA' by Norman Garstin – *The Studio,* vol.23 No.100 July 190l.).

Forbes had a remarkably close relationship with his mother Juliette de Guise; she visited him frequently in Brittany and Newlyn, and he wrote to her each day. These letters and notebooks (now deposited in the Tate Gallery) record in detail his activities and comments upon his fellow artists in Newlyn. In January 1884, fresh from Brittany, he wrote to her from the Union Hotel, Penzance as he

STANHOPE FORBES

Singular attempt to cross the Channel by a young Artist.

sketch in a letter to his mother, December 1883.

TATE GALLERY ARCHIVES.

searched the Cornish Coast for a new painting venue: 'You will be astonished to read the above address, I expect, but you know my unsettled nature and will soon realise that I am on a kind of tour round the country in search of a more picturesque place than Manaccan.' He had walked over to Helston, and then to Porthleven, which he found attractive. 'So that, unless I prefer a place called Newlyn within a mile of this town which I have just come over to see, I shall probably put up at Porthleven... I sleep here tonight, go over first thing tomorrow morning to Newlyn, judge it, return then to Falmouth again with baggage and back again to whichever place I decide upon finally.' (Undated letter)

On 25 January 1884, having decided to stay in Newlyn, he wrote c/o Mrs Tonkin, Gwavas Terrace, 'Newlyn is a sort of English Concarneau and is the haunt of a great many painters.' This resemblance to Concarneau cemented his attraction to Newlyn. He had worked well in Concarneau, and the two towns were very alike. Both were working seaports with the bustle of waterside activity and the movement of large fishing fleets. Both had beautiful natural settings – Concarneau with its large protected natural harbour enclosing its ancient fortified town the 'Ville-Carré'; Newlyn within the great curve of Mount's Bay and the medieval background of St Michael's Mount. Both towns had already been discovered by painters, many of whom Forbes already knew personally or by reputation:

> *The man I returned from Brittany with last year, Suthers has been here all last summer and Todd, the young fellow that fell in love, and got engaged... at Quimperlé last year is here and offered to share a sitting room with me, I declined this however, for I know but little of him. I have however, found very nice rooms and a studio... (built by a painter here out of an old sail loft) for 15/- a week including attendance, cooking, lights and in fact everything but coal and food.* (letter dated 25 January 1884).

Models were readily available: 'The girls are quite pretty in spite of their rather ugly English costume – sixpence an hour is the tariff – higher than in France of course.' (25 January 1884). Sustained by the presence of other artists in the town, Forbes was able to work as he wished in the open air. Even so there were difficulties, for the inhabitants of Newlyn were still not accustomed to artists working in the streets.

> *To plant one's easel down in the full view of all, and to work away in the midst of a large congregation needs a good deal of courage; but it takes even more to boldly ask some perfect stranger to pose for one under such very trying conditions. But our principles demanded it, and convinced of their virtue, I strove always to be consistant to them...* ('Cornwall from a Painter's Point of View', from the *Annual Report of the Royal Cornwall Polytechnic Society*, 1901).

The community in which Forbes found himself was based wholly upon fishing, a family trade that pervaded all aspects of Newlyn life. The steep streets leading down to the harbour were a scene of continuous activity; women and children bringing fish up from the boats in heavy baskets, or 'cowals', and younger children following to pick up the spilled fish. Home and industry were inextricably mixed, and a distinct type of courtyard building had evolved. The ground floor was given over to fishing gear, with a wide door on to the street to admit a cart or fish barrel. This led into a granite-paved yard, usually with a well, for washing fish and for household use, and open slate-roofed sheds called 'fish cellars', for preparing fish and storing fishing gear. In the cool cobbled fish cellars the pilchards were cured and packed with salt for dispatch to the Mediterranean countries where there was a good market.

Situated between the cold waters of the North Sea and the warmer Gulf Stream, Newlyn had a considerable natural advantage as a fishing port. The boats were Mount's Bay luggers, of between thirty and forty feet long, a small 'cuddy' or cabin to the fore, and an otherwise open hold for fish and lockers for the gear. Many of the Newlyn men owned their own boat or sailed with others

Stanhope Forbes painting in a Newlyn Street.

from the same family who did. Although the boats were small, the voyages were long, and trips of three months were not unusual. The fishing year began with mackerel, fished locally and as far away as the Scilly Isles until Easter. Then came herring, which took the men to Irish waters and to the East Coast fishing grounds in June and July. In the late summer, pilchard shoals came on the warmer waters and were caught in seine nets off the southern and northern coast of Cornwall. Boats went regularly to the great autumn fishing grounds of herring off the coast of East Anglia and Yorkshire, and then in search of the mackerel and other cold water fish, to northern and eastern waters, usually returning to Newlyn by early October for 'Paul Fest', a major local event, celebrated in the parish church of St Pol-de-Leon in the nearby village of Paul.

The shoals of fish seemed inexhaustible. Stanhope Forbes wrote of the prosperity of the town in 1884:

> *Never has there been such fishing known, and were it not that fish are so cheap the people would all be rolling in money. Boats are bringing in as many as 12,000 mackerel and the great difficulty is to find means of packing these large quantities. The salesmen's bell is heard each minute, and the beach is always crowded with buyers.* (letter from Belleview, April 1884).

In early February Forbes started a painting of 'The Shoot' which he described as 'a sort of little waterfall where the people all come to wash, to fetch water, etc.' However he found the weather too poor for outdoor working and made studio studies instead. By mid February he had conceived the idea of a large painting to be called 'The Arrival of the Boats with the Fish and the People Crowding Round on the Wet Sands'. In his letters he continuously refers to the 'wet sands': 'I cannot imagine anything more beautiful than this beach at low water. If I can only paint figures against such a background as this shining mirror'. (17 April 1884). He made several small oil studies for the painting, and an ambitious start on an enormous canvas, nine feet by five-and-a-half feet. But even for Forbes this proved too difficult to handle, fighting with the east wind on

STANHOPE FORBES

Beach Study, 1884.

oil on canvas, 135 x 180mm.

PRIVATE COLLECTION.

STANHOPE FORBES

Two Studies for 'Fish Sale on a Newlyn Beach'.

oil on panel, each 200 x 150mm.

DAVID MESSUM FINE ART.

the cold slippery beach. By June he had redesigned the picture and ordered a new canvas to the more modest five feet by four. The struggle to achieve on canvas the strong feeling that he had for the scene took the late summer and autumn, and progress was slow. He realised that 'painting out of doors in England is no joke and the picture will be a long weary job.' (9.6.84.). He experienced many setbacks and made a number of major alterations to the painting. In September he added a donkey cart in the distance, and in October, 'I have put in a new head with a yellow straw bonnet, and it has greatly improved the composition.' (23.10.84.). By December the painting was nearing completion and he was prepared to admit that it was 'a long way the best picture I have ever painted' but it was still not finished and now bad weather was more of a problem. 'I sallied forth to have another go at the large picture. I got blown about and rained upon, my model fainted etc...'(11.12.84.).

The painting – now called 'Fish Sale on a Newlyn Beach' – was finished in January 1884. It depicted a glistening beach at low tide, a heavy sky over a slate-blue sea. The fishing fleet is moored off-shore, and fish are being unloaded and offered for sale on the beach. The high horizon is cut by the angled pattern of the sails of the working boats, recently come to moorings from the fishing grounds; some have not yet lowered their heavy square mainsail, a few are still at sea, hull down on the distant horizon. Smaller boats bring the catch ashore, threading between the moorings towards the large group of men and women gossiping and exchanging news of the day, as they wait upon the beach to unload. As Newlyn goes about its daily task on this clear cool day, there is no drama, but a timeless quality in the frieze of figures silhouetted against the expanse of drying sand which mirrors the many blues, greys and greens of the sky and sea. There is detail and character in the relaxed and confident stance of the gossiping women, and the assurance of the young fisherman, conscious of his masculinity, who poses nonchalantly by the water's edge. The old fisherman has a heavier tread as he carries fish up the beach to the auction.

Forbes later described his intentions for the painting:

From the first I was fascinated by those wet sands, with their groups of figures reflected on the shiny surfaces, which the auctioneer's bell would gather around him for the barter of his wares... It was there that I elected to paint my first Newlyn picture, and out on that exposed beach, for many a month, struggled over a large canvas... Yes those were the days of unflinching realism, of the cult of Bastien-Lepage. It was part of our artistic creed to paint our pictures directly from Nature, and not merely to rely upon sketches and studies which we could afterwards amplify in the comfort of a studio. ('A Newlyn Retrospect' by Stanhope Forbes, *The Cornish Magazine* Vol. 1 1895).

As a theme, the fish auction or figure group on the beach is by no means unfamiliar. Several painters of the Norwich School used it for east coast subjects, as did the Dutch and French painters. A recent version that Forbes may have seen was John Singer Sargent's 'The Oyster Gatherers in Cancale' (1877), which depicts a procession of women and children moving across the wet sands towards the oyster beds, viewed against the sea and sky, and the veiled reflection of the figures in the glistening sand. The painting received wide attention when it was shown at the Paris Salon in 1878, and later at the Fine Art Society in London. In its use of light and strongly silhouetted figures and the general handling of the subject, the painting had many points of similarity with Forbes' 'Fish Sale'.

The Newlyn painting was a *tour de force* of sustained observation. It described the basics – who, where, time of day and condition of weather and season – with a planned precision that moves from the long perspective of the distant sails to the shimmering still life of fish, pearly white and grey, lying before us on the drying sand. It expresses the truth of appearance with clarity and accuracy of observation, a simple and familiar scene is described as a series of closely observed pictorial events, painted *en plein air*, and freed from the conventions of studio-based academic painting,

The painting was well shown at the Royal Academy in 1885, but first reaction was restrained. Claude Phillips writing in the *Magazine of Art*, called it 'good honest prose free from sentimentality', but went on to criticise the perspective, ending cautiously, 'French technique has it would seem something to do with the success of this work, and it will be necessary to examine others by the same hand before venturing to predict the exact place the artist will take.' Later writers were more enthusiastic, 'it rang out with its fresh vibrant note of sincerity', said Lewis Hind in his full length tribute to Forbes. ('Stanhope A. Forbes, A.R.A.' by C. Lewis Hind, *Art Journal* 1911). Alice Meynell, the first critic to write a major article on the Newlyn artists, said 'Stanhope Forbes' "Fish Sale" manifests the finest quality of natural art. It is a triumph of true pictorial visition. And to see pictorially the simple truth of nature is the first of arts.' (*Art Journal*, 1889). Her husband, Wilfred Meynell, also a writer on art and an enthusiast for Newlyn painting, later reminded his readers: 'Who can forget its gradations of greys, its air of pearls? It was a picture which besides being delightful in itself, awakened expectations, and those expectations have since been realised. If it did not make an era in English Art, it began to make one.' (Wilfred Meynell, *Art Journal* 1892). However it was Norman Garstin who best captured in words the effect of this freshness and directness of approach, and the welcome contrast it made to an Academy so steeped in convention:

> *The fresh vitality of it seemed like a wholesome breeze from the sea breathed in a studio reeking with oil and turpentine, while its brilliant new technique fell upon the younger painters as a revelation.* (Norman Garstin 'The Work of Stanhope A Forbes ARA', *The Studio,* Vol. 23 1901).

The 'Fish Sale' was the only painting by Forbes at the Royal Academy in 1885, but it indicated a direction for his work, that of the large figure-group. More importantly it was a turning point in the development of *plein air* painting, and public acclaim for the picture also encouraged other artists in Newlyn. Forbes was recognised as an innovator and his leadership was accepted in the growing community, and from that time the Newlyn artists began to be seen as a group with a considered point of view, likely to change the direction of English painting.

There was constant movement in Newlyn as artists came and went. They visited Newlyn as they had done the ports of Brittany, to paint for a few weeks or months, returning for a winter's work in London or the Midlands. But increasingly they came to stay. By the time Stanhope Forbes arrived in 1884 the first settlers were already firmly established. Walter Langley and his young family were at Pembroke Lodge in Newlyn Town, Edwin Harris was living at Cliff Castle (a house later owned by Forbes). This was the year in which the greatest number of artists came to Newlyn for the first time. They included Ralph Todd and Leghe Suthers, who was to visit regularly for ten years; Henry Tuke from Falmouth; Frank Bramley and Fred Hall. who were soon followed by

STANHOPE FORBES

*Fish Sale on
a Newlyn Beach.*

oil on canvas, 1060 x 1520mm.

CITY OF PLYMOUTH MUSEUM AND
ART GALLERY.

another of Verlat's students, Norman Garstin. From Paris came Chevallier Tayler, the painter of historical tableaux, and A. H. Rheam. The *Cornishman* reported that by September there were no less than twenty-seven artists residing in Newlyn.

As the colony grew, so it found its own momentum and reasons for existence:

> They found friendship and the camaraderie of the ateliers of Paris and Antwerp, a sympathy with each others intentions, a mild climate suitable for out-of-door work, a grey-roofed village overhanging a lovely bay – these were the determining causes that led the young artists setting up their easels hard by the Cornish sea, and the same causes, ended by that cumulative sedative called habit, have held many of them there ever since. (Norman Garstin, *op. cit.*).

In the narrow streets of Newlyn good lodgings were not always available; one of the best and most used by the artists was Mrs Madden's house, Belleview, which stood back from the village on Chywoone Hill, far enough above the harbour to avoid the reek of fish, yet with fine views of the bay. Stanhope Forbes came there in April 1884: 'The rooms are very good, especially the sitting room which is large and looks towards the sea... but the great attraction of this place is the situation which is worth anything in this relaxing and fishy place...' He appreciated Mrs Madden's attentive housekeeping but her

religious views did not coincide with his own brand of free-thinking aetheism: 'she is a strict Sabbatarian, who considers even letter writing to be a breach of the Lord's Commandment...'. Accordingly he was not able to paint on Sundays. 'I am told Mrs Madden would turn me out bag and baggage if I were to paint or otherwise break the day. Apart from this, she is a nice old dame, and the first week's bill was moderate – £1.4.0, ten shillings for the rooms fourteen shillings for goods.' (1 June 1884).

In a series of letters to his mother, Forbes recounted the daily gossip of Newlyn, 'The Langleys came back a week ago and are in high glee, for he has sold his picture for 400 guineas.' (Belleview, undated). 'I know everyone in the place – lots of pretty girls, and babies for the Governor (his father) to talk to – you can visit these folk, see them in their houses, contrast them with the Bretons'. (21 July 1884). 'Fletcher has just arrived, and is going to dwell in this house, but we are to have separate rooms.' (6 August 1884). 'They are flocking in here every day.' (16 September 1884). In July 1885, 'A new man Detmold, a very clever painter who arrived here in this house, and Craft is also back. Bodilly I see much of. He is great on the fishing.' (14 July 1885). All of this news is interspersed with reports of dinners with the Harrises, musical evenings, further arrivals and departures. Ingram was there in October 1886; in 1887 Tayler was back. Napier Hemy, the sea painter from Falmouth, stayed there and Craft returned for a few days. In May '87 'A jolly little party' – Craft, Detmold and Forbes. Forbes recalled the feast to celebrate Langley's temporary departure from Newlyn '... we shall all miss his vivacity and high spirits at our social gatherings'. As the members left Belleview at two in the morning, they formed a line and marched through the village headed by Langley with his

A group of Artists from Newlyn, photographed, probably, in Autumn 1884.

Left to right standing:
Frank Bodilly, Fred Millard,
Frank Bramley,
William Blandford Fletcher,
William Breakespeare,
Ralph Todd,
Alexander Chevallier Tayler,
Henry Scott Tuke.

Left to right seated:
William Wainwright,
Edwin Harris, Stanhope Forbes.

banjo singing 'as we went home by the light of the moon.' (18 April 1886). In June 1887 Stanhope Forbes gave up his rooms with Mrs Madden. For the three years he had been at Belleview it was the centre of a convivial and hard-working band of artists.

Not all of the artists who came to Newlyn had the abilities or the ambitions of Langley, Bramley or Forbes. Ralph Todd (1856–1932) had studied at the South Kensington Schools, where he won several major prizes, and came to Newlyn in 1883 after some years in Paris, the Netherlands and Belgium. He was the eldest son of a wealthy family but his father disapproved of him becoming a painter and refused to give him financial support.

When Forbes arrived in Newlyn, he and Todd became close friends. They dined together twice a week and kept Sundays free for walking. Forbes was sympathetic to his friend's difficult financial circumstances, but had a low opinion of his work as an artist. 'Todd poor fellow, in an awful state and I cannot open his eyes. He has no art in him and were he to paint for ever would do no real good work'. (Forbes always referred to him as 'Todd poor fellow'). Later Forbes wrote: 'Todd poor fellow is in a bad way... with I believe 6d in the world. It is I believe a hopeless case. His father does not answer his letters – his last communications have been to the effect that he might pawn the shirt off his back and paint signboards for he would do nothing for him'. (March 1884).

In spite of extreme financial difficulties, Todd persevered with his work, and his paintings, especially in portraiture, began to improve. He was relieved to have his work accepted by the Academy for the first time in 1895 with the painting 'Early Morning – the Latest News'. This apparently led to a family reconciliation. Forbes found him 'in good spirits and going up to town shortly to paint his father's portrait' (19 May 1885). But the success did not last and he showed at the Academy on only two further occasions, both with somewhat ominous titles 'A Darkened Hour' (1882) and 'The Prodigal's Return' (1883). The latter painting was ambitious and depicted the returning son who finds that his father has died before he reached home and he weeps tears of repentance and self-reproach upon the coffin. The bereaved mother holds out her arms to him in forgiveness. Todd treats this hackneyed subject, with a portentious seriousness perhaps influenced by his own experiences with his father.

Todd was a close friend of Fred Millard with whom he shared a studio in Newlyn near the corner of the Rue des Beaux Arts, which F. W. Bourdillon described: 'You looked across the steep road, over a wall into a field generally blooming with cabbages and fruit trees, in the lower corner of which was planted the wooden shanty which serves Millard and Todd as a studio, and along the top of which, on a sort of raised terrace, was a fine and flourishing forest of the common or garden rhubarb.' (letter to his sister 8.8.1850). However their friendship was badly damaged because they were in competition for the affections of the same lady.

Todd's best work was quiet landscape views of Newlyn, market scenes and groups of fisher folk. He developed a considerable skill in watercolour and Forbes remarked upon his 'astonishing progress' in this medium. (1.2.86.). He used a stippling technique popular with other members of the Newlyn group, particularly Langley, but his figures have a woodenness and lack of refinement that distance them from Langley's. Todd showed in the Academy only three times, in 1885, 1887 and 1893. He exhibited regularly in Birmingham, where his work found favour and at the Royal Institute of Painters in Watercolours, the New Watercolour Society and the Royal Society of British Artists.

Todd lived in Newlyn for nine years, and then for most of the remainder of his life in nearby Helston, finally moving to St Keverne on the Lizard peninsula.

Another member was Fred Millard who in 1880 was one of a group of artists, including Blandford Fletcher, painting *en plein air* in Belgium and northern France. With his friend Henry Tuke, Millard became a fellow student at Lauren's studio in Paris in 1881–82. He was photographed with the other English students at Laurens looking younger and less confident than his companions. Perhaps this was symptomatic of the minor role that he was to play in Newlyn.

Forbes mentions his arrival in Newlyn in April 1884, 'a man named Millard from Reigate who is a friend of Todd', describing him as 'a decent fellow and an acquisition to our society'. Millard was a friendly if somewhat unremarkable character who took part in social occasions, and only once raised Forbes to confess to 'Feeling very very jealous of people like Millard who are settling down and marrying'. (27 May 1886). (This was at a time when Forbes' own marriage plans, in respect of Elizabeth Armstrong, seem to have been giving problems). Little of Millard's work in Newlyn is known, and what survives is not of high quality, although he had work accepted in the Academy in 1885, 1887 and 1888.

William Teulon Blandford Fletcher (1859–1936) trod the same paths as other Newlyn artists but because of his early departure from the town shared little in their successes. He was born into a solid and successful Nonconformist family, and his father, a Freeman of the City of London, was a prosperous linen draper. At the age of sixteen, despite family opposition, he entered the South Kensington School of Art, at the same time as the somewhat older Walter Langley. Fletcher won the silver medal and the Queen's prize and was encouraged by the newly appointed Director, Edward Poynter, to continue his training in Europe. Fletcher joined Verlat's Académie Royale in Antwerp, for:

> *Living in those days was cheap in Antwerp, a bed-sitting room (which was all most students could afford) with coffee and 3 buttered rolls for breakfast (known as 'pistolets') costing but 20f to 25f per month. Dinner at a very tolerable hotel could be obtained for 40f a month. Supper was prepared on the bed-sitting room stove and consisted merely of coffee with sugar (but rarely milk) and bread and cheese or butter. (William Teulon Blandford Fletcher, A Painter of Village Life, by Nancy Hood, Oxford 1986).*

For several summers Fletcher joined the groups of English artists in the country districts of northern France painting at Quimperlé, Pont-Aven, Dinan and Mont St Michel. Some of his best figure studies were done on these early visits. On one such visit he met, and was greatly impressed by Bastien-Lepage, who was then working with his own students. His first exhibit at the Royal Academy in 1884, 'The Kitchen Garden in November', was a painting of Brittany.

After his European training it was natural for Blandford Fletcher to join Forbes, who he had come to know in Brittany, and other friends in Newlyn. He came in August 1884, took rooms with Mrs Madden at Belleview and stayed eight months, working with great determination on a large painting entitled 'Dame Grigson's Academy'. The picture is of a Newlyn courtyard in which a village teacher, Dame Grigson, gives lessons to her small group of children in the sun. As in Forbes' painting there is exploration of character and gentle social comment, and a similar attention to the details of everyday life, but it

RALPH TODD

Newlyn, 1884.

oil on panel, 300 x 445mm.

PRIVATE COLLECTION.

FRED MILLARD

Cornish Girl with Basket of Primroses, 1884.

oil on canvas

ROYAL CORNWALL MUSEUM, TRURO.

lacks the strength of composition and the fluent figure painting that Forbes had by now achieved. 'Dame Grigson's Academy' was exhibited at the Royal Academy in 1885, the same year as Forbes' 'Fish Sale'.

It is difficult to understand Fletcher's decision to leave Newlyn when this picture was finished, at a time when the tide of public attention was beginning to run in favour of the Newlyn artists. Perhaps it was comparison with Forbes and the feeling of unwelcome competition that made him look for other venues more in tune with his vision of rural England. In May 1885 he left Newlyn for Berkshire with Chevallier Tayler. Forbes was sorry to see him go, and he referred to Fletcher as 'the best comrade I know'. (31 May 1885). However, he kept in touch with his friends in Newlyn, particularly Tuke, Bramley and Chevallier Tayler, and was drawn into the discussions that led to the formation of the New English Art Club. One of his letters to Chevallier Tayler asked: 'What do you think of the English Art Club business? I keep getting letters and circulars, some of them so ambiguous I can't make nothink of nothink out of this'. (W.T.B.F. *Memoirs, op.cit.*).

For some years Fletcher travelled in the South West of England, mainly in Berkshire in the Vale of the White Horse, painting gentle paintings of the life of the villages and the quieter country backwaters, in soft earth colours and greys. He continued to show at the Royal Academy, but his work achieved little notice and only limited success. In 1894 he married, and his wife joined his travelling life. Later they settled in Abingdon where he lived for the last part of his life, a withdrawn and somewhat morose man, until his death in 1936.

WILLIAM BLANDFORD FLETCHER

Dame Grigson's Academy, 1885.

This is Fletcher's major Newlyn painting on which he worked for most of a year. Taken from a photograph of the only known surviving print.

oil on canvas, 1100 x 1500mm.

PRIVATE COLLECTION.

At first Stanhope Forbes welcomed Henry Detmold (1854–1924) and described him as a 'clever painter' when he moved into Belleview in July 1885. However on further acquaintance he decided 'I shall never make a chum of him' and referred to him as 'that disagreeable fellow'. Detmold was not a popular man, he disagreed with Bateman, and soon fell foul of Forbes. This friction between the two artists grew even deeper when they became rivals for the affections of Miss Armstrong, and in April 1886 Forbes writes 'I shall have to play my cards with great care.' Later that year Forbes was annoyed to see that a painting by Detmold, which had been rejected twice by the Royal Academy, now hung 'on the line'.

Little is known of Detmold's life, but it is thought that he had a European training with considerable periods of study in Dusseldorf, Brussels and Munich, and in Paris at the studio of Carolus-Duran. In later life he made frequent trips abroad, as his many paintings of Algiers and San Remo in Italy testify. He was known as a Francophile, and often visited Paris. From 1882 to 1898 he became a regular exhibitor at the Royal Academy, he also had a long connection with the Royal Birmingham Society of Artists with whom he exhibited over the same period.

In 1889, in Alice Meynell's comprehensive article on Newlyn, Detmold's painting 'Departure of the Fishing Fleet' received favourable comment. The arrangement of the painting is obviously similar to that of Forbes' 'Fish Sale' – a high horizon, boats about to sail on a calm sea 'the sails soon to be absorbed by the warm and tender mist', and a group of figures in the foreground. But Detmold had adopted a high viewpoint, a grassy cliff-top overlooking the sea, rather than the wet sands of Forbes. The figures which Detmold includes are those who are left behind when the fleet goes to sea - the women and children and one old man whose fishing days are over, but in 'whose garments a whole career was written in their attitude'. Alice Meynell found the painting of the sea, with its beautiful lucid surface 'an intricate and yet distinctly impressionary study'. (*Magazine of Art* 1889 p.140).

In 1892 the *Magazine of Art* described Detmold as a prominent member of the Newlyn School, and acknowledged his success at the First Exhibition of the New English Art Club. Detmold's talents were described as:

accurate in drawing, reticent in colour, subtle in tone, he was yet charged in his earlier days, with being too precise and photographic. These faults have now disappeared, and along with a diligent and fruitful study of atmospheric effects of sea and of sky, and with greater ease and facility of execution, have come a more poetic method of realising nature, and a happy combination of the modern teaching of the Schools of France and Holland.

Detmold probably left Newlyn shortly after the article was written. For some years he had a studio in London and later he lived in Hastings.

Work by the Newlyn artists was now seen frequently in the London galleries, and Newlyn became more clearly identified as an artists' colony. Painters working in the steep streets of the town, or on the quays ringed with a crowd of curious onlookers, were a common sight. The artists' group took on a more settled existence, with time for relaxation and enjoyment. There was a strong sense of community among the artists, and they devised their own pleasures and pastimes. In summer there was walking and fishing, and excursions by wagonette to picnic in Lamorna Valley, or to St Ives to visit other artists. In winter they gave supper parties, or social evenings at which music played an important part. Few of the 'good' houses were without a piano, and a number of the artists became proficient performers. Forbes greatly enjoyed these occasions and taught himself to play the cello which he had acquired as a property for his painting 'The Village Philharmonic' (1880).

When the Newlyn artists began to be recognised as a group, it was their French influence that was most often remarked upon. Earlier academic painting in England emphasised the importance of preparatory drawings which described the form shape by shape, or modelled surface against background, worked-up compositions which tended to be rigid and sterile. Colour, light, surface and texture were all sacrificed for ease of organisation, and the complexities of nature were reduced to formulae. The new message of the *plein air* painters brought more direct and testing ways of observing nature, contending with all the subtleties of changing light and movement and demanding a continuous effort of detailed examination. They preferred grey days, when the sun was behind clouds, in order to work for as long as possible without strong changes of light and shade. The human figure presented special problems however, and sometimes elaborate arrangements were necessary, with individual figures posed one by one on the open beach, on the pier, or in a cottage interior. Where this was not possible, theatrical arrangements might be made in the studio, often using elaborate set pieces and furnished interiors, but still with the human model.

*Plein-air*ism, the message that Stanhope Forbes brought to Newlyn from France, was described as 'a combination of Gallic clarity and British level headedness'. ('Stanhope Forbes' by C. Lewis Hind, *Art Journal*, Christmas 1911). It was not a revolt against academic conventions but rather an instinctive desire to work directly from the human figure in its everyday environment or, as Forbes put it from 'nature'. 'Nature' he said 'is hard to beat! I advise you to approach her with reverence and to take what she gives you and be contented'.

The young artists were fired with the same enthusiasm: to work in the open air and to record the life of their own time – people at work, or in their homes. Newlyn appealed to them for the same reasons as the villages of Normandy and Brittany – it was somewhat old fashioned and picturesque and had a similarly timeless quality. The Newlyn artists felt a sense of high ambition, part of the the same endeavour that had moved the great masters of the past, who had left such a fine record of the time and places in which they had lived and painted.

— 4 —

FRIENDS FROM THE SLADE

There was a vitality about the newly formed Slade School of Art in London. Any lack of tradition was more than made up for by the verve and liveliness of its students and it attracted some of the most talented of the young generation, including a number who came to Newlyn: Henry Tuke, Thomas Gotch, Percy Craft, Alexander Chevallier Tayler and Frank Wright Bourdillon were among them. The Slade School, founded in 1871 as part of University College, London, offered the most enlightened training then available in England. Under its first Professor, Edward Poynter, it modelled itself upon the French system, which gave the students greater freedom and purpose. Drawing from the figure held a central place in the curriculum, together with direct painting from the figure and copies from the old masters.

HENRY TUKE
Self Portrait, 1879.
etching

In 1875 Edward Poynter left the School to revitalise the South Kensington Schools. The Slade's close connection with France was further reinforced by his successor, the French realist painter Alphonse Legros (1837–1911), and its character changed. In the 1860s Legros had been at the centre of advanced artistic movements in Paris, one of the circle of younger artists around Manet and a close friend of Whistler and Monet. His teaching was based upon observation and the training of visual memory, and his own paintings were mainly peasant scenes and the work of the country – realism compounded with morality – which expressed the grim sadness in the daily monotony of labour. His social awareness affected many of the students who worked under him. Two of these students, Henry Tuke and Thomas Gotch, witnessed the demonstrations of portraiture that Legros gave. His poor command of the English language was more than compensated for by his ability to provide such evidence of his skills, and in the 1870s he toured Great Britain doing one hour portrait demonstrations in public.

Henry Tuke (1858–1929), was an unusually gifted student who entered the Slade in 1875 at the age of sixteen. Tuke was born into a Quaker medical family from York; his father Daniel Hack Tuke, was a leading authority on psychological medicine. His practice was in Whitby and it was here that he met and married Esther Maria Stickney, known as 'Essy'. Soon after Henry's birth, because of a breakdown of Dr Tuke's health, the family moved to Falmouth, to a house at the western end of Woodlane, where their daughter Maria was born in 1861. A later move to a larger house in Florence Terrace, with a view over the bay, gave Henry one of his earliest memories as he watched the vessel *Marmion* wrecked in a great storm one Sunday morning. In this educated household Henry had a free outdoor life, bathing and boating, long walks in the countryside and excursions to other Quaker houses of friends – to Penjerrick where kind old Robert Weare Fox and his redoubtable daughter Anna Maria lived, or to Penmare where Alfred Lloyd Fox would show the children his treasures from Palestine. However to provide greater opportunities for the education of the children, the family moved to London.

At the Slade Henry Tuke soon attracted attention. In 1877 he was awarded a Scholarship of £50 which allowed him to go abroad for the first time, to Belgium and France, and to make a summer painting visit to Normandy and Paris. He greatly admired French painting and showed a particular aptitude for painting from the figure and portraiture. In l879, while still a student, he had his first success at the Royal Academy with a small painting 'The Good Samaritan' and an etching.

Tuke's friends at the Slade included Joseph Benwell Clark, William Strang and George Percy Jacomb-Hood, but the most important friendship of these early years was with an older student, Thomas Gotch (1854–1931) who came later to the School. One of four sons from a wealthy family in Kettering, Northamptonshire, manufacturers of boots and shoes and with interests in banking, Thomas worked for a time in the family business, before coming to London to study at Heatherly's School of Art. Here he met and formed a lasting friendship with a fellow student Caroline Burland Yates, they were to meet later at the Slade School. Thomas studied in Antwerp for a few months before joining the Slade for the next two years. He and Tuke became close friends, they went for long walks in the countryside together, shared their love of music and admired the work of Burne-Jones and Whistler at the first exhibition of the new Grosvenor Gallery. In the summer of 1879 they travelled to Falmouth to sketch, fish and bathe. Gotch visited Caroline Yates who was staying in Newlyn and both students formed an attachment for the town which lasted for their lifetimes.

That autumn Gotch and Tuke became members of the 'Pioneers', a club formed by Henry Tuke's brother Willie as a meeting place for medical students and art students, who held 'Free Discussions and Social Intercourse'. Tom Gotch spoke on 'Life and Art', but the existence of the club was threatened when more radical and taboo subjects such as 'Free Love' were discussed, leading to the withdrawal of the more timid female members. At this time the outrageous personalities of Tite Street, Oscar Wilde and James McNeill Whistler, were the talk of London. George du Maurier had caricatured them in *Punch* and their 'aesthetic' doctrines had been parodied by W. S. Gilbert in his new comic opera *Patience* which opened in 188l and which mocked the 'greenery, yallery' style of decoration and dress advocated by Wilde.

This description of the young Tom Gotch by a fellow student reflects the sophistication in the London art world:

> *Gotch stood out among the students; not excluding those girls whose limp costumes had "greenery, yallery, Grosvenor Gallery" tints and hues. We regarded him as a true Tolstoyan, always eager to do everything for himself except cooking his own meals during his long hours of work in the horrid life-class. He wore one suit of clothes that was a genuine costume, designed, cut out and made by himself – knee-breeches and an original tunic in Burnell serge, peacock blue in colour, choicely piped and lined with cashmere of an art green. Yet it looked quite alright; for Gotch, then very young, was golden-haired and fresh complexioned.* (Walter Shaw Sparrow *Memories of Life and Art Through Sixty Years*, p.100–101).

In the autumn of 1880 Gotch and Tuke went their separate ways. Caroline Yates was already in Paris at Julian's Academy. Thomas Gotch followed. Their friendship developed rapidly and in the following year, whilst on a visit to Newlyn, they were married. Returning to Paris, Caroline continued her studies at Julian's Academy. Thomas preferred the more testing and heady atmosphere of J. P. Laurens studio. To his friend Tuke he wrote:

I like Laurens, he is very original in composition and interests himself in it. The noise, the heat, the smoke and the students generally, depress me beyond measure, and I am played out pretty soon every day, but one learns... (Maria Tuke Sainsbury *Henry Scott Tuke, A Memoir*).

In April 1882, with Caroline expecting their first child, the Gotches moved to Brolles, on the outskirts of Paris, a rural neighbourhood, where they could work out of doors. Their daughter Phyllis was born there. The following year Caroline's poor health brought them back to England and they decided to spend that summer painting in Newlyn. Gotch converted a fisherman's loft into a studio and they began to work.

Henry Tuke meanwhile had returned to Italy, which he had visited in the previous year. After five years at the Slade, but still only twenty-two years old his painting advanced considerably in the home of the great humanist tradition. From the winter of 1880 until the following summer he worked in the streets and galleries of Florence, with visits to other northern Italian towns. He made copies of Titian's 'Holy Family and St Anthony' and Corregio's 'Madonna'. Tuke wrote to his sister Maria 'I am going in heavily for naturalism now... It is a very odd thing that I have been much more influenced since I came here by Mr Lemon, than by the old masters. He is a first-rater.' (Maria Tuke Sainsbury, *op.cit.*). Arthur Lemon (1850–1911) was an older painter living in Florence who had been brought up in Rome. He was an expatriate Manxman who had spent some years in America as a cowboy and cattle dealer and was an advocate of *plein-air* painting.

Tuke and Lemon spent the summer months on the coast, at Pietra Santa near Livorno, painting the white cattle, the low woods and the sun-browned boys playing and bathing in the sea. Tuke wrote in his diary 'We have done several nude boys on the beach which is more useful than anything for me.

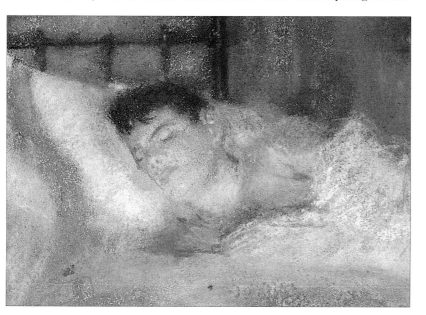

WILLIAM WAINWRIGHT

Portraits of Thomas and Caroline Gotch, 1882.

watercolour, each 175 x 110mm.

On each portrait is inscribed 'A Souvenir of 1881' – the year of Tom and Caroline Gotch's wedding.

PRIVATE COLLECTION.

HENRY TUKE

Ambrose, 1888.

pastel, 160 x 220mm.

TUKE COLLECTION, ROYAL CORNWALL POLYTECHNIC SOCIETY.

They sit till they are incapable of sitting any more and are richly rewarded with twopence'. (Maria Tuke Sainsbury, *op.cit.*). In later years Tuke's paintings of the nude in sunlight became his best known subject, although in Victorian times the naked human body was a matter of shame unless covered by the cloak of classical allusion.

Towards the end of the year Tuke followed his friends to Laurens' atelier in Paris, joining Tom Gotch and others including Fred Millard, William Wainwright, Jacomb-Hood and von Glehn. Tuke entered into the rich and varied life of Paris, his painting broadened and he took every opportunity to work out of doors in the country around Paris and the coast. He became friendly with the painter Jacques Emile Blanche, whose father was a doctor in Passy, and occupied a studio in their house. There he met such notable personalities as Puvis de Chevannes and Oscar Wilde. He also came to know John Sargent in Paris and made visits to Bastien-Lepage, where he saw 'many things of surpassing beauty'. He was part of a civilised and sophisticated group of young artists, already conscious of their achievements and of the value of working directly from nature. These were years of apprenticeship, absorbing new principles in painting, which they would soon carry back to England.

Tuke returned to England in 1882, and in September travelled to Devon on a painting holiday with his friend Jacomb-Hood. Hood later recalled how Tuke in his methodical and persevering way worked steadily on a largish canvas in full sunlight, painting a village lad asleep in the boughs of an apple tree, the blue sky and sea beyond. This painting was shown in the following year at the Paris Salon under the title 'Un Jour de Paresse' (A Lazy Day). (Jacomb-Hood *With Brush and Pencil*, Murray 1925).

Tuke made his first extended visit to Newlyn in 1883 at the suggestion of Tom Gotch who was already there on a painting visit. He stayed in Philip Harvey's house in Trewarveneth Street overlooking the bay. Between September and November he completed several paintings, mainly in and around Philip Harvey's sail loft and cellar, with the Harvey family as models. Tuke wrote to his sister 'I have found a very fascinating cellar under our house, which is alive with subjects; there are lots of nets and boat's "appurtenances", and I have a lad making a schooner, while a maid converses with him.' Another painting 'Dinner Time' done in the sail loft was of a boy about to eat a pasty:

> The model has the fine name of Ambrose Ruffignac, of a family of French extraction. If you have got so grand as to keep a tiger (house boy) he would do very well, he is very paintable and has a nice Cornish accent. I am painting the portrait of Philip Harvey and his cousin Tom, in exchange for two boats they are making me, one for sailing and one a model... (Maria Tuke *op.cit.*).

Portraiture was a major part of Tuke's work in those early years, and a ready source of fees. For the winter he returned to London to arrange sittings in a borrowed studio, and at the end of May took the overnight train back to Newlyn. By now Stanhope Forbes and Chevallier Tayler had joined the group of artists, and Tuke spent the summer in his usual way, painting out of doors, sailing, bathing and enjoying pleasant social evenings. He wrote '... Newlyn is looking more bewitching than ever, I only wonder why I didn't come down sooner, it is now simply reeking with subjects...' (Registers). In all Tuke painted only six or seven paintings in Newlyn plus two portraits (of Philip and Tom Harvey) and some pastel sketches, but for the months that he was there he was an important member of the group. He was rapidly making a reputation in

London through his connection with the picture dealer C. W. Dowdeswell, whose portrait he had painted, and who was increasingly selling work by the Newlyn artists from his gallery in Bond Street. Stanhope Forbes who was painting 'The Fish Sale' was encouraged by Tuke's enthusiasm for this painting, in his turn he described Tuke as 'the best of painters in Newlyn'. On the cliffs he painted a double portrait of Philip and Janie Harvey, and one of Sarah Ann Stevenson in Walter Langley's orchard. One of Tuke's last Newlyn paintings was painted from his first boat 'Ripple' which he bought in Newlyn, and another 'Summer Time' shows two local boys, John Wesley Kitching, stripped to the waist, and John Ruffignac Cotton, sitting in Philip Harvey's punt 'Little Argo' 'As I carried it about all the boys would call out "There's John Wesley all naked!"' wrote Tuke. There was a sad sequel to this which Tuke also recorded 'Kitching was killed or drowned at Cowes in the Autumn of 1905 and one of his shipmates was tried for murder but acquitted. Another shipmate who was concerned hung himself in his yacht' (Registers).

In appearence Tuke was not unlike a sailor – sturdy, broad shouldered, with dark hair and moustache, a suspicion of a sea roll in his walk and a watchful manner. He was unconventional by the standards of the day, and relaxed in his attitude to work. He was a swift worker, rising early and painting before breakfast, so there was always time for sailing or swimming. To be in a boat on water was a continuous attraction, and formed his major subject, together with the figure, usually male and nude. He was sociable and was welcomed by a large circle of friends in London, Falmouth and on his visits to Newlyn and St Ives.

Part of that summer was spent with a painter friend from St Ives, William Ayerst Ingram, on a chartered yacht, *Verbena*, from which the two artists made watercolour studies of the sea and ports from the Needles to Falmouth. Some of Tuke's first sketches done afloat were made from this boat. In the painting 'Any Orders My Lord?', the steward of the *Verbena* stands in the doorway between the saloon and the fo'c's'le; Tuke is shadowed in the mirror. The following winter was again spent in London, where Tuke worked on portraits, a number of which were shown at the Academy in 1885. Tuke was now able to command the very respectable sum of one hundred guineas for a full-length portrait.

In May 1885, after a further visit to London to work on portraits, Tuke again took the train to the west, but this time stopped in Falmouth 'to look for new pastures'. He walked out to Pennance and found lodgings in a cottage amidst the ruins of the old arsenic works which overlooked the bay between Swanpool and Pennance Point. This was to be his home for the rest of his life. He returned to Newlyn for brief visits, and remained on good terms with a number of the Newlyn artists, but he was no longer identified with them. When asked about this he referred to the artists' group in Falmouth and said: 'No; we consider ourselves quite a distinct branch of the brotherhood, and we are a congenial set too'. (Flora Klickman, 'The Life Story of a Famous Painter', *Windsor Magazine* 1895).

The Gotches were among the first artists to visit Newlyn, but did not move there for several years; most of their time was spent in London. Thomas Gotch's earliest known painting of Newlyn was 'Mental Arithmetic' (1883), painted on a sketching visit, out of doors on the slip. It is a study of age in which an old fisherman looks quizzically at a cup of tea offered by a young girl.* The

---

* This painting was sold to a relative of Tom Gotch who lived in Australia, and who later presented it to the National Gallery, Melbourne.

HENRY TUKE

Jack Rolling on the Julie of Nantes, 1888.

oil on panel, 235 x 140mm.

THE TREHAYES COLLECTION.

following year the Gotches made the long journey to Australia, where Thomas Gotch had a family connection in Melbourne. Both Thomas and Caroline exhibited their work there, and Thomas was involved in the formation of the Anglo-Australian Society of Artists, which later became the Royal British Colonial Society of Artists.

Returning to England they again visited Penzance where they met Stanhope Forbes for the first time in December 1885. The following summer they met again in Newlyn, at a reception given by Frank Bodilly, whose wife was a sister of Caroline Gotch. Forbes later recorded that he found Gotch 'a weak sort of creature' (18.7.86), and he was equally critical of Caroline, 'I do not think that I shall like her as well as Mrs Bodilly. She's more lively, but somehow "je ne coutonne pas a elle"'. Forbes later compared Gotch to an unmade bed, and Caroline as 'very aesthetic (a term of criticism) and untidy'. Despite these poor first impressions Forbes came to appreciate the Gotches' hospitality and friendship, and accepted Caroline's eccentricities.

In 1886 Thomas Gotch was greatly occupied with the formation of the New English Art Club and its first exhibition in April that year. He and Caroline appeared in Newlyn briefly in the summer, and for a longer period in the autumn, but the repercussions of the first exhibition of the New English Art Club was the chief subject of conversation among the artists, together with the scandalous activities of Whistler and his 'gang'. Whistler had become President of the old established, but moribund Society of British Artists. He presented a 'loyal address' to the Queen in her Golden Jubilee year and earned the Society the title of 'Royal', but his autocratic behaviour and radical approach to the Society's exhibition greatly angered the older members. Gotch at first admired Whistler's contributions to the Society, but later had an important difference of opinion with him over the hanging of the exhibition. The ensuing arguments and acrimony may have had much to do with the Gotches' decision to take up more permanent residence in Newlyn. In July 1887 they moved into the Malt House.

Thomas Gotch was reflective and inward-looking, he often appeared dreamy and unworldly, but his wide-ranging imagination challenged the more pedestrian aspects of realist painting. During his first years in Newlyn, Gotch had accepted the discipline of *plein air* painting, and found his subjects as others did, in domestic scenes and coastal and harbour views. A typical painting of this time is 'Sharing Fish' (1891) in which a group of women on the beach share out the catch beneath the sea wall. This work clearly recalls Forbes' 'Fish Sale', it too depicts a group of women in shawls and aprons and the glistening fish upon the sand. Gotch's model for the younger woman was a Newlyn girl Mary Rowe, who had posed as the bride in Forbes' 'Health of the Bride'. But Gotch's picture lacks atmospheric qualities and by comparison with Forbes' painting, is unconvincing in its realism. The best of Gotch's early work in Newlyn is seen in his many delicate landscapes, in oil and watercolour. His figure paintings also show considerable technical skill but at this time he was not able to develop that imaginative symbolism that he would later capture.

THOMAS GOTCH

Cottage Interior with a Woman Peeling Potatoes c.1888.

385 x 230mm.

PRIVATE COLLECTION.

After her arrival in Newlyn, Caroline Gotch continued to paint and her studies of women and children such as 'Girl Among Chrysanthemums' have delicacy and simplicity, but she was less successful with the more complex figure groups that she occasionally attempted. However she went to considerable pains in creating these groups. Her painting 'In The Midst of Life We Are In Death' (1891) is a cottage scene in which the grieving family gather round the body of a drowned young seaman. For this Caroline Gotch had photographs taken of local people somewhat stiffly taking the poses required by the artist. This painting was exhibited at the Royal Academy in 1891 and later at the prestigious exhibition of paintings from Cornwall held in the Nottingham Museum and Art Gallery in September 1894.

Alexander Chevallier Tayler (1862–1925) was the son of an Essex solicitor. He went to the Slade at the age of seventeen and later became a close friend of Stanhope Forbes. Both came from professional backgrounds, but as Forbes described 'not overburdened with worldly wealth'. Chevallier Tayler was fortunate in gaining a scholarship (which was rare at this time) to the Slade. His two years there were followed by two years in Paris and Normandy, mostly in company with his friends from the Slade, Tom Gotch and Henry Tuke. He was in Paris, at Laurens' Atelier in 1881–82, and may also have spent some time at the studio of Carolus-Duran whilst Forbes was there.

Tayler's first painting to be exhibited at the Royal Academy was 'Interior of a Country Druggist's' painted in 1884, shortly before his first visit to Newlyn. In Newlyn Tayler joined Forbes and Blandford Fletcher at Belleview. Forbes wrote 'Tayler has turned up with all his goods and chattels and so far all is harmony in the little menage.' (2l September 1884). This first visit lasted about a month, but Tayler returned in the following February to work on his Academy submission (which was unsuccessful), and in May he left again to accompany Fletcher on a

CAROLINE GOTCH

Paul Church, 1881.

A student painting done in the year of her wedding to Tom Gotch.

ALAN SHEARS FINE ART.

CAROLINE GOTCH

In the Midst of Life we are in Death, 1894.

Illustrated in the catalogue *Cornish Painters of Newlyn, St Ives and Falmouth 1894*, Nottingham Art Gallery, No. 50.

CAROLINE GOTCH

Photograph of a studio set up for *In the Midst of Life we are in Death*, 1894.

Painters of Newlyn, St Ives and Falmouth 1894, Nottingham Art Gallery, No. 50.

ALAN SHEARS FINE ART.

painting trip to Berkshire. Although they had only recently become friends, Tayler's company was missed by Forbes:

> *for he improves each day on acquaintance, and I have found living in this manner so infinitely more pleasant than when alone, that I quite dread it. True I shall have Fletcher, but he is a bit morose, and has not the cheerful influence of the other man.* (2 October 1884).

In the first years Tayler's visits to Newlyn were short but he was a popular figure and Stanhope Forbes made many friendly references to their joint excursions and social occasions – and to Tayler's large appetite. His only weak point, in Forbes' opinion, is that he will go to church. But Tayler had little success with the sale of his work, although he was willing to offer paintings at ridiculously low prices. Forbes did all he could to help and wrote to a dealer friend:

Poor Tayler he has no luck at all, never sells anything. There are so many in the same plight, but few I should better like to succeed... I suppose he has not that same grit you were referring to the other day. I wonder why the men without it seem so much more likeable... Fortunately there are better things than doing fine pictures and becoming famous.' (3l May 1885).

Tayler's first two paintings from Newlyn to be exhibited at the Academy were both shown in 1886. They were 'Not Lost but Gone Before' and 'Portrait of F. W. Bourdillon'. In the following year – described by Forbes as 'a triumph for Newlyn' – Tayler's large painting 'Bless O God, These Gifts To Our Use', was well shown. It portrays the quiet consolations of domestic family life. In a Newlyn cottage interior a family group is assembled for supper and grace is being said. This is not a household depleted by loss, for the seafaring husband is there, as are three generations from the aged grandparent to the baby in the

Albert Chevallier Tayler and Henry Tuke *(right)*.

cradle. The painting delicately describes the play of light from the cottage window falling upon the surfaces of the room – the white tablecloth, the women's garments and the various tones of walls and floor. In its moral message, restrained treatment and quiet tonality, it is closer to Bramley than to Forbes. Alice Meynell had this painting in mind when she wrote in the *Art Journal* in 1889: 'It is in their studies of interiors no less than in their open-air work that the Newlyn school prove their love of truth'. The economy and precision of Tayler's early portraits and paintings of seated girls has some of the tranquil quality of Dutch figure painting, but his touch is not certain and the delicacy sometimes becomes thin.

In June 1887, Tayler was sponsored by the London dealer Arthur Tooth on a painting visit to Venice. This acknowledgement of his work was an excuse for a celebratory supper party, and the following evening he was seen off by the Newlyn artists from Penzance station. Forbes recalled: 'He was in high glee for he had played in a cricket match in the afternoon, and made top score, so he is leaving Newlyn with very pleasant recollection.' (14 June 1887). From his early days in Newlyn, Tayler had been increasingly drawn to the Roman Catholic faith, perhaps influenced by Wainwright and Bourdillon, who were both Catholic. Tayler was converted, probably in 189l, and from this time many of his paintings have religious themes.

One of Tayler's most ambitious paintings comes from the following year. It is 'The Departure of the Fishing Fleet, Boulogne', painted as a commission, a complex figure painting set on the quayside in Boulogne. It is a scene of bustle

ALBERT CHEVALLIER TAYLER
Girl Shelling Peas, 1886.
oil on canvas, 370 x 265mm.
PENZANCE AND DISTRICT MUSEUM AND ART GALLERY.

ALBERT CHEVALLIER TAYLER

*The Departure of the
Fishing Fleet, Boulogne,*
1891.

CITY OF BIRMINGHAM
MUSEUM AND ART GALLERY.

and activity in which the silhouetted figures are seen against the reflections of
the wet cobbled quay. The tonal structure and shifting reflections, and with the
shining fish in the foreground, are all reminiscent of Forbes' 'Fish Sale'.
Another subject from his French visit, 'La Vie Boulonnaise', was exhibited at the
Royal Academy in the same year.

Later Tayler's most popular subjects were convivial dinner parties and other
scenes of domestic celebration, alternated with religious subjects. These were
not liked by his fellow artists and Stanhope Forbes, who had previously always
supported Tayler, was criticial of the painting 'Gentlemen, the Queen' exhibited
at the Academy in 1894:

> *Chevallier Tayler turned the brothers Cornish into smart young guardsmen,
> drinking the King's Health at the mess or as guests at a dinner party
> exchanging toasts with old Doctor Montgomery over a glass of port.* (Forbes. A
> paper read at Penzance Library 26 January 1935).

Yet Tayler's work earned him success at the Academy and he was a regular
exhibitor. In 1904 he was made an Associate and six years later an Academician.
By this time he was again living in London, having been an irregular resident of
Newlyn until 1895 or 1896.

Frank Wright Bourdillon (1851–1924) had a short painting career of about
twelve years, most of it spent in Newlyn. His romantic imagination and
fascination with stirring tales of Elizabethan seafarers, was the mainspring of
his work. He was born in India, where his father, a civil servant in the East India
Company, hoped that he would become a coffee planter. However Frank

showed an early interest in art, developed from his study of birds, and was encouraged by a family friend in England to become an artist. He was already thirty-one when he came to London to train at the Slade and his doubting brother (appropriately named Thomas), questioned the wisdom of this:

> To an outsider it seems a very long hill that an artist has to climb and beginning so late in life is a disadvantage – but no doubt a fair living can be obtained if he does not get quite to the top of it.' (Letter to Emily 6 December 1883).

Frank Bourdillon became a student at the Slade in about 1882, probably shortly after the departure of Thomas Gotch and contemporary with Percy Craft, who became a firm friend. After a year at the Slade Bourdillon studied for a further year in Paris, where he worked hard, but he was uncertain about his true vocation and expressed doubts that were eventually to lead him away from painting. From Paris he wrote to his sister:

> I used to think painting was a mere matter of hammer and tongs, or that if one only kept one's nose long enough on the grindstone one was bound to attain a certain edge at last. Work and study as hard as any galley slave, but picture making wants something more, and if the poor wretch has either the blues or megrims, he'd be far happier splitting nails in the backwoods and more usefully employed chopping firewood in the back kitchen. (February 1884).

In July 1884 he returned to England and began to address himself to the more professional problems of picture-making, and to search for subjects that might prove attractive to the selectors of the Royal Academy. He worked on a large costume piece called 'The Bailiff's Daughter from Islington' (the title taken from an eighteenth century ballad), based on the ancient theme of lovers – a squire's son and a bailiff's daughter, separated by the differences of their social positions. He found the work difficult, and wrote: 'To hammer away at studies as at the Slade or in Paris was a grind but to have to evolve a picture – my eye! its the very mischief.' (November 1884). This painting was rejected by the Royal Academy in 1885, but after extensive re-working, was accepted the following year.

Bourdillon came to Cornwall in May 1886 and spent eight months painting at Polperro before moving to Newlyn. Here he lodged with Mrs Madden at Belleview and he was soon a friend and fishing companion of Stanhope Forbes. In 1888 his painting 'Check' was exhibited at the Royal Academy. It depicts a domestic interior – not a fisherman's cottage, but a more sophisticated home in which father and son play chess. Bourdillon's figure studies were interspersed with delicate, finely observed landscapes, noticeably similar to those of his friend Norman Garstin. However it was the romantic legends of the sea that stirred Bourdillon's imagination, and he found new excitement when he moved to lodgings in a farm house called Trewarveneth near to the Ring and Thimble stone on the top of the hill above Newlyn:

> This bit of sea-view was of value this morning for when I got up I saw far out on the horizon a number of our 'nautics' and hurrying downstairs for a glass, I spotted no less than 20 of our lovely war-ships straining in magnificent array across the glistening summer sea till they disappeared one after the other round the Lizard point. This is now the period of the sham fight after the great review at Spithead. I had no means as yet of ascertaining whether these ships were part of the attacking or defending squadron. How I wished I could have got out amongst them. (July 1889).

FRANK BOURDILLON

The Jubilee Hat, 1887.

oil on canvas, 900 x 675mm.

PRIVATE COLLECTION.

In spite of his doubts, Bourdillon was ambitious for his work and critical of the more pedestrian painters in Newlyn. He wrote:

> *If I can, God helping me, realise these scenes, they may not be so saleable, but I am quite sure they are better worth doing than a pretty girl doing nothing in particular on a window seat, or even an old woman cleaning the fire irons!* (1 April 1890).

Increasingly he became engrossed in the saga of Elizabethan seafaring, and painted out of doors a remarkable reconstruction of a sword fight under the title 'On Bideford Sands', which depicts the duel between Will Carey and Rose's Spanish lover, at the moment when Sir Richard Grenville intervened between the combatants. This painting marked the high point of his career. It was

FRANK BOURDILLON

A Duel on Bideford Sands, 1889.

oil on canvas

ART GALLERY OF NEW SOUTH WALES.

FRANK BOURDILLON

Photographs of costume poses for *A Duel on Bideford Sands by* .

ALAN SHEARS FINE ART.

exhibited at the Royal Academy in 1889 and sold in the following year to the Melbourne National Gallery of Southern Australia, for the good price of £260. Bourdillon wrote 'I am very thankful for this, it will help me clear through this year and into next without drawing on dear old Jas.' [his brother]. (4 July 1890). With renewed confidence he began to gather material for another seafaring picture based on Tennyson's account of the wars with Spain.

A romantic zeal for the past coupled with religious enthusiasm marked Bourdillon from his Newlyn colleagues. 'History painting' usually related to biblical or classical subjects was an acknowledged part of Reynold's 'general style' in painting and was generally accepted throughout the eighteenth and nineteenth centuries. What gave strength to Bourdillon's ideas was that these were interpreted through direct painting from nature. His Elizabethan set pieces were constructed and painted in the open air, in carefully chosen settings, with models dressed in period costume. When he could not work out of doors he made studio reconstructions. As Forbes remembered:

A stranger entering a fish cellar at that time might have been surprised to find a fight in progress and two Elizabethan gentlemen with drawn rapiers engaged in fierce combat – for Frank Bourdillon was painting his clever picture 'A Duel on Bideford Sands'. (Stanhope Forbes. A paper read at Penzance Library 24 July 1935.)

Bourdillon also took photographs of costumed models arranged in the poses of the paintings to give greater realism to his portrayel of action.

In the summer of 1890 Bourdillon moved into his new studio in the Meadow in Newlyn, a handsome two-storey building shared with Norman Garstin. In the autumn he set up a stage there to paint costume interiors, of which he wrote: 'it is a speculation and I hope I shall find lots of costume pot-boilers in it; perhaps being able to paint a big picture or two out of it; or of course I would not go to the expense'. With characteristic humility he defended his preference for historical subjects. 'You see I am rather drawn to this costume work for down here there are lots of clever fellows who do the village business so much better than I can.' (29 October 1890). He produced a succession of seventeenth-century dramas with such titles as 'From the Spanish Main' (1891), 'Aboard the Revenge' (1891) and 'Sink Me the Ship, Master Gunner' (1892). The last title, taken from a ballad by Tennyson, is Sir Richard Grenville's deathbed scene, as he commands the sinking of his broken ship rather than see it taken by the Spanish.

Bourdillon's work showed originality and high technical skill, and he was reasonably well treated by the Academy. However, he had difficulty selling his paintings and constantly doubted his artistic ability, doubts which were fed by his devout Christianity. He was also affected by the arrival in Newlyn in 1888 of John Mackenzie, a printer and illustrator, who formed the Newlyn Industrial Class to promote employment for 'fisherlads' through the teaching and manufacture of metalwork, enamelling and embroidery. Together Bourdillon and Mackenzie gave a considerable part of their time to Bible studies and spiritual work with the poorest members of the community. They helped with the Seaman's Rest and were active members of Paul Church. In the spring of 1892 Bourdillon wrote 'It has been the happiest winter I have spent here'. Only part of that enjoyment came from painting however, for he was increasingly concerned with the spiritual welfare of the people of Newlyn. The artists proved more difficult to reform. Bourdillon wrote:

It is glorious being allowed to use one's studio for the dear Lord – but I want to be filled with love for Him that I may be ready to go anywhere in His service. As you will believe, Mackenzie and I are both praying that some of our artist friends may be brought to know the love of Jesus, but they are not so open to influence as the simple fisherfolk. (30 March 1892).

In June 1892 he recorded his decision to become a missionary, gave up painting and after taking orders he returned to India, where he married a fellow missionary, and worked for some years before returning to England. He passed the remainder of his life as a curate in Ramsgate.

Forbes later remembered Bourdillon with great affection:

When Dilla, as we used to call him, first arrived, he was keen on his art and on sport and fishing but gradually the more serious matters of life absorbed him and claimed all his mental activity and he left us to go as a missionary to India... The finest tribute that I have ever heard was once paid to him by a friend of mine, Henry Detmold. There had been a boating accident in Mount's Bay and at a re-union of painters in one of our lodgings, the talk turned upon drowning and someone observed 'Oh, you know of course no one ever sinks until all the sins he has committed pass through his mind'. 'What a ghastly idea', said Detmold, 'I shall be bobbing about in Mount's Bay for a week! But', he added, 'Dilla will go down like a stone'. (Stanhope Forbes, A paper read at the Passmore Edwards Gallery, Newlyn, 3 June 1939.)

William Banks Fortescue (c.1855–1914) was born in Southport, Lancashire, as was Leghe Suthers. Fortescue was an engineering designer in Birmingham before studying art in Paris, and in 1883 or 1884 he travelled to Venice. Fortescue was in Venice at about the same time as Bramley and Suthers and he may have been with them there for they had known each other in Birmingham. In 1884 Fortescue exhibited a group of Venetian scenes at the Royal Birmingham Society of Artists. He had begun to show with the Society six years before, and did so regularly until the end of the century, exhibiting in all about one hundred works. He was made an associate member in 1884 and a full member in 1899. It was probably Fortescue's acquaintance with other artists from Birmingham who had already visited Newlyn that directed him there, for by 1885, he was in Newlyn and living at Belleview. Stanhope Forbes found him convivial company and wrote 'I kept my birthday last night having Hall and Bramley and Fortescue to dinner... they talked till midnight at which time I entered my twenty-ninth year'. Fortescue featured in many of the artist's musical evenings, playing the cello, and accompanying Bateman on the flute and Mrs Bateman on the piano. No doubt he also performed the clog dance he had learned in Birmingham, which Fred Hall caricatured, portraying him as a jovial moustachioed figure in a raincoat and clogs, a cello under one arm and square-ended paintbrushes in the other hand.

In 1887, Fortescue had three works accepted at the Royal Academy. All were Cornish subjects, and at least one was hung 'on the line'. From then on he exhibited landscape and figure paintings at the Academy, at the Suffolk Street Galleries and elsewhere in London. He also kept in touch with his native town of Southport, where he exhibited in the Spring Exhibitions from 1886 to 1897.

Fortesque saw the working people of Newlyn in a manner very similar to Langley. One of his best known paintings, 'The Fish Fag' (1888) depicts an old woman carrying a heavy 'cowal' or fish-basket on her back returning from the

WILLIAM BANKS
FORTESCUE

*Planting Brocolli,
Cornwall.*

oil on canvas, 1200 x 900mm.

DAVID MESSUM FINE ART.

boats with a small boy, over the wet glistening sands. Although the subject is directly after Forbes' 'Fish Sale' the painting is drier and more modelled, executed with a square brush. 'Words of Comfort' (1894), in which a wrinkled old woman finds consolation from her Bible, was described by the *Western Morning News* (29.3.1894) as his best painting. Most of Fortescue's work was from the figure, well observed and precisely deliniated in oil and watercolour.

Fortescue kept in touch with Newlyn for the rest of his life, although in 1890 he moved to nearby Paul, and later to St Ives. As he left the Newlyn he found more pastoral subjects in the countryside, one example is 'A Ploughing Match – Cornwall', shown at the Academy in 1891. In later years his work developed in a more open and colourful manner, sharing that move towards Impressionist colour affected by many of the St Ives painters.

The witty and observant Irishman Norman Garstin (1855–1926) was already thirty-one years old when he determined to try art as a profession. He was born at Cahirconlish, County Limerick, where his father was a colonel in the English Army; his mother, Mary Hastings Moore was an educated Irishwoman related to George Moore. Following Norman's birth, his mother suffered a form of paralysis which permanently crippled her. His father later committed suicide, and Norman was brought up by grandparents in Ireland and then by guardians. He was educated as a gentleman, but lacked direction and had limited means. He started to train as an engineer in Cork, but as his professor noted 'his drawings were more accurate than his calculations'. He entered an architects' office in London. However he soon became bored with this ordered life, and set out for the diamond fields of South Africa. 'I turned my T-square into a pick axe and sailed away to seek my fortune' he said. He went to the Kimberley Mines, where he met Cecil Rhodes, at that time young and unknown, and it was Rhodes who took Garstin to Cape Town where he became sub-editor of the *Cape Times*. He spent six years in South Africa where he saw a great deal of the country and developed his skills as a writer, but fortune eluded him and he returned to Ireland.

Soon after his return he lost the sight of his right eye in a riding accident. Paradoxically it was after this that Garstin decided to make a career from art, which up to that time had been a hobby. In 1878 he went to Antwerp, to study at Verlat's Academy working alongside Frank Bramley, Fred Hall and other English students, and painted in the Belgian countryside. Then he moved to Paris, and for three years was in the studio of Carolus-Duran, living a Bohemian existence in the Hotel St Malo, off the Boulevard Montparnasse, with a circle of English colleagues, including Henry Detmold and Chevallier Tayler who were to become close friends in Newlyn, and Millie Dow who later came to St Ives.

Garstin was in Paris from 1880 to 1882, the period of the fifth, sixth and seventh Impressionist exhibitions. The public were at last becoming receptive to the work of artists they had previously rejected, and Garstin recognised that important new directions were opening up. He also met Degas and possibly Manet. In 1884, before coming to Newlyn, he noted in Manet's work 'a delicious brightness and happiness... he lets in light and air.' ('Edward Manet', by Norman Garstin, *Art Journal* 1884 p.110).

The earliest surviving paintings by Garstin from this period are 'Among the Pots' (c.1882) painted in Belgium and 'Church of St Michael, Quimperlé, Brittany' (1882). Both have a clear organisation, but they are sombre, reflecting his northern academic training and lack that lightness and feeling for colour he later achieved. More adventurous are the many small paintings done shortly afterwards in London, with such titles as' St Paul's Churchyard', 'Thames Scene', 'King's Bench Walk', 'Across the River St Paul's', all lightly brushed sketches with a narrow colour range from umber to light ultramarine.

Garstin was a tall and imposing figure with a native Irish elegance, a charming companion, and a nervous but eloquent talker. He began to exhibit in 1882 at The Walker Art Gallery, Liverpool, the following year he showed at the Royal Academy and in other exhibitions. He moved his home several times in England and Ireland during the next four years, and travelled abroad to Hyeres in the south of France (1883), Venice and Tangiers (1885) where he found Morocco 'an Arabian Nights existence where anything could happen'.

It is possible that he included a visit to Newlyn, for the date of 1884 has been given to a light and gentle study painted from The Meadow. This superb miniature is a domesticated version of impressionism. Across the expanse of long grass, seen in the change of colour of late autumn, a young girl collects dried heads of sorrel; behind her the ground falls away to the rocks of Newlyn and the blue mists of Mount's Bay.

In 1886 Garstin returned from Ireland to England and shortly afterwards married Miss Dochie Jones from Bedford. In his own succinct words 'I came home, married, and settled in the West, for the first three or four years at Newlyn, and then we moved into Penzance!' ('The March Hare Interviews Norman Garstin. Newlyn. *The Paperchase* Summer Number, 1909.) At about the time of his arrival in Newlyn, the funds from his father's estate, which had kept him in reasonable comfort during his long period of travelling abroad, ceased, due to mismanagement by his guardians. He was declared bankrupt and to supplement his wife's small income he taught, wrote and took groups of students on study visits abroad.

The Garstins were well received in Newlyn, and became popular members of the artists' group. Dochie Garstin won a reputation for kindness and good works in the village, although she suffered from poor health. They lived in Newlyn for four years, in a house called Mount Vernon. Here their first son Crosbie was born in 1887. Norman Garstin took one of the newly built studios in Bateman's 'Meadow', shared with Bourdillon. He retained this when in 1890 the family moved to Penzance for the birth of their second son Denys, as 'Newlyn cannot afford accommodation for their now enlarged family'. (FWB October 1890). Crosbie Garstin was to become a poet and writer of distinction, and Denys (who later changed to his name to Denis which he thought less affected) published two books both of which were well received, but this early promise was extinguished in the First World War when he was killed on the British expedition to Archangel in Russia. It was the Garstin's daughter Alethea, born in 1894, who inherited her father's talent as an artist. Entirely taught by him she was to make her own major contribution to painting in Cornwall.

The most robust painting of these years by Norman Garstin is undoubtedly 'The Rain it Raineth Every Day' (1889). Here, along the wide rain-soaked expanse of the promenade between Newlyn and Penzance, a few figures of women and children struggle beneath umbrellas. Rain and spray make the glistening promenade a mirror, reflecting the widely spaced figures beneath a leaden sky, precisely set around an empty centre in this modelled greyness. A flash of spray dashes across the flattened space of mist and rain which recedes to the buildings flanking the promenade – the Queens Hotel, the rising terraces of the town and the distant tower of Penzance Parish Church. The picture is a sympathetic record of Norman Garstin's home town seen in a believable space and time. It is also a major painterly statement, built with certaincy and precision, yet with the lightest of touches. Frank Wright Bourdillon, who saw it before it was sent to the Royal Academy in 1889, called it 'a stunning picture'. The *Cornishman* more prosaically said that it 'conjures up thoughts of influenza' (28 March 1889). In spite of the undoubted strength of 'The Rain it Raineth' it was not accepted at the Royal Academy, perhaps because of its evidently French style of tonal painting. Forbes wrote 'I regret very sadly that Garstin's and Bateman's pictures are crowded out at the last moment... we are all very sorry for Garstin who can ill-afford to loose any chance of selling.' (3 May 1889).

Some forty works of Garstin's were shown at the Royal Academy during his lifetime, and his pictures were exhibited in Glasgow, Manchester, Birmingham and Liverpool. However it was mostly his smaller sketches – studies of sea and landscape that captured the transient effects of light – rather than the more elaborate figure compositions demanded by the Academy, that attracted the attention of dealers and collectors.

Garstin's paintings have a feeling for space and atmospheric colour that single them out from his contemporaries. In his questioning intelligence he looks forward to a more modern period. His best paintings are small landscapes which have more of Whistler than Forbes, plus a French strength of colour, a sense of time of day and a preference for the mood of sunset or early morning.

An inveterate traveller, Garstin took every opportunity to work when he was abroad. In 1886, shortly after his marriage, he painted a number of small panels whilst visiting cousins in Canada, and on a later visit in 1892, he recorded and illustrated the opening of the Canadian Pacific Railway. His description of the great landscapes of Canada is in language as brightly coloured as his impressionist studies:

> *I cannot touch the sunset, it is too much, the pageant too swiftly changing, from the gaudy moment when the whole sky is streaked and splashed with molten gold, down to that softer time when the rising shadow of the earth with puritan tints draws its discreet veil over the western orgies of colour that marks the royal masque of sunset.* ('Days & Nights in the North West' in 'C.P. Railway Part l: The Prairie' by Norman Garstin, *Art Journal* 1892, p.169–175.)

Garstin's talent for writing found expression in *The Studio*. From 1895 onwards he was a regular contributor with a feature 'Studio Talk', in which he sympathetically chronicled the work of the Newlyn and St Ives artists and he wrote major articles on individual artists associated with the area, including Stanhope Forbes, T. Millie Dow, Laura Knight and A. J. Munnings.

In 1899 Garstin conceived the idea of taking small groups of students on sketching tours to the continent, to centres used by earlier generations of artists, 'everywhere from Quimperlé to Delft', at a time when such organised

parties were most unusual. Garstin found them financially rewarding but exhausting and they took him away from Newlyn for considerable periods so that he was unable to develop his work on a major scale. He was undoubtedly a good teacher, and was remembered by a number of students who achieved distinction, including Harold Harvey, a native of Penzance, and the New Zealander Frances Hodgkins who later made her own special contribution to the modern movement. His success as a teacher led to a proposal to form an art school in Newlyn, to be taught jointly by himself and Stanhope Forbes. During one of Garstin's absences abroad, Forbes opened the Newlyn school on his own. This led to a cooling of relations between the two men, but later Garstin opened his own school called 'The Newlyn and Penzance Art Student School'.

In spite of the many diversions produced by teaching and writing, Garstin created a substantial body of work, and he remained open-minded and optimistic. When asked in 1907 for his opinions on art he replied:

My chief theory on painting is not to have a theory. Painting is purely a personal matter... What we are chiefly interested in is less the thing depicted, than the personality of the painter who did it. One is always anxious to see another man's outlook.

Norman Garstin and his family moved to Penzance in 1895 and until his death in 1926 lived at 4 Wellington Terrace. His obituary in *The Times* remembered him as 'a man of general artistic and intellectual ability rather than a powerful artist. He was a man of unconventional ideas, often taking the unpopular side of a question'. (*The Times*, 24 June 1926).

Elizabeth Armstrong (1859–1912) had begun to make her reputation as an artist before she came to Newlyn in 1885, showing work at the Royal Academy and the Royal Institute of Watercolour Artists. She had also made the acquaintance of Whistler and Sickert, mainly through her interest in the art of

NORMAN GARSTIN

The Rain it Raineth Every Day, 1889.

oil on canvas, 928 x 1600mm.

PENZANCE AND DISTRICT MUSEUM AND ART GALLERY.

etching. Elizabeth Armstrong was born in Ottawa, Canada, the only daughter of a Canadian government official who died when she was young. Her childhood was lonely, for she was brought up apart from her older brothers. She was educated in England, living with her mother in Chelsea next door to the ageing Rossetti. As a young student she went to the South Kensington Schools and then to New York to continue her studies at the Art Students League. Here she met American artists who had worked in Paris, and discovered Millet and Bastien-Lepage. Three years later, chaperoned by her mother, she travelled to Europe – first to Munich, which she found an unhappy place, and then in 1882 (still with her mother), went to Pont-Aven, where she met Edwin Harris and a number of the American painters. (Stanhope Forbes, was then in nearby Quimperlé, but they did not meet for a further three years). Elizabeth Armstrong later spoke of her time at Pont-Aven with great fondness:

A lively picturesquely clad Bohemian group of men and women, who might themselves have been worthily set in a canvas by a Zorn or a Kroyer, lingering at the bord as the day's experiences were narrated and the latest theory advanced, and the flow of talk went merrily along under the swinging lamps. (Mrs Lionel Birch *Stanhope A. Forbes A.R.A. and Elizabeth Stanhope Forbes A.R.W.S.*).

In the summer of 1884 Elizabeth was painting the Dutch landscape with other students from the Art Students League, near Zandfoort. American and Canadian artists had made the Netherlands one of their main goals in Europe and in Canada the Hague School painters enjoyed great popularity, as did the paintings of the earlier Dutch masters. Elizabeth was one of a group of American and Canadian students working with the American artists Robert F. Blum (1857–1903) and William Merritt Chase (1848–1916) who had taught her in New York. The influence of Dutch painting and the memories of the misty Dutch landscape had a lasting effect upon her work, as is evident in the many small panels of clear, concise colour such as 'Dutch Scene' (1884) or 'Zandfoort Fishergirl' (1884).

Elizabeth was attracted to Newlyn by reports of the successes of the newly formed group, and in November 1885 visited with her mother. Her first impressions were poor, for 'it was not at all a place in which women stood any chance of developing their artistic powers.' ('Mrs Stanhope Forbes' *The Queen, The Ladies Newspaper,* 18 Oct 1890). Stanhope Forbes soon met her and duly recorded their first meeting:

On Friday night I went round to the Harrises and was introduced to the young lady artist Miss Armstrong. She cannot be said to be pretty but is a nice intelligent and ladylike girl. I had a very long and interesting talk with the Canadian girl about Pont-Aven and all my old friends there, for she, Miss Armstrong, was staying at Julias's whilst I was at Metayers. (19 November 1886).

A sequel to this first meeting soon occurred:

I was walking with her one day very shortly after her arrival and crossing Newlyn Bridge I saw old Sam Plummer leaning aginst the parapet, so thinking he might be useful to my young friend as a model, I introduced her, whereupon he roared out in a voice like a foghorn, loud enough to be heard in Penzance, "So that's Miss Armstrong they do say you and she are going to be wed." (1939).

STANHOPE FORBES

Self Portrait 1889.

oil on canvas

This portrait and the one of Eizabeth (opposite) *was painted in the year of their marriage.*

NEWLYN ART GALLERY

Elizabeth stayed on in Newlyn and by the early summer it is clear that Forbes has a high regard for her. He was also aware that she was a person of independent views, and dedicated to her painting. 'She is one of the most energetic and industrious girls I have ever seen, and that is better than a dowry of two or three hundred a year.' He also admired her professionalism. 'She has sold her pictures at the Grosvenor and British Artists and etchings at the Royal Academy' (l June 1886). He particularly praised her etchings, quoting Napier Hemy's views that they are as good as any that are done at that time. Soon Forbes was talking of an engagement, and wrote to his mother asking for a cheque for £15 to buy a ring. (13 June). But still Elizabeth was not yet Mrs Forbes, and Stanhope is desperate for this to take place, preferably in Newlyn, as he feels that the opulence of the Forbes' residence in London could be an awful ordeal for Elizabeth. He confesses to his mother 'That you should know and love the girl I hope to make my wife, is now my constant thought.' (July 1886). It was finally arranged for Mrs Forbes to come to St Ives for a summer holiday, Newlyn was unsuitable for his mother: 'If you saw the oceans of mud and the sort of place generally', whereas St Ives was well equipped for visitors with good hotels, and the bathing from Porthmeor Beach was better than any other.

Elizabeth Armstrong (and her mother) spent much of the summer in St Ives, and Forbes was there a good deal, working on studies for 'Their Ever Shifting Home', the painting that he would show in the Royal Academy the next year. This was an ambitious painting of a group of gipsies moving slowly through the village of Newlyn from Paul Hill. A young woman carrying her child heads the procession, followed by men on foot leading their caravan. The walking figure of the girl, set against the grey tones of the village street, cuts the painting vertically. The movement is carried upwards by bare trees to a high horizon with its frieze of distant figures; the low viewpoint and vertical emphasis is reminiscent of Bastien-Lepage. The painting was assembled from its components. Forbes painted the figure of the girl first, for he was concerned that she might have her next child before he had finished painting her. He moved on to the background, and in November 1886 wrote that 'I have almost finished my roofs. Keyed up the sky and repainted the trees, but hardly touched the ground for I can get better roads than the one over there. It has no nice wheel ruts in it and that I must go for on Paul Hill I expect.' (3.11.1886). The gipsy van which 'quite makes the picture!' was put in in February 1887, and the group of gipsies came later. It was difficult to get them to stay, and there were times when Forbes gathered an audience of a hundred waiting while he hurriedly painted. The picture was well shown at the Academy in 1887 but Forbes was disappointed with its reception. He wrote to Elizabeth Armstrong 'I had heard very few complimentary remarks and it seemed to me to astonish nobody. It looked very bad to me.' (26.4.1887).

The friendship between Elizabeth Armstrong and Stanhope Forbes caused considerable speculation within Forbes' family. Forbes' Aunt Annie wrote from St Ives in September 1886:

STANHOPE FORBES

Portrait of Elizabeth Armstrong, 1889.

oil on canvas

NEWLYN ART GALLERY.

We had such a pleasant day at Newlyn and I like Mrs Armstrong very much, we paid a visit to all the studios... I fear love making and painting don't go together, Stannie has not done much of the latter and oh! to say he is silly over Miss Armstrong is to say nothing he is too foolish and does not care who sees him. If I were Miss Armstrong I should box his ears... I liked Miss Armstrong very much

ELIZABETH FORBES

School is Out, 1889.

oil on canvas, 1050 x 1160mm.

PENZANCE AND DISTRICT MUSEUM
AND ART GALLERY.

but if anything she is less religious than her intended husband which to me is dreadful... It is most amusing the friendship that exists between these artists and they are in and out of each others rooms and houses at all times of the day. (Letter from St Ives, September 1886).

The one cloud in the relationship was Elizabeth's acquaintance with Sickert and Whistler, who shared an interest in etching and who admired her work. In November Elizabeth was in London, Forbes wrote 'I have had a long talk today with Thomas Gotch about Whistler I really can hardly bear to think that very likely you are going to meet him tomorrow' (November 1886). A few days later 'I hope sincerely you have seen the last of him for some time, however amusing he may be'. Forbes admitted to being prejudiced against Sickert, whom he had never met, for he detested the school to which he belonged, and he could hardly contain the dislike he felt for the Whistler 'gang'. 'I cannot find words strong enough to show my contempt for them. I feel sure a time will come when you will see it too, but my prayers do not go up to those who were instrumental in drawing you into the clique'. Elizabeth did little etching after her marriage because of the lack of facilities in Newlyn, and perhaps because of Forbes' antagonism.

Elizabeth was not resident in Newlyn until her marriage in 1889, although she was a frequent visitor. She worked in London, and made many visits to St Ives. In January 1887 she returned with her mother to stay at Cliff Castle in Paul, where she worked for the forthcoming exhibition of the New English Art Club and completed a large picture, 'Suspense', for the Royal Academy. Later that year she borrowed Percy Craft's St Ives studio and wrote to Stanhope Forbes. 'I have taken Mr Craft's studio here, and have made up my mind to do several things before leaving St Ives. I certainly like the place better than Newlyn.'

She found subjects in the local life of the area, and discovered a theme that she would make particularly her own – the village children. She chose to depict the domestic side of village life to which she naturally responded, rather than the grimness portrayed by some of the other artists in Newlyn. She painted with a delicacy and clarity that few of the Newlyn painters, including Stanhope Forbes, could rival, and although much of her work was small in scale and less dramatic in subject, her skill was no less evident.

In 'School is Out' (1888) exhibited at the Royal Academy in 1889, Elizabeth gives a precise yet sympathetic description of the children as individuals, and their relationship to their long suffering teacher at the village school in Paul. This is a wholly enjoyable painting of the schoolroom at the end of day. The clock reads one minute past four and the children gladly close their books and gather their belongings, ready to stream from the schoolroom into the warm summer afternoon; older girls in pinafores and bonnets help the younger ones, and mothers call for their offspring. The painting has great warmth and observation of the children's character. It is full of incident and delicately painted.

STANHOPE FORBES

The Health of the Bride,
1889.

oil on canvas

THE TATE GALLERY.

It was a protracted engagement for Stanhope and Elizabeth. Both were heavily occupied with their work, and there were financial difficulties. Their marriage did not take place until 1889, when Forbes had a further success at the Royal Academy with 'The Health of the Bride'. The subsequent purchase of the painting by Sir Henry Tate for the substantial sum of £600 brought the means for them to marry. Forbes wrote from Newlyn, 'I myself will be rather occupied down here – no less a matter than my own wedding. It was inevitable after painting the picture'. (Letter to Henry Tate, 16 July 1889). This work was later to be part of the gift to the nation of sixty-eight pictures which led to the formation of the Tate Gallery.

In 'The Health of the Bride' Forbes portrayed an intimate family affair – the wedding group toasting the shy young pair at the centre of the table. An older man at the head, the bride's father, has finished his speech and accepts the compliments of a friend of the groom, a merchant seaman. Grandfather takes the two grandchildren on his knee, and all of the family enjoy the scene from their different perspectives. The masts of sailing ships and signs of the port's activity are seen through the window. Wine and beer have been drunk and the cake waits to be cut. The colour scheme echoes the intimacy, soft greys and whites with a few points of warmer colour. This scene of celebration was painted from studies made in the local inn and from friends of the artist who sat in his studio. Stanhope and Elizabeth Forbes' own wedding followed shortly afterwards. A detailed report was provided by Frank Bourdillon:

> *I can today report on Forbes' and Miss Armstrong's wedding... the date was yesterday 6th, the hour 2pm and the place St Peters Newlyn – The bride's dress was (I believe) a walking dress of white cashmere with satin lacings and fancy hat trimmed with lilies of the valley. The Bridesmaid wore white cashmere and fancy hat alike trimmed with sage green and crushed strawberry. Mr Lacksyz (the Vicar of Newlyn) performed the ceremony and General Pearl Yates graced the occasion with his accustomed dignity... After the ceremony was over all adjourned to the 'marine retreat'. There we discussed the cake and other unwholesome delicacies until Forbes and his wife went off to Plymouth by the 6.35pm in 'first class' style and a heavy shower of rice. As we were nearly all artists and their connections (all our own crowd and the married men from St Ives) the company (I hope you will admit it) could not fail to be entertaining.* (Bourdillon's Letters, 7 August 1889).

5

AN INTERNATIONAL COMMUNITY

At about the same time that the artistic colony was established in Newlyn, another, and in many ways similar, group of artists came together in St Ives. They too had been trained in France, and had been converted to the doctrine of *plein-air*ism. As each centre became established, they developed different characteristics and attracted different personalities. The figure painters of Newlyn found home-grown success at the Royal Academy, whereas, from the first, St Ives was more international in its outlook, and its artists were drawn towards the more experimental position of the New English Art Club. There were rivalries between the two artist groups, but there were also many friendships and movement between them.

Norman Garstin compared the attractions for a young artist of Newlyn and St Ives:

The distance in mere miles between the two art colonies is insignificant; a moderately good walker finds it a pleasant afternoon's trudge over the breezy moorland, bright with gorse and furze, and ominously strewn with boulders and extinct mine chimneys, while the sea stretches away behind and before him... Newlyn looks east – there are no sands, the fringe of the sea is not very alluring; and the sun soon sinks behind the hill on which the village lies, but this gives the figure-painter an admirable opportunity for placing his personages in shadow with a grey or glowing background of sea, hence many of the Newlyn motifs. St Ives, on the northern coast, has a north-east to a north-western aspect; the sun comes gleaming over the water in the morning on the one hand and sinks gleaming into it on the other hand in the evening; big waves come tumbling over white sands, and the foam is dyed in turns with all the colours of the spectrum; out of the windows of their foam-spattered studios the St Ives artists can watch the sea pranking itself in all the many tinted garments of the day and evening, and so they become impressionistic and sensuous in colour... (Norman Garstin, writing as N.G. in *The Studio* vol.VI No.33, December 1895.)

The luminosity of light, reflected on all sides by the sea, gave St Ives a Mediterranean brilliance. The intricate pattern of houses, fish lofts and alleyways and the life of its harbour, backed by a coast of outstanding natural beauty held an infinite fascination for artists. One of the first artists to settle in the town, H. Harewood Robinson, wrote of it before it was a residential colony:

St Ives had before then been visited summer after summer by painters of greater or lesser note, who hailed from London and elsewhere, and who used St Ives as a temporary sketching ground. The fishermen 'down along' have still stories to tell of 'Squire' Hook (The Royal Academician whose seascapes still delight us), of the late Mr Henry Moore, R.A. (who, alas! painted the last of his blue rolling seas last year), of Mr Whistler and many others.' ('St Ives as an Art Centre' by H. H. Robinson, from *Historical Sketch of St Ives and District* compiled and published by W. Badcock, 1896.)

St Ives in the last years
of the nineteenth
century.

PHOTOGRAPH BY GIBSON, BY
PERMISSION OF ANDREW LANYON.

'Squire' Hook, was the much respected Royal Academician James Clarke Hook (1819–1907), whose connections with the area went back to the early years of the nineteenth century. He left school at fourteen with a prize for drawing and received advice from none less than John Constable. In the 1850s he came into his own, a vigorous painter of sea and coast, and was voted into Royal Academy membership to the place vacated by James Ward. A number of his most important coastal views of the Cornish coast were purchased by Sir Henry Tate and formed part of the original collection of the Tate Gallery. Henry Moore R.A. (1831–1895) [a Yorkshire man like his later namesake] was also an acclaimed marine painter, noted for his large-scale views of the open sea and the effects of light and weather. He adapted the principles of Pre-Raphaelite painting to a looser and more direct handling, with a fine sense of colour, working up and down the South Coast with many painting visits to Cornwall. Other names remembered by Robinson as 'old frequenters' of St Ives are R. W. Allen, W. H. Bartlett, and the French lithographer Emile Vernier who came to St Ives probably in 1885. His prints of the town and its surroundings enhanced its reputation among artists.

The beginnings of St Ives as a residential art colony could be marked by the visit of James McNeill Whistler and his two young assistants Walter Sickert and Mortimer Menpes, in the winter of 1883–84. Throughout the last quarter of the nineteenth century the tempestuous James McNeill Whistler (1834–1903), strutted across the stage of British art, always in the limelight and always provocative. An American, he had been brought up in continental Europe where his father, a Major General in the United States army, was recruited by Nicholas I, Emperor of Russia, to build the railway from St Petersburg to Moscow. Whistler was a small man, self-absorbed, with sparkling black eyes and a head of dark curls, sophisticated and vain. His extraordinary talent, coupled with a blistering wit, was to make him a central figure in London and Paris.

Whistler trained in Paris with Charles Gleyre, where he was attracted to the doctrine of Realism and the art of Courbet, whose pupil he became. In 1861 he spent three months on the coast of Brittany, one of the first of the young American artists to paint there, and produced a major painting 'Alone with the Tide', boldly executed in the manner of Courbet. Whistler long remembered it, 'A beautiful thing – painted in Brittany – blue sea – long wave breaking – black and brown rocks – great foreground of sand – and a wonderful girl asleep'. But he soon repudiated this earlier influence. In 1867 he wrote to his friend Fantin:

JAMES MCNEILL WHISTLER
Self Portrait.
chalk drawing
CHELSEA ARTS CLUB.

> *That damned realism made such a direct appeal to my vanity as a painter, and, flouting all traditions, I shouted, with the assurance of ignorance, 'Vive la nature!' Nature, my boy – that cry was a piece of bad luck for me...*

In the 1860s and 1870s his work advanced towards atmospheric colour, brevity of detail and rejection of incident. He sought to capture the drama of revealed beauty, seen in a fleeting glimpse at dawn or dusk. The aesthetic of 'art for art's sake' that he advanced was at the opposite pole of the straightforward naturalism of Forbes and the Newlyn artists. In his 'Ten O'clock Lecture' delivered in 1885, Whistler stated the argument which later led towards abstraction:

> *Nature contains the elements, in colour and form, of all pictures, as the keyboard contains the notes of all music. But the artist is born to pick, to choose, and group with science, these elements, that the result may be beautiful.*

In the 1880s Whistler was at the height of his powers, and had produced some of his most important pictures. Based in London he had become an important contact with Degas, Monet and the Impressionist painters, but he was recovering from a serious setback to his career. He had suffered notoriety and public rejection following his lawsuit of 1878 with John Ruskin. Ruskin had seen a painting by Whistler on display in the Grosvenor Gallery called 'Nocturne in Black and Gold – The Falling Rocket' (an impression of a firework display at Cremorne Gardens). John Ruskin, then elderly and almost certainly deranged, objected to the title and to the price asked, which he considered ourageous for a sketch. He published his opinions in one of his monthly 'Letters to the Workmen and Labourers of Great Britain':

> *Sir Coutts Lindsay ought not to have admitted works into the gallery in which the ill-educated conceit of the artist so nearly approached the aspect of wilful imposture. I have seen and heard much of Cockney impudence before now; but never expected to hear a coxcomb ask two hundred guineas for flinging a pot of paint in the public's face.*

Whistler brought an action for libel against Ruskin, and there followed a trial that was more notable for its comic misunderstandings than for its display of justice. The most remembered exchange was between Whistler and Ruskin's

Council, Sir John Holbers. Whistler was asked how long it had taken to 'knock off' the picture. He replied 'two days'. Holbers responded 'The labour of two days, then, is that for which you ask two hundred guineas'. 'No', replied Whistler, 'I ask it for the knowledge of a lifetime'. Whistler was successful in law, but was awarded the derisory damages of one farthing. Ruskin, a wealthy man, had his costs borne by his friends and admirers. Whistler received no such assistance and public ridicule coupled with his own autocratic behaviour at the trial angered his patrons and drove them away. Whistler found himself destitute and in May 1879 he was declared bankrupt. His house in Tite Street, called the White House, designed to Whistler's own specification and furnished with a superb collection of oriental pottery and *objets d'art* was sold and his collection dispersed. It was during the period in which he was endeavouring to re-establish his reputation that Whistler made his working visit to St Ives, to produce small landscapes and marine paintings for an exhibition at Dowdeswell's Bond Street gallery.

Walter Richard Sickert (1860–1942) was then a young man who had recently decided to leave the acting profession. He was thoroughly Europeanised in his background, born in Munich in 1860 into a family of professional artists who later settled in England. His father, a Dane from Schleswig-Holstein, was a painter and graphic artist who had worked in Germany and France, his mother, half English, half Irish, had lived for many years in Dieppe. Before choosing art as a career, Walter Sickert had a short period as an actor, playing minor parts in provincial touring companies. At the age of nineteen he met Whistler and was totally overwhelmed by his single minded enthusiasm: 'Such a man! The only painter alive who has first immense genius, then conscientious persistent work striving after his ideal, knowing exactly what he is about and turned aside by no indifference or ridicule.' (letter from Sickert to Alfred Pollard Baron). As a result of this meeting Sickert abandoned his acting career and studied for a few months at the Slade School. Whistler persuaded Sickert to leave the Slade and work under his direction, possibly to score off his old anatagonist Legros, the Slade Professor. Whistler's words were 'you've wasted your money Richard, there is no use in wasting your time too'. For six years Sickert became an apt and willing studio assistant for Whistler, and during this time turned from a young actor with a gift for caricature, into a hard working professional artist with an additional gift for the written word.

The third member of the part was Mortimer Menpes, a talented and sophisticated graphic artist, born in Australia, who, with Sickert went on ahead to St Ives, to prepare for the visit of Whistler. The party stayed for about three months at a small lodging house, 14 Barnoon Terrace, overlooking the harbour. 'Whistler loved St Ives, the boats, the sea, the fishermen all fascinated him... he did much good work there'. (Mortimer Menpes). Sickert was also highly appreciative of Whistler's 'pochades':

> *Never was instrument better understood and more fully exploited than Whistler has understood and exploited oil paint in these panels. He has solved in them a problem that had hitherto been insoluble: to give a result of deliberateness to a work done in a few hours from nature.* (Robert Emmons *The Life and Opinions of Walter Richard Sickert* Faber and Faber 1941).

Whistler would be out before breakfast making swift colour sketches, mostly views of the sea and sky seen from the beach. Sickert wrote enthusiastically that 'He will give you in a space of nine inches by four inches, an angry sea, piled up and running as no painter ever did before....'. (Baron *op.cit.* p.11). The movement of the sea was an endless fascination, Whistler wrote to his friend Godwin from St Ives: 'The country you know never lasts for me long and if it had not been for the sea I should have been back before now'. He recorded its changing appearance in such paintings as 'Angry Sea', 'Cliffs and Breakers' and 'Low Tide'. Colours are subdued, 'Silver and Grey', 'A Grey Note – Village Street' (a view of Market Place, St Ives). Whistler's paintings of the Cornish coast are not ambitious or experimental, but his presence in St Ives and the silvery tonality of his painting was to affect many of the painters who later worked there.

Sickert and Menpes assisted Whistler – preparing his panels, mixing his paints and cleaning his brushes. Sickert also made a number of paintings but only two small panels, which owe a great deal to his master, are known to exist, 'On the Sands, St Ives' (1884) a view of figures on a beach and 'Clogdy Point Cornwall' (1884). Soon after this visit to St Ives, Sickert left Whistler's service, and went to Paris where he renewed an earlier acquaintance with such Impressionist painters as Degas, Renoir and Monet. In 1885 he moved back to London and became friendly with a number of other young artists trained in Paris or associated with Whistler. Sickert was a natural leader, and before long was centrally involved in art activities in London which brought him into direct opposition to the Newlyn artists.

Other artists were soon attracted to St Ives:

A small studio (which has long since gone back to its original state of ruin) had been constructed by the Hon. Duff Tollemache out of a disused and ruinous building at Carn Crowse, and in 1885 Mr and Mrs Harewood Robinson and Mr William Eadie had studios made (in the one case out of an old wooden carpenter's shop, and the other out of an old out-house), and settled in St Ives as winter residents. The following summer a number of painters swooped down on St Ives with the intention of making it their abode and field of labour. (H. H. Robinson op.cit.).

H. Harewood Robinson, who wrote these notes, arrived in 1885 and had previously worked in Concarneau and Fontainebleu and was to be identified with St Ives for many years to come. He painted atmospheric views of sea and coast, he was a frequent exhibitor at the Royal Academy and became President of the St Ives Arts Club. The Honourable Duff Tollemache (1859–1936), a member of the Tollemache family of Helmingham Hall, Suffolk, had studied at the Royal Academy Schools and in Paris and Brussels. He exhibited many scenes of Cornwall and the Scilly Isles at the Royal Academy between 1883 and 1895. William Eadie was a winter resident of St Ives from 1885 onwards: he painted fishing scenes and domestic interiors.

St Ives soon rivalled Newlyn as the English equivalent of the art colonies of northern France, and by the late 1880s more than sixty painters, including Americans, Australians, Scandinavians and others, worked there for a few weeks or months in the winter before returning to their continental haunts. The town was well equipped to accommodate visitors. The Porthminster Hotel offered golf, tennis, bathing, sea fishing and a darkroom for photographers. The Tregenna Castle Hotel, overlooking the bay, boasted that the winter temperature in St Ives was, on average, only four degrees less than in Rome. Queens Hotel in the High Street had the best stabling in the town. In addition

JAMES MCNEILL WHISTLER

St Ives, c.1883.

watercolour

FITZWILLIAM MUSEUM,
UNIVERSITY OF CAMBRIDGE.

there were no less than fifty-seven houses with apartments to let. However the town did not always treat the artists kindly. In 1890 the St Ives newspaper reported that a Japanese painter had set up an easel on the quay and began to paint. He was assaulted by local children, who threw stones at him not because he was Japanese, but because he was painting on a Sunday.

In autumn 1888 an artists' club began to meet in the studio of Louis Grier, an Australian painter who with his brother Wylie had settled in the town. The studio, known as the Fo'c's'le, was the scene of many light hearted gatherings on Saturday nights, usually with music and charades and attracted more than sixty members:

> *On fine nights the large doors at the end of the studio would be opened and then we would have a series of nocturnes that would have merited the artistic appreciation of Mr Whistler. The lights of the incoming herring boats, the rippling waves dancing, the lanterns' reflections and right in the foreground, the wet scintillating sand, and the group of hurrying fisherfolk, made a scene of great beauty.* (Louis Grier, 'An Artists Club', *The Studio,* vol.V. 1895).

In the late spring, many of the painters returned to Paris or London and this first informal club closed. By the following autumn Louis Grier had decided that he required the uninterrupted use of his studio. However such was the pressure for a permanent meeting place that in August 1890, largely through the efforts of H. Harewood Robinson, the St Ives Arts Club, was formed and premises were found on Westcotts Quay. The granite building of the club formed part of the sea wall, overlooking the boulder-strewn beach. Grier described it as 'a room with curious windows in the most unexpected places all on different levels, and with a quaint Dutch-like roof, with here and there a skylight, and here and there a swinging window'. (Grier *op.cit.*). The upper floor, which became the club room, was reached by an external ladder, and had been a net loft. It was weatherboarded and tarred and the tiny windows on all sides gave glimpses of sea and town. The ground floor continued to be used as a carpenter's shop during the early years of the club's existence, its wood shavings were a constant hazard until it was decided to replace oil lamps and candles

THE HON. DUFF
TOLLEMACHE

After the Catch, c.1885.

oil on canvas

IPSWICH MUSEUM.

WALTER SICKERT

Clodgy Point, 1883–84.

oil on panel

THE HUNTARIAN COLLECTION, GLASGOW.

The painting is shown in its original 'Whistler' frame.

with gas. To assist the less athletic members it was agreed that 'a rope be provided for the stairway, and at the end of the rope, a piano'.

Membership of the club was limited to practitioners in the arts, broadly interpreted to include architects, authors and musicians. *Although it was above all a social meeting place, the club's rules were strictly observed, and would-be members who failed to meet the professional requirements were black-balled. At an early general meeting it was resolved that 'on the evenings of Tuesday and Thursday the Club shall be reserved for the exclusive use of ladies, and on the evenings of Monday and Wednesday for the exclusive use of gentlemen. At all other times the Club shall be open to all members'. This was soon relaxed in favour of more general use of the club.

*According to W. A. Williams, past president and secretary of the St Ives Arts Club, the group who formed the club included Adrian Stokes, who became the first President, Marianne Stokes, E. W. Blomefield (Treasurer), Louis and Wylie Grier, William Holt Yates Titcomb, H. Harewood Robinson and Mrs Robinson, William and Mrs Eadie, Folliot and Mrs Stokes, Simmons, Docker, Davis, Lomax, Jevons, Fox, Bosch, Reitz, C. G. Morris, Bertram, Bell, Roller, Bishop, Detmold, Thomas and Caroline Gotch and the Misses Hayes, Ford and Cameron. Information from 'The St Ives Arts Club 1890–1961', in *The St Ives Scrapbook* by S. Canynage Caple. pub. St Ives 1961.

A net loft in St Ives,
c.1910. One of the many
fish lofts in the town
which later became
studios.

PHOTOGRAPH BY PERMISSION OF
ANDREW LANYON.

The St Ives painters were a more lively crowd than their fellows in Newlyn. Social life was expansive and generous. Discussions, drawing classes and demonstrations were arranged in the Arts Club, and Saturday nights were reserved for entertainment and conversation, encouraged by good wine. The Australian brothers Louis and Wylie Grier enlivened the early meetings of the club. Louis Grier (1864–1920) produced carefully constructed impressions of the sea and of the harbour crowded with the sails of the fishing fleet, with a silvery tonality which owed much to Whistler. His prolific painting was sometimes the subject for criticism, 'it was said in Downalong that he painted by the mile and cut off by the yard'. He had come to St Ives in 1884* and was a conspicuous figure in the town usually dressed in check knickerbockers of a generous cut and a flowing black cloak. The earlier work of Wylie Grier (c.1825) included many portraits, but he later painted atmospheric landscapes, with such titles as 'A Golden Autumn Eventide' (1888), 'Light Lingers on the Lowland' (1894) and 'Silver Night' (1896). Both artists exhibited intermittently at the Royal Academy from 1886 onwards.

*The dates of the arrival of Grier and of other early artists at St Ives are from *St Ives, Portrait of an Art Colony* by Marion Whybrow, Antique Collectors' Club, 1994.

Members of the St Ives
Arts Club, 1895

PHOTOGRAPH BY J. C. DOUGLAS.
ILLUSTRATION FROM *THE STUDIO*
VOL. 5, APRIL 1895.

Left: *F. W. Brooke.*
Back: *Alexander.*
Standing: *M. A. Jameson, J. Bromley.*
Left facing: *L. Grier,*
W. E. Osborn, J. H. Titcomb,
C. G. Morris, W. H. Y. Titcomb.

The Americans were outgoing, boisterous and slangy. Lowell Dyer (1856–1939) from Boston was noted for his wit and frequently acid comments. He took up permanent residence in St Ives and became a staunch supporter of the Arts Club. He was known as a Swedenborgian, probably because his father was a minister in the church established by Swedenborg, the eighteenth-century Swedish mystic. Lowell Dyer's paintings of children portrayed as angels have a heavy symbolism in accord with the revival of Medievalism that occurred in the last years of the nineteenth century, and which is reflected in the work of other artists in the area, such as Dow and Gotch.

The St Ives Arts Club,
Westcotts Quay.

Adrian and Marianne Stokes came to live in St Ives in 1886, each with an established reputation. Adrian, 'a sensitive and glowing colorist' as described by C. Lewis Hind, was thought to be one of the most promising landscape painters in Britain, and he had been a regular exhibitor at the Royal Academy for ten years. Marianne was a figure painter, and already one of her most important paintings 'Madonna, Light of the Earth' had been purchased by The Walker Art Gallery, Liverpool. With painting trips abroad and periods in London, they were to make St Ives their home until the late 1890s.

Adrian Stokes (1854–1935) was born in Southport, Lancashire, the son of an Inspector of Schools. It had been intended that he should enter the Navy, but a change of Government policy lost him his nomination and he entered a firm of cotton brokers in Liverpool. Already he had begun to draw seriously, and soon gained entry to the Royal Academy Schools, which he left in 1875, the year before Stanhope Forbes – three years his junior – began as a student.

As a young man Stokes was much influenced by Whistler and sought his advice:

The Fo'c's'le, the studio
of Louis Grier in St Ives.

PHOTOGRAPH BY W. TREVORROW.
ILLUSTRATION FROM *THE STUDIO*
VOL 5, APRIL 1895.

ADRIAN STOKES

*St Ives Harbour,
Moonlight.*

oil on canvas, 485 x 560mm.

DAVID MESSUM FINE ART.

*Before I went to France, I had several times the privilege of visiting the
brilliant Whistler in his studio; and no great artist was kinder, when talking to
a youngster, than he was to me. On one occasion – rather hoping that he would
tell me to go to Paris – I asked him where he studied. His answer came like a
flash 'Wherever I happened to be'.* (Adrian Stokes, *Landscape Painting,*
Seeley, Service & Co. 1915 p.3l).

In spite of this typically contrary advice Stokes went to France:

*not, at first, to Paris but to the country of France, where I associated with many
gifted and enthusiastic students, both French and American, and some of the best
French landscape painters of the day... and a vast new prospect seemed to open out.*

At Fontainebleau he came into contact with the most talented of the artists
working there, Corot, Courbet, Rousseau, Daubigny and others. At Pont-Aven
he became friendly with Stanhope Forbes and in 1883 he met the young
Austrian artist Marianne Preindlsberger whom he married the following year.

This was Marianne's second visit to Pont-Aven. Two years earlier she had
gone there with a fellow student from the Atelier Colorossi in Paris, Helene
Schjerfbeck, from Finland, who later worked in St Ives. During her earlier stay

LOUIS GRIER
Marshland.
St Ives Town Council.

in Pont-Aven Marianne began her first Salon painting, 'Tired Out' (1881–82). It was of a Breton girl sleeping by the stream from which she has come to draw water, painted in the manner of Bastien-Lepage.

Whilst at Pont-Aven, Adrian Stokes had become friendly with the highly talented and successful Danish artist Peder Severin Krøyer. Soon after their marriage, Adrian and Marianne Stokes visited Krøyer in Skagen, an artists' colony which had formed in the remote northern tip of Jutland in Denmark. A Danish friend of Krøyer, Karl Masden, who later became director of the Skagen Museum, wrote this uncomplimentary description of Stokes: 'Typical John Bull, fat, like a bulldog, who painted landscapes – featuring sand dunes and sheep – which were typically English colour and sentiment'. Marianne, by contrast, was described as a delightful personality and a very gifted painter. Whatever their faults they became great friends with Krøyer, who painted their portraits in 1886.

The Stokes came to Cornwall at the invitation of Stanhope Forbes, probably in 1886. It is difficult to picture the solidly built and normally reserved Adrian Stokes, as he entered into the spirit of a convivial evening's charade at the Fo'c'sl'e. Louis Grier described him as 'one of England's hopes in Landscape Art, chirping about on settees and things as "Little Tom Tit" guised in simple drapery, with a seven-foot matchstick under it by way of a tail; while a six foot genius from Boston stalked him with a mighty gun'. The hunter in this scene could have been either Frank Chadwick or Lowell Dyer, both from Boston (from Louis Grier 'A Painters Club', *op.cit.*). The Stokes first lived at Lelant, and later at 15 The Terrace St Ives, with a studio in Virgin Street, later destroyed by fire. They were a popular and successful couple. In 1890 Stokes was elected as the first President of the St Ives Arts Club, and because of the illness of the elected candidate Leslie Stevens, he continued as President for the following year. He was again President in 1896.

Adrian Stokes remained a staunch supporter of Whistler, of Japanese art, and above all of Corot and the earlier French landscape painters. He also had a high regard for the Impressionists. He remembered a phrase of Whistler's 'The first moment is the artist's moment', referring to the artist's immediate response to nature, and he was of the opinion that this more clearly described impressionism than the process of painting by divided colours. During his time in Cornwall the naturalism of his earlier work became a more decorative abstraction from landscape, with the colours of autumn or sunlight as a means of expression. He also became a fine sea-painter, 'The Harbour Bar' (1883) and

HUBERT VOS
Portrait drawings of Adrian Stokes and Marianne Stokes.
Reproduced in 'Newlyn and the Newlyn School' by W. Christian Symons for the *Magazine of Art* 1890.

MARIANNE STOKES
(née Preindlsberger)

Tired Out.

oil on canvas

'Off St Ives' (1890), were of the St Ives fishing fleet off shore, low on the horizon under a vast sky. In 1888 he received national recognition when his painting 'Uplands and Sky', an evening study of the Hayle River, was purchased from the Royal Academy by the Chantry Trustees.

Marianne Stokes (1866–1927) remained principally a figure painter, with children as her favourite subject. From 1885 she exhibited regularly in the Royal Academy. Her exhibit in 1886 was 'Childhood's Wonders' which depicts the fascination of three young children watching the blind groping of three newly-born puppies. It is a delicate portrayal of infancy, enlivened by realistic rendering of texture and detail. Three years later she exhibited a scene of bereavement entitled 'Go, Thou Must Play Alone My Boy, Thy Sister Is In Heaven' (1889). Like Elizabeth Forbes in her later work, she was increasingly drawn to medieval themes. *The Studio* in 1899 reported that

> *Mrs Adrian Stokes' eyes are frankly turned on the older Italians... she is contriving an armoured knight embracing a fair lady, a queen if one can judge from her headdress and her stately robe, the whole set in a dim wood of tall trees.* (*The Studio* Vol.Xlll, No.61, April 1895).

The Stokes left St Ives towards the end of the century, before making an extended visit to Holland to prepare work for an exhibition held at the Fine Art Society in 1900. After this they made London their base, with many visits to France, Italy and Austria. In 1903 a study by Adrian Stokes of the Austrian Tyrol, 'Autumn in the Mountains' was bought for the Chantry Bequest. He was elected ARA in 1909 and became RA in 1919. His later work was a more decorative form of landscape painting, often in tempera, a technique which lent itself to more colourful treatment. He also developed a considerable skill as a watercolourist, and became a leading member of the Royal Watercolour Society.

In its early years as an artists' colony St Ives was remarkably cosmopolitan, the painters moving between the ateliers of Paris and Antwerp and the artist communities of northern France and Scandinavia. The American artist Howard Butler (1856–1934) wrote to his father from St Ives:

> *There are many artists here – lately there has arrived a young lady from Finland – she has a wonderful talent and is a most interesting person altogether, although unfortunately lame – there is also a Russian lady here – neither speak any*

*English, but both are fluent in French. We have in our colony in addition to the
Finn and the Russian, an Austrian, a German, a Norwegian, a Swede, an
Irishman, a Scot, a Canadian, four Americans and several Englishmen – we
had a Greek who we are glad to have got rid of...* (Howard Butler, letter to his
family quoted in *The Good and Simple Life, op.cit.*, p.159).

The four Americans were Edward and Mrs Simmons, Alexander Harrison and
Butler himself.

The Simmons came to St Ives early in 1886, and were captivated by the place.
Edward rented a net loft, overlooking Porthmeor Beach, installed a skylight, and
by the summer he and three other painters were working there. He felt that:

*Going from Concarneau to St Ives was like moving from the thirteenth to the
seventeenth century. No more thatched roofs, no more floors of beaten earth, no
more manure piles in front of the houses. The roofs are of slate, topping little stone
houses, with quite proper floors...* (*The Good and Simple Life, op.cit.*, p.153).

His enthusiastic description of St Ives and the photographs he sent back
brought more Americans from Concarneau.

Simmons' early life had been adventurous. As a boy in Concord,
Massachusetts he had known Thoreau. He graduated from Harvard and went
West, first to Cincinnati as an oil salesman, and then to teach in a frontier school.
He studied art at the Boston Museum School, leaving for France in 1879, where
he enrolled with other Americans at the newly established Julian's atelier. His
work was accepted by the Salon in 1882, and he soon moved to Concarneau
where he became a central figure among the early group of Americans and made
the acquaintance of many visiting English artists, including Frank Bramley,
Adrian Stokes, Edwin Harris and Stanhope Forbes. Simmons remained in St Ives
until 1891, when he returned to the United States.

Howard Butler came to St Ives a few months after Simmons and described it as

*more beautiful than any of the French ports. Here the water is pure as crystal,
the old town is fully as picturesque as Honfleur; the fishermen are splendid models
– the coast is rugged and the sea heavy – colour exceedingly rich – the only
drawback – as on the coast of Maine – the sea fogs.* (Howard Butler, letters to his
family 1886–87 in the Archives of American Art, quoted in *The Good and Simple
Life, op.cit.*).

During the previous year he had studied art in Paris and worked in several
of the artists' communities in France. After a week in St Ives he found lodgings
at the top of the town, away from the fishy smells of the harbour. He too created
a studio overlooking Porthmeor beach from an old fish loft; in two days he cut a
window in the roof and white-washed the interior. He entered fully into the life
of the area and observed the changes that the influx of artists brought to the
town. On his first visit he stayed in St Ives until September 1887, and on later
visits he noted that in the space of nine years a whole row of twenty-four lofts
had been converted into artist's studios.

Another couple who came from Concarneau were the American Frank
Chadwick and his wife Emma (née Löwstadt). Emma was the first of many
Scandinavian artists to work in St Ives. She had trained in Paris and gained a
medal in the Salon of 1877. Her husband, from Boston, was less talented but
enjoyed private means. They were a lively couple who joined in the social life of
St Ives and Newlyn. In 1887 Stanhope Forbes reported that they had come over
to Newlyn for a ball that had been arranged among the artists. Chadwick wore a

EDWARD EMERSON
SIMMONS *(opposite)*.

Awaiting his Return.

oil on canvas, 533 x 387mm.

PRIVATE COLLECTION.

*Painted in Brittany before his
first visit to St Ives.*

'More singular costume than ever, a white waistcoat, a black "paget coat" and a folding top hat', this last caused much amusement among the girls in Newlyn. (*The Good and Simple Life* p.163 *op.cit.*). The Chadwicks remained in contact with their friends in Grez-sur-Loing, and when they left St Ives at the end of the 1880s, they returned to Grez where they lived for the rest of their lives.

The most distinguished of the American artists in St Ives was Alexander Harrison (1853–1930), who came in 1899 and stayed at the Tregenna Castle Hotel. He found many old friends and acquaintances in the town, particularly Adrian and Marianne Stokes and the Simmons, whom he had known in Grez-sur-Loing. Harrison had established a considerable reputation through his work in Brittany – and some notoriety through his paintings of the nude in the open air. The best known of these 'In Arcadia' (1885) [now in the Louvre, Paris] depicts three girls, posing in dappled sunlight filtering through the trees of an orchard. He was also much respected as a painter of the sea, and became absorbed with painting twilight and nocturnal effects of sea and sky, for which he relied on memory, a practice shared with Whistler and by later marine painters in St Ives. His large painting 'The Wave' of 1885 was seen as a *tour de force*. It was based upon a series of memory sketches prior to the finished work. He began with an 'ebauche', a small study with only a few tones, which recorded the effect at a certain hour that he wished to achieve. This was to get the mood throughout the work. Between this study, of five by ten inches, to the final painting, nearly ten feet long, were six or seven graded studies, each gaining in strength. This painting was a great popular success and was later purchased for the Pennsylvania Academy of Fine Arts.

Harrison had won the friendship and respect of Bastien-Lepage and had arranged a lecture visit to the United States for him, but because of the early death of the French master, these plans never materialised. Harrison, Butler and Simmons were part of the early group of American artists in Concarneau, vividly described by Blanche Willis Howard in her book *Guenn* written in 1881. In this novel she sympathetically described the artists' colony and its Bohemian way of life as well as the traditional superstitions, customs and dress of the Breton peasants. Many of the characters are well-known Concarneau figures, drawn from life – the hero, Hamor, is Edward Simmons. Just as many artists came from Concarneau, so St Ives increasingly took on the character of an international artists' colony.

The Swedish artist Anders Zorn (1860–1920) and his young wife Emma Lamm spent the winter of 1887–88 in St Ives. Zorn later had great international success and became Sweden's best known painter of the late nineteenth century. Born in Mora, a remote northern village in the province of Daforna, Anders Zorn was the illegitimate son of a wealthy businessman, brought up by his mother, a peasant woman. He identified strongly with his working class origins and celebrated its simple values in his greatest paintings. As a student at the Royal Academy of Fine Art in Stockholm, Zorn had begun to paint with conviction and originality, and showed an instinctive response to watercolour, which he used with great vigour. He made an extended visit to Europe – first to 'that rather big village London', where he found enormous wealth and bad art. In Paris he felt more at home, but soon he was in Spain where he was intoxicated by the evocative atmosphere and made many paintings of gipsy girls. He returned to London in 1884, established good contacts with the expatriate Swedish community and began to exhibit and sell his work.

Zorn's time in St Ives came at an important period in his own development. He was an artist of considerable physical presence. His friend Edward Simmons described him as 'a man with great hypnotic quality, who did not talk much, but dominated without speaking'. Zorn became friendly with the English painters particularly Adrian Stokes and his Austrian wife Marianne and with the Scandinavian artists Helene Schjerfbeck and Bernt Gronvold who were also in the town. His overtures of friendship to his compatriot Emma Chadwick who he had known in student days were not returned. She received him coldly and appeared to have difficulty in speaking Swedish.

Zorn was an extraordinarily gifted painter who worked from landscape subjects and from the figure with equal ease. He found his models among the seamen and their families near his studio in Downalong, and captured the strong light of St Ives in pearly translucent colour. He had earlier worked mostly in watercolour but was continuously searching to free this medium from the precision and detail with which it was often associated. Edward Simmons records watching Zorn wash off a large watercolour by throwing pails of water over it, in order to 'bring it together'. To achieve the scale and solidity that he required for figure studies he began use oil paint. One of his first large oil paintings was of a young St Ives couple, leaning on a stone parapet gazing at the full moon rising over the town, the harbour and panorama of St Ives below them. Zorn described this as 'a fisherman and a girl flirting in a way which I believe unique to England'.

Despite his feeling for the natural beauty of St Ives, Zorn and Emma were conscious of the strong social divisions and cramped, dirty conditions that existed in the town. Emma was also shocked to find that boys of eighteen or nineteen years were made to marry fourteen year old girls to keep them from being corrupted. The Zorns left St Ives in the spring of 1888 to see his painting 'Fisherman, St Ives' (1888) safely to the Paris Salon. (The painting was later purchased by the French Government and is now in the Musée des Beaux Arts.). They settled in Paris and became part of that celebrated circle that

ANDERS ZORN

Mr and Mrs Anders Zorn, 1880.

etching

REPRODUCED IN *THE STUDIO,* VOL. XII, NO. 61, APRIL 1898.

ANDERS ZORN

Boats in St Ives, 1887.

ZORN MUSEUM, SWEDEN.

ANDERS ZORN

St Ives, Cornwall, 1891.

etching

The etching is of the same subject as his painting 'Fishermen of St Ives', 1888, purchased by the French Government.

included Antonin Proust, Albert Besnard and Auguste Rodin. Zorn also made the acquaintance of the Impressionist painters and became friendly with Monet.

The 'talented young lady from Finland... unfortunately lame', mentioned by Howard Butler, was undoubtedly Helene Schjerfbeck (1862–1946), one of a small group of Finnish painters who had trained at the Atelier Colorossi in Paris, and later worked in Pont-Aven where she had become friendly with Marianne Preindlsberger (later Stokes). Helene Schjerfbeck was lame from childhood but she possessed a unique talent and after a continuous struggle against ill health and poverty, she later became one of the best known women in Finnish art. She was never to marry, although it was rumoured that she had at one time been engaged to an Englishman and was recovering from her broken engagement at the time of her first visit to St Ives.

Helene Schjerfbeck was in St Ives from July 1887 to the early part of the following year, and again in 1889 with her Finnish friend Maria Wiik. In St Ives she found many 'veterans' from Pont-Aven and Concarneau and rented a studio from Harewood Robinson. She also attended drawing classes given by Adrian Stokes, several times a week. Her painting had a delicate openness and spontaneity that enabled her to tackle subjects ranging from a sympathetic portrait of a sick child in 'The Convalescent' (1888) [awarded a Gold Medal at the Paris International Exhibition in 1899], or the dark glow of the bread ovens in St Ives in 'The Bakery'. In 1917 Helene Schjerfbeck had her first exhibition in Sweden and from then on her work met with increasing success.

Maria Wiik (1853–1928), also Finnish, was a fellow student at the Finska Konstreningen, and followed Helene Schjerfbeck to St Ives. Maria then went to the Académie Julian in Paris and studied under Puvis de Chevannes; the two girls were also together in Pont-Aven. They shared a preoccupation with mental and physical illness and solitude, characterised in the work of other Scandinavian artists, notably Edvard Munch. In St Ives Maria painted a study of youth and old age, 'Out in the World', a tender description of a young girl, who, whilst attending the sick bed of her aged relative who is nearing the end of her life, anticipates that moment when her responsibilities for the invalid will end, and she must fend for herself.

This cosmopolitan group of artists brought great liveliness and vigour to St Ives, but as few became long term residents, their work passed unremarked in English art circles, although much of it was outstanding. Soon however the town began to attract a number of older British artists of assured reputation.

One such artist was Alfred East (1849–1913) who translated his feelings for nature into broad and atmospheric paintings in which landscape became a metaphor for nature's own strength. He came late to painting yet was an enormously popular landscapist and a prominent Royal Academician, and was knighted for his services to Art. East was born in Kettering, Northamptonshire. His parents were opposed to painting as a career and it was not until he was thirty-one that he was able to start his training. For three years he studied in Paris, at the Ecole des Beaux Arts, and then at the Académie Julian, where he was taught by Fleury and Bouguereau. Like his contemporary Thomas Millie Dow, East worked at Grez-sur-Loing, and his first strong influences are 'the men of 1830', the French landscapists, particularly Corot and Rousseau whom he met in Barbizon.

The tranquility of East's landscapes was deeply satisfying to the British public. If they contained few surprises, they committed no offences. He first exhibited at the Royal Academy in 1883, a Barbizon landscape entitled 'The Dewy Morning', and from then until his death he exhibited each year. He was also innovative as an etcher, drawing directly on the plate out of doors and became one of the early members of the Royal Society of Painter Etchers.

Throughout his life East was deeply conscious of his English heritage, and drew on a tradition that owed much to the intimacy of nature achieved by Constable and Turner. 'His streams and skies, his ariel foliage, his orange autumns, his pearly moonlight nights, will be the joy of successive generations' (catalogue to the Alfred East Memorial Exhibition 1914). He worked thoroughly on particular themes, studying the elements of landscape with great care, seeking always to broaden his approach. Trees, hills and woods were

HELEN SCHJERFBECK

*Boys on the Shore
by St Ives,* 1887.

oil on wood, 825 x 1050mm.

PRIVATE COLLECTION, HELSINKI.

drawn and re-drawn from different points of view until he became fully acquainted with their form and colour, and could select those aspects that most inspired him. His exhibition at the Fine Art Society in 1895 consisted of many paintings of the same scene painted from dawn until moonrise – an examination of changing light similar to Monet in his series of paintings of poplars, haystacks, and of the façade of Rouen Cathedral.

East was a natural teacher and wrote a number of articles and books on landscape painting. In 1906 he advised:

> *You should always be a sketcher, morning, noon and night. I have sketched skies every morning for months together, and have got to know something about skies. I have sketched trees for years and in this way I have learnt something about trees... how they live, to see how they grip the earth and how the sap finds its way up through the trunk and into the leaves... Look at nature with the eyes wide open and you will see the big facts; and a thousand little mistakes, no matter how carefully painted will never make one big truth.* ('On Sketching from Nature: a few words to students', by Alfred East. *The Studio* Vol.37 No.155, 1906).

Alfred East was resident for long periods in St Ives in the years around the turn of the century, and many of his annual submissions to the Academy came

MARIA WIIK

Out in the World, 1887.

oil on canvas, 465 x 365mm.

THE MUSEUM OF FINNISH ART.

ALFRED EAST

Autumn, 1907.

REPRODUCED IN *THE STUDIO*
VOL 37, NO. 155 FEBRUARY 1906.

either from Cornwall, the Cotswolds or the Lake District. Lewis Hind gave a description of East painting at St Ives:

'Figures,' he said to me one day, 'should merely be partakers in the colour harmony. I'll show you'. And he led me to his studio where there was a six foot canvas of a gorgeous decorative landscape laid in Southern France – his 'Faith' picture. He began to paint quickly on sky, hilltops and trees, and at intervals, with full brush, his hand dropped to the foreground, and smudged there blobs of colour. As he worked he would turn from time to time, to shape these blobs into contours, and they gradually became a procession of peasants winding up towards the hills. (C. Lewis Hind *Landscape Painting*, Chapman-Hall 1924).

Given such talent and industry, it was inevitable that East should rise to a position of leadership at the Royal Academy. He was elected A.R.A in 1899, and four years later he was awarded the 'Grand Order of the Corona' of Italy with the title of 'Cavaliere'. He was knighted in 1910 and in 1913, two months before his death, he became an R.A. A memorial gallery with a large collection of his work was created in his home town of Kettering.

When the Scottish artist Thomas Millie Dow (1848–1914) took up residence in St Ives in about 1890, he was a mature artist and his work was well respected. He had been associated with the 'Glasgow Boys' in the early 1880s, when he gradually changed from Lepage-inspired naturalism, to a more symbolic use of subjects from myth and legend. His unusual combination of *plein-air* painting with classical or allegorical themes, drew Dow away from the direct realism of his Scottish contemporaries and he was one of the first to leave Glasgow.

ALFRED EAST

Pencil sketch, 1903.

REPRODUCED IN *THE STUDIO* VOL 37, NO. 156 FEBRUARY 1906.

Son of the town clerk of Fife, Dow had embarked upon a legal training, but abandoned it to work in Gérôme's studio at the École des Beaux Arts with Carolus-Duran. Dow's work was delicate with a light atmospheric touch; restrained and decorative rather than vigorous. He painted landscape and still-lifes with soft colour harmonies which have much in common with those of his friend Norman Garstin. Garstin wrote:

these harmonies of colour remain with us, thrilling us with that plaintive pleasure which is the last gift of all beauty. His pictures touch us as a summer evening touches us, as a melody heard over still water. (Norman Garstin 'The Work of T. Millie Dow'. *The Studio* Vol.X April 1897).

Dow exhibited his work little in this country, but more often abroad, including Munich with the Secessionists. His work was held in high regard by his contemporaries. George Henry, one of the most advanced and rebellious of the 'Glasgow Boys', described two of Dow's landscapes as:

the most beautiful things I have ever seen. I don't know of any other Fellow who has managed to make one feel on seeing these pictures so much of the spirituality of nature. They are intense in this way. One especially seems to make you creep with the strong quietness and mystery of nature. They are pictures that will probably never see a public exhibition, at least until there is a revolution in art. (Undated letter probably written in the autumn of 1885, quoted in *The Glasgow Boys* by Roger Billecliffe, John Munroy 1985).

In Scotland Thomas Millie Dow had married Florence Pitcher, who had previously been married in India and already had two daughters. They later had another daughter and five sons. The move to St Ives was partly to help the asthma of one of the boys. In 1889 they visited St Ives and six years later they bought Talland House, a spacious villa, set in a steep garden of about half an acre, then owned by the writer Leslie Stephen, the editor of *The Dictionary of National Biography* and father of Virginia and Vanessa (later the writer Virginia Woolf and the painter Vanessa Bell).

Millie Dow shared that spirit of internationalism that affected many of the St Ives artists. He had spent several summers during the early 1880s in the village of Grez-sur-Loing, the artists' colony outside Paris, frequently visited by Bastien-Lepage and many visiting British and American artists. The portrait of Dow, by his great friend William Stott, painted in Grez, is very much in the tradition of Whistler.

Another close friend of Dow's, from Gérôme's studio in Paris, was the American Abbot Henderson Thayer (1849–1921), the son of a physician brought up in the country of New Hampshire and Vermont. Thayer was a natural draughtsman and became a well-known portrait artist. Many of his paintings of women and children are idealised, often portrayed as angelic beings in attitudes of blessing or reconciliation. In his lifetime he received great adulation, his figures were compared to Botticelli and he was described as 'one of the artistic heroes of the nineteenth century in American Art'.

In 1884 Millie Dow visited Thayer in the United States and they painted from the landscape in the Hudson Valley. It is probable that Thayer returned with Dow to Cornwall, for in the same year he was reported as living at 5 Bellair Terrace, St Ives (Whybrow, *op.cit.*, p.212). In Cornwall Thayer painted portraits of Millie Dow's children and several landscape studies.

Alfred East

Photographed on his election to the Royal Academy. The Art Journal, *which published the portrait in 1899, described it as 'very tardy recognition'.*

WILLIAM STOTT
(OF OLDHAM)

*Portrait of my friend
TMD.*

oil on canvas

NATIONAL GALLERY OF MODERN
ART, SCOTLAND.

ABBOT H. THAYER

Portrait of Elsie Pitcher
(Stepdaughter of Thomas
Millie Dow), 1898.

oil on canvas, 625mm x 500mm.

PRIVATE COLLECTION.

THOMAS MILLIE DOW

*Porthminster Beach
from The Island, St Ives.*
oil on canvas, 900mm x 1200mm.
PRIVATE COLLECTION.

THOMAS MILLIE DOW

Souvenir of Spring.
watercolour, 240mm x 255mm.
PRIVATE COLLECTION.

6

THE ROYAL ACADEMY AND THE NEW ENGLISH ART CLUB

In the 1870s the Royal Academy reigned supreme. It had recently moved to newly extended premises in Burlington House, Piccadilly, and in 1869 the first Summer Exhibition was held in the handsome new galleries. These larger exhibitions brought a considerable increase in popular attention, and immediately became part of the London summer season. It was the ambition of every young artist to be accepted in the open competition of the Summer Exhibition, for if a work received public attention and was favourably commented upon by the press, its sale was assured. Membership of the Academy, with the right to hang five works in each of its exhibitions, brought a degree of financial security. The most successful artists were those who painted set pieces from history, especially the triumphs of Empire: large-scale paintings which reflected the wealth and aspirations of Victoria's reign. Portraiture was also favoured, both as a social and an artistic convention, and if the sitter was famous this was an added attraction.

The Academy was dominated by a group of Olympian giants who directed popular taste and sentiment. The classicists Frederick Lord Leighton (President from 1878 to 1896 and the first English artist to be awarded a Baronetcy), Sir Lawrence Alma-Tadema and Sir Edward John Poynter (President 1896–1918 and also made a Baronet); the great populist William Powell Frith and, from the ranks of the Pre-Raphaelite Brotherhood, Dante Gabriel Rossetti, William Holman Hunt and George Frederick Watts, and the latter-day Pre-Raphaelite, Sir Edward Burne-Jones.

Leighton's work found a ready response among the newly prosperous merchants and industrialists of England and as his reputation mounted he was richly rewarded. His first success was 'The triumphal procession of Cinabue's "Madonna" through the streets of Florence' , which was favourably received by John Ruskin, and was bought by Queen Victoria for the princely sum of 600 guineas. Subsequently his paintings fetched huge sums and in 1879 his sculpture 'Athlete Struggling with Python' was bought under the terms of the Chantry Bequest for £2200.

The vast size of his paintings was designed to overwhelm, 'Captive Andromache' purchased by Manchester City Art Gallery in 1889 was 160 inches long. The measure of Leighton's public acclaim was his magnificent house and studio in Holland Park, elegant and richly decorated, and packed with superb works of art collected on his extensive travels. His achievement and wealth were rivalled by the naturalised Dutch painter Lawrence (Lourens) Alma-Tadema (1836–1912) who converted his house in St John's Wood into a Pompeian palace. His art was dedicated to the accurate reconstruction of Roman life and spectacle in a manner that would soon be the province of the Hollywood film industry.

A late flowering of the Pre-Raphaelite artists gave a strange romanticism to Victorian art. Dante Gabriel Rossetti (1828–1882) retained an extraordinary magnetism and in the last twenty years of his life explored a private medieval dream world of heavenly and earthly love and the idealisation of female beauty. George Frederick Watts (1817–1904) dealt with the imponderables of Faith, Hope, Love, Life and Death, in large allegorical paintings and earned a handsome living from flattering portraits of beauties and celebrities. John Everett Millais (1829–1896) was elected to the Royal Academy in 1863. He left behind his idealistic allegiances to the Pre-Raphaelite Brotherhood and became a fashionable painter of portraits and history pieces. He too was awarded a Baronetcy and in the last few months of his life was elected President of the Royal Academy. On his death the Presidency went to that other glittering classicist who dominated the official art circles of the end of the century Sir Edward Poynter, painter, sculptor, monumental decorator and a fine draughtsman, whose work ranged widely across ancient history. Poynter held almost all of the public positions of note, becoming the First Slade Professor at University College, the Director of the Schools of South Kensington, and for a period of twenty-two years President of the Royal Academy. For eight years he was also the Director of the National Gallery.

The best and worst of the Academy at this time was described by W. P. Frith (1819–1909) in his large painting 'The Private View of the Royal Academy 1881' (page 117), which portrays a gathering of celebrities of the day – statesmen, poets, judges, philosophers, musicians, painters and actors – all of whom have come to see and be seen. In the foreground with a group of eager worshippers, is Oscar Wilde, apostle of the beautiful. Well known artists whose work is being discussed anxiously await his pronouncements. In the centre of the composition Sir Frederick Leighton is in conversation with Lady Lonsdale, who sits with Lady Diana Huddleston and Baroness Barnett Coutts. Mr Gladstone shakes hands with Sir Stafford Northcote; Professor Huxley, the Archbishop of York, Herr Tenniel, George du Maurier, Ellen Terry and others are also faithfully represented.

A further extension of Academy influence was the right to purchase works of contemporary art from the substantial funds of the Chantry Bequest. 'The National Collection of British Fine Art' acquired by this fund was transferred to the Tate Gallery on its formation in 1897, but the selection of work for purchase remained for many years in the hands of the Academy.

The growth of the prosperous middle-class brought a new popular audience for a more intimate kind of painting, smaller in scale and more human in expression. The favoured subjects were not the grand classical themes but simple moral or descriptive scenes. This new market brought about the development of new galleries and dealers in London and other cities, and a good living for growing numbers of artists capable of providing what John Ruskin unkindly described as:

bright little watercolours which could not look other than pert in ghostly corridors, and petty in halls of state; but they gave an unquestionable tone of liberal-mindedness to a suburban villa, and were the cheerfullest possible decorations for a modest-sized breakfast parlour opening on a nicely mown lawn. (John Ruskin Notes on Samuel Prout and William Hunt, 1879–80.)

Societies of artists such as the Institute of Painters in Oil Colours and the Royal Society of British Artists were very active, and municipal galleries opened, particularly in the northern towns. Considerable interest was shown in the sales of foreign and English pictures, and price lists were published regularly. Pictures costing more than 1400 guineas were thought to be extraordinary, such prices were usually received for Reynolds, Romney, Turner and Constable. At the sale of Lord Leighton's effects, seventeen pictures from his collection fetched above this figure, the highest price going to a block of four fine Corot's sold for the great price of 6000 guineas. But it was still very difficult for a young artist to make a decent living. Stanhope Forbes complained 'it is perfectly impossible to make more than £200–300 a year'.

In London one of the very few alternative showing places to the Royal Academy was the Grosvenor Gallery built in New Bond Street by Sir Coutts Lindsay, a wealthy art lover and dealer who had poured great sums of money into creating an elaborate setting for the finest work of the day. The creation of the gallery was itself a criticism of the highly conservative attitude of the Royal Academy, which did nothing to encourage the work of young artists. Work shown in the Grosvenor was very much the personal choice of Sir Coutts Lindsay and it was his policy to present a broader view of contemporary art than did the Academy. The principal artists who exhibited in the opening exhibition in May 1877, were Burne-Jones and Whistler, together with G.F. Watts and Albert Moore, each showing major groups of recent work, and hung in a well lit and spacious great hall. The walls were covered with red damask, and below them a dado of dark green velvet. The panelled ceiling had been painted a deep blue and was decorated with phases of the moon and stars by Whistler, oriental rugs, pottery, plants and fine furniture completed the setting. Henry Tuke saw this exhibition whilst still a student at the Slade. He recalled the impact of Burne-Jones' 'Merlin' and the regular 'arrangements' and 'harmonies' by Whistler and the portraits of Legros. For the artists of Newlyn and St Ives the Grosvenor Gallery provided a London audience for their work and for a number of years this highly influential gallery attracted the attention of the critics and the public. The last exhibition at the Gallery was held in 1890, but as this closed so others were coming into being.

In the 1880s and 1890s the Royal Academy was largely hostile to imported ideas, particularly those of French *plein-air*ism, which appeared to threaten its position. Henry Tuke was disappointed when his paintings were rejected by the Royal Academy in 1883, and spoke for many young artists when he wrote that: 'It is not to be wondered at when the hanging committee consists of men going rapidly down hill, and two already arrived at the bottom'. (Maria Tuke Sainsbury, *op.cit.*) Tuke had already exhibited at the Paris Salon in the two previous years, he had executed a number of portrait commissions and had attracted the friendship and support of the Bond Street dealer C. W. Dowdeswell. In 1883 much of the work by the younger group was rejected on the grounds that they were too 'French'. Most of Tuke's friends shared the same fate, although they had previously shown in the Summer Exhibitions and had evident talent. These wholesale rejections resulted in a decision by the younger artists to free themselves from dependence upon the Academy.

Even while they were students in Paris, the younger artists had felt the need for a new society, run by painters for painters. The first formal meeting took place in January 1886, with fifteen artists present including a number from Newlyn: Stanhope Forbes, Thomas Gotch, Henry Tuke and Percy Jacomb-Hood. Others included Fred Brown, S. J. Soloman, W. J .Laidby and Philip Wilson Steer. All had trained in France and they first considered calling themselves 'The Society of Anglo-French Painters'. Later they decided to assert their national identity by taking the name 'The New English Art Club'.

The London dealer Martin Colnaghi agreed to arrange the club's first exhibition in the premises of the Royal Institute of Watercolour Painters in Pall Mall, which had been re-vamped and named the Marlborough Gallery. However, it became clear that Colnaghi, who was a dealer in old masters, lacked conviction in terms of the more forward looking members. When he toured the artists' studios he was alarmed by the sight of Henry Tuke's painting of nude boys and he withdrew two weeks before the start of the exhibition. Fortunately one of the members, W. J. Laidby, had the means to finance the exhibition and it opened, a week later than intended, on 12 April 1886. By then the club had attracted a membership of fifty artists, forty-three of whom exhibited. The French influence was clear; many of the subjects were peasant and genre scenes, and the distinctive square-brush technique which many artists had adopted was much in evidence. The *Pall Mall Gazette* was appreciative of the innovative work, reporting that:

> *The desire of the new school is to vindicate the soundness of emigrating English feeling and sentiment upon what is known as French technique – French only because no adequate attention is paid to the teaching of technique out of France. (Pall Mall Gazette 13 April 1886.)*

Lord Leighton, then President of the Royal Academy, was less complimentary. He declared 'The second year will try these men and the third probably disband them'.

Henry Tuke had been nominated for the selection committee but to his relief he was not on the final list of members who were elected. The day after the show opened he fled to Falmouth, to race his boat *The Lily*, the joy of his life. He showed two paintings at that first exhibition, 'Basking' (1885), a clothed boy lying on a beach and 'Bathers' (1885), the first of the many large-scale, open-air painting of the nude for which he was to become famous. 'Bathers' was painted on Maenporth beach, Falmouth. It contained three principal figures and

HENRY TUKE

Bathers, 1885.

SKETCH REPRODUCED IN THE *PALL MALL GAZETTE* OF THE PAINTING EXHIBITED AT THE FIRST EXHIBITION OF THE NEW ENGLISH ART CLUB IN 1896.

two small ones, all painted from the same model, Arthur Shilling. Tuke recorded that, 'I am almost tired of painting the same boy but in the bathing picture I consider him quite impersonal, the vehicle of splendid fresh colour and form'. (Maria Tuke Sainsbury *op.cit.*)

During the first exhibition, Stanhope Forbes' friend La Thangue proposed that the club should open itself to every artist in Britain, and be run by a committee elected by practising artists who would select work by open competition. He further suggested that a circus should be used to house such a great exhibition. His proposals were put to the members in a flood of letters and received support from some members, but not from Forbes or the other Newlyners. Finally the matter was put to a general meeting, and voted down. La Thangue resigned, and it was agreed that for the next exhibition larger premises would be sought in the Egyptian Hall, Piccadilly.

One important change that was agreed was that any artist could exhibit two works if invited to do so by two members of the club. It was by this means the Impressionist camp gained admission and finally ascendency of the New English Art Club. The Impressionist group included a number of artists who had been closely associated with Whistler, including Sidney Starr, an original member, Mortimer Menpes and Walter Richard Sickert. Whistler was to have great influence on the New English Art Club, but he remained apart from it, leaving it mainly to the younger artists, many of whom had been his pupils. He exhibited in a number of the annual exhibitions, where his work was treated *hors concours* as was that of other distinguished artists including Degas, Monet, Legros and Renoir.

At the second exhibition in June 1887, nudity was again an issue. This time it was not the work of Tuke that caused controversy (he showed a sailing picture, 'The First Boat In'), but Theodore Roussel, the club's secretary, who was criticised for his painting 'The Reading Girl' (1887) which depicted a nude girl in a studio setting, seated on a folding chair reading from a journal. The ordinariness of the scene aroused critical fury: 'There has been no attempt to idealise the figure, it is simply a portrait of a rather underfed woman who is content at a shilling an hour to be naked and not ashamed', wrote a reviewer. Philip Wilson Steer was also criticised by the *Magazine of Art* for his painting of three women bathers at the seaside called 'A Summer's Evening' (1888): 'These ladies came down to bathe unclothed... they are about three quarters life-sized, and very indecent'.

Walter Richard Sickert became a member of the club late in 1887. His friends Frederick Brown, Philip Wilson Steer, Sidney Starr and Theodore Roussel were already well established members and together they set out to change the attitudes of the New English in line with their own more radical sympathies for Impressionism. By this time Sickert had freed himself from Whistler's influence and had found new subjects in the London music hall, which, for him, rivalled the ballet and theatre themes of Degas. However, he aroused the open hostility of the founder members of the Club, including many of the Newlyn painters, who objected to his subject matter – scenes of the music hall and low life of London and Paris. Sickert's 'Gatti's Hungerford Palace of Varieties – Second Turn of Miss Katie Lawrence', exhibited at the club in 1888, was thought to be sensational. Stanhope Forbes wrote to Elizabeth Armstrong:

I was astonished to find the Impressionists in great force... I am sure you will be astonished with Sickert's picture... I only hope it is not in any way a reflection of the painter's mind. Tawdry, vulgar and the sentiment of the lowest music hall... unless the Whistler influence is stamped out, the club will go to the bad. (letter dated 31.3.1888).

THOMAS GOTCH

Destiny, 1896.

oil on canvas, 2500 x 1900mm.

Exhibited at the first exhibition of The New English Art Club 1886.

THE ART GALLERY OF SOUTH AUSTRALIA.

Forbes' own contribution to that exhibition, called 'Palmistry' (1888) was criticised as trivial, 'A young man in evening dress talking nonsense far too seriously over a girl's hand, or rather hands, for he apparently requires them both'. (*Magazine of Art*, 1889).

The strongly-voiced opinions of Sickert and his friends soon began to antagonise other members of the club who complained that only second-best pictures were being sent in to the annual exhibitions, and after a particularly vigorous meeting in which Sickert proposed that each member be required to send in only their best work, he wrote:

Our friends, ie, the Impressionist nucleus in the N.E.A.C. have all advised that my name must not this year appear much in proposing or seconding people, as my work is said to be most unpoplular with a dull but powerful section of the

HENRY TUKE

August Blue, 1894.

oil on canvas, 1200 x 1820mm.

THE TATE GALLERY
(CHANTRY BEQUEST).

N.E.A.C., the people whose touch is square, and who all paint alike and take their genealogy, I believe, from J. P. Laurens. (Letter to Emile Blanche in *The Life and Opinions of Walter Richard Sickert* by Robert Emmons, Faber & Faber, London).

This expression of open hostility to the Newlyn painters was fiercely resented. Forbes and Gotch were still on the selection committee, but so were Steer and Roussel, and it was clear that Sickert was intent on making the New English into an Impressionist club. In his role as London Editor for the *New York Herald*, Sickert again attacked the Newlyn artists, this time for their exhibits at the Royal Academy:

Again and again we find canvasses which have nothing to recommend them to the critic but a heavy travesty of the touch of second-rate French painters, praised for truth, which are full of untruths of value.

Frank Bramley came under particularly fierce attack from Sickert. Bramley had shown 'Winter' in the Club's first exhibition. a small study of an elderly man tranquilly resting before a warm fire and reflecting upon the past. In the second exhibition he had shown the important picture 'Weaving a Chain of Grief' (1887) which had attracted much favourable attention. Perhaps because of this success it received particular criticism from Sickert. He was enraged by Bramley's further success at the Academy with 'A Hopeless Dawn' (1888) and its subsequent purchase by the Chantry Bequest. 'I would sentence admirers of

Mr Bramley's transportive studio realism to no more form of correction than a condemnation to live three weeks with "A Hopeless Dawn"', he wrote. (Robert Emmons, *op.cit.*)

Sickert continued to conduct a personal and highly vituperative attack on the work of the Newlyn painters, seizing upon the central principle of *plein-air* painting for his most caustic criticism:

The sun moves too quickly. You find that the grey weather is more possible and end by never working in any other. Grouping with any approach to naturalness is found to be impossible. You find that you had better confine your compositions to a single figure. And with a little experience the photo-realist finds, if he be wise, that the single figure had better be in repose.

He went on to demolish the fabric of naturalism, replacing this with his own feelings for pictorial values:

Your subject is a real peasant in his own natural surroundings, and not a model from Hatton Garden. But what is he doing? He is posing for a picture as best he can, and he looks it. That woman stooping to put potatoes in a sack will never rise again. The potatoes, portraits every one, will never drop into the sack, and never a breath of air circulates around that painful rendering in the flat of the

FRANK BRAMLEY

Weaving a Chain of Grief, 1887.

oil on canvas, 900mm x 1125mm.

Exhibited at the second exhibition of the New English Art Club in 1887.

DEPARTMENT OF HERITAGE.

authentic patches on the very gown of a real peasant. What are the truths you gained, a handful of tiresome little facts, compared to the truths you have lost? To life and spirit, life and air? (W. R. Sickert 'Modern Realism in Painting', Andre Theurit *Jules Bastien-Lepage. A Memoir*, T. Fisher Unwin 1892).

The polarisation within the New English Art Club that resulted from these attacks led to the withdrawal of the Newlyn painters. They resigned *en masse* in 1890 and from that time gave their full support to the Royal Academy. Many of the St Ives artists were also members of the New English Art Club. They included Millie Dow, Arthur George Bell, Henry Detmold, Emanuel P. Fox, Alfred Hartley, Adrian and Marianne Stokes, Alfred East, Julius Olsson, W. H. Y. Titcomb and Moffat Lindner. Because they were naturally more inclined to the views of Whistler and his followers, they retained their membership and continued to exhibit with the club until well into the twentieth century.

The Academy had retained a strong attraction for the Newlyn painters. Even during their period of revolt, as members of the New English Art Club, many continued to exhibit there, and soon were pleased to accept membership. Stanhope Forbes, in common with many of his generation, was highly suspicious of the Academy. He believed it to be a corrupt institution, 'universally and rightly detested' but he argued that 'The Royal Academy is so bad in every way... that perhaps it will not be so hard a fight as we imagine' (letter to William Forbes 15.2.87).* In December 1886 following his success with 'A Fish Sale on a Cornish Beach' Forbes was invited to serve on a Provisional Committee drawn from artists inside and outside the Academy, and including some of the most senior Academicians, to look into ways of reforming it.

It was their success at the Royal Academy that established the Newlyn painters in national opinion, and many of the paintings were constructed in ways calculated to attract such success. Forbes continued to paint large-scale works, specifically designed for the Academy's annual exhibitions, and from which he had consistent success with such important paintings as 'Off to the Fishing Ground' (1886), 'The Village Philharmonic' (1887), 'The Health of the Bride' (1888), (bought by the Chantry Bequest), and 'By Order of the Court' (1889). In 1892 he was invited to become an Associate member of the Academy. The *Magazine of Art* saw his election as 'embracing the daring and the unconventional', and a rebuttal of those who criticized the the Academy for being prejudiced and conservative. Forbes saw his election as bringing new blood to the Academy. He became a full Academician in 1910.

Other Newlyn painters also had considerable success in the Academy exhibitions. Henry Tuke exhibited his largest picture 'All Hands to the Pumps' in 1889. It measured four feet by six, and had been painted on board the *Julie* in Falmouth Harbour. A painting of ten figures in crowded action, it was hung 'on the line' and was bought from the Exhibition by the Chantry Bequest.

---

* Forbes had exhibited at the Royal Academy regularly since 1878, while he was still a student at the Royal Academy schools. In 1885 he had an outstanding success with his most ambitious painting to date 'A Fish Sale on a Cornish Beach' (1884). He described it in 1886, as 'A triumph for Newlyn'. In fact it was a triumph which Newlyn shared with St Ives, but nevertheless a triumph for the painters of Cornwall. Important pictures were exhibited by the Newlyn artists – Elizabeth Armstrong, Frank Bourdillon, Frank Bodilly, Frank Bramley, Percy Craft (soon to move to St Ives), Henry Detmold, Norman Garstin, Leghe Suthers and Stanhope Forbes, who produced one of his most vigorous figure studies 'Off to the Fishing Grounds'. The St Ives artists who showed were Wylie Grier, Marianne Stokes (but not Adrian), William Titcomb and Alfred East, with Henry Tuke from Falmouth.

Four years later, Tuke was paid an almost unprecedented compliment when a second of his paintings, 'August Blue' (1893–4) was bought by the Bequest. Another large work, this was Tuke's most typical and popular painting, a picture of pure pleasure – sun and nudist beauty. It depicts boys bathing from a boat called *August Blue* (a quotation from Swinburne's 'Sundew'). Tuke's election to the Academy came later. He was made an Associate member in 1900 – an event celebrated in London, and in Falmouth where a banquet was held in his honour by the Falmouth artists in the Polytechnic Hall, decorated with flags and bunting. He was not made a full member until 1913, three years after Chevallier Tayler.

In 1888 Frank Bramley's 'A Hopeless Dawn' achieved notable success at the Academy, and was bought for the Chantry Bequest. In the next year he exhibited 'Saved' and in 1891 'For Such is the Kingdom of Heaven' – both attempts to blend Newlyn realism with pathos and sentiment, although less successfully in the public estimation.

The art press supplied its readers with detailed information about the artists of Cornwall. The first major article on Newlyn was written by Alice Meynell and published in the *Art Journal* in April 1889. She describes the newly developed colony as 'a little centre, a core, at the Royal Academy, although it was still a kind of secret, known only to a few.' Mrs Meynell noted that

> *some Newlyners abide in St Ives and some at Lelant and that one dwells in a boat off Falmouth. But in common they work with sincerity and directness, they have devoted themselves to the subtle study of light rather than to the obvious study of colour and they have style.*

In the following year the *Magazine of Art* produced a substantial article entitled 'Newlyn and the Newlyn School', written and illustrated by W. Christian Symons. He described in affectionate detail the village and its activities, and noted that the colony had now been in existence for about nine years. From 1893 onwards the newly formed magazine *The Studio* regularly contained notes on affairs in Newlyn and St Ives. These were contributed by Norman Garstin, writing usually as NG in the column 'Studio Talk'.

By 1896 the *Art Journal* saw Stanhope Forbes as the undisputed leader of the Newlyn painters, commenting that:

> *Only a few of the most extreme opponents of the Newlyn influence would deny to Mr Stanhope Forbes a place among the most prominent of the younger artists of the present day. He is without a doubt, the centre and rallying part of the colony... popularity has come to him because he has painted subjects, one after another, which appeal to the sympathies and sentiments of large sections of the public.*

Paintings from Newlyn and St Ives were often exhibited together outside Cornwall. In 1888, for example, the London dealer Walter Dowdeswell visited artists in both communities to buy pictures for his well known Bond Street gallery. He found the most interesting work in St Ives, and was greatly taken with Adrian Stokes and his gifted wife Marianne. In 1890 he arranged 'An Exhibition of Pictures by Artists residing in or painting at Newlyn, St Ives, Falmouth, etc. in Cornwall', and three years later the large 'Fisheries Exhibition' was devoted to paintings of the sea and fishing. Tom Gotch as

STANHOPE FORBES

Off to the Fishing Grounds, 1886.

oil on canvas, 1560mm x 1650mm.

WALKER ART GALLERY, LIVERPOOL.

Secretary of the London Committee, used his influence to attract work by all the best sea painters working along the coast.

The most extensive review of painting from Cornwall filled the splendid premises of the Nottingham Castle Museum and Art Gallery in September 1894. The exhibition 'Cornish Painters of Newlyn, St Ives and Falmouth' consisted of two hundred and twenty three works by some fifty artists. Almost all the Newlyn artists were represented, some by a large number of works, but Newlyn artists accounted for only about a third of the exhibitors. Those from St Ives, and the few others who had settled in Falmouth, were now in the majority. The Newlyn work was very strong however, Forbes' four paintings included two of his best – 'The Village Philharmonic' (1887) and the more recent 'Forging the Anchor' (1891), which was used as a frontispiece for the handsome catalogue. Bramley showed five paintings including 'A Hopeless Dawn' (1888), which was already firmly established as one of the most popular paintings of the decade. The *Magazine of Art* reported 'Some of the Newlyn Men may lean to what is called "Impressionism" and others to a style admitting to a comparatively minute finish of detail; yet all, above all other qualities seem to aim at this justness...'.

An equally broad view of art in Cornwall was given to a London audience in an exhibition at the Whitechapel Gallery in 1902, which spanned fifty years and included such early visitors as J. C. Hook, Alfred East, Henry Moore and

John Brett. It was remarked that only three of the Newlyn painters were still there – Walter Langley, Stanhope Forbes and Ralph Todd. The painters of St Ives were described by the *Magazine of Art* as 'the talented little company who have settled in this picturesque old world village...', and it was noted that '...the full strength of the St Ives School of Landscape has yet to be realised'. (*Magazine of Art*, 1902.).

7

CHANGES IN NEWLYN

Percy Craft painting on The Terrace, Belleview, c.1885.

As St Ives began to gain in importance as an artists' colony, the town of Newlyn was in a state of change. By the early 1880s it had developed considerably as a fishing centre but still lacked suitable shelter for its growing fleet. The small harbour, that had existed since medieval times, gave only limited protection to a score of boats, and at the first sign of worsening weather the fleet had to run to shelter in Penzance. The need to improve facilities in Newlyn had been given tragic impetus in 1880 by the loss of the lugger *Jane*, returning to Newlyn from the North Sea. Within sight of home she was rolled over by a heavy sea and broke in two with the loss of all seven men aboard. A proposal was drawn up to create a modern large harbour and fishing port in the most sheltered corner of Mount's Bay, below Newlyn Town, to be open at all times of the year. Capital was found locally, in the form of bank loans.* On St Peter's Day, 25 June 1884 the foundation stone was laid for a pier 700 feet long, to give protection from southerly gales, and a lighthouse. Two years later the river was diverted in order to build a longer pier which encircled the harbour area of Newlyn to an extent of 40 acres, and gave shelter to the fishing fleet at all states of the tide. This second part of the work, which was completed in 1894, included the building of a harbour road to connect the two parts of the town. It was backed by sheds for the sale of fish, covering for all time the slips and little beaches that had served as landing places for the smaller boats and provided subjects for the painters.

These changes gave Newlyn considerable advantage as a fishing port, and it soon surpassed St Ives as the chief fishing port in Cornwall. In the 1880s and 1890s there was a great expansion in pilchard and mackerel fishing, but there was also the threat of invasion from 'foreign' fleets – steam drifters from the East coast of England that intruded into Cornish waters. Newlyners, who were strict Sabbatharians, did not fish on Sundays, and the men from the north-east found that by breaking the Sabbath they could command the Monday fish market. Matters came to a head in the 'Newlyn Riots' of 1886 when Newlyn fishermen demonstrated violently against Sunday fishing by the Yorkshire fishermen.

As Newlyn became more prosperous so new terraces and groups of houses began to appear in the upper part of the town, changing its appearance and losing for ever that timeless quality that had attracted many of the artists. For many, Newlyn became less interesting, less 'picturesque'. New artists continued to come however, and new interests developed. In February 1885, shortly before the departure of Blandford Fletcher, Forbes noted the arrival at Belleview of Percy Craft and his young wife Alice Elizabeth. It was their first visit to Newlyn although two years earlier Craft had exhibited a painting at the

---

* Loans were made totalling £53 000 from the Bolitho bank – Thomas Simon Bolitho was a leading supporter of the harbour project, and another substantial loan came from a Penzance bank. The project received no support from the Government or local industry, and the fishermen formed a co-operative to pay off the debt with a levy on fish of twopence in the pound.

Royal Academy called 'The Huer, Cornwall, Shoot' (1883), a fishing scene, probably painted in St Ives. It showed the pilchard fishermen preparing to 'shoot' a net to surround a shoal of fish that had been spotted by the 'huer' or caller, who directed the boats from the clifftop. It was a theme to which Craft returned on a number of occasions.

Percy Robert Craft (1856–1934) had spent his early years in pursuit of a stage career and for a time he had been an actor with the Old Stock Company of Plymouth. Ill health forced him to give up acting, but he retained his fascination with the stage, and kept his stage name 'Robert Percy', taking every opportunity to perform as an amateur. He also showed early talent as an artist, and studied at Heatherly's Academy in London and the Slade, where he won gold and silver medals. He did not have the benefit of a contintental training however, an omission that affected the later development of his work. Although his paintings were frequently shown at the Academy from 1882 onwards, Craft had litle success in selling them. In Newlyn he became a good friend of Forbes, and they worked in adjacent studios. Two years after his arrival, Forbes recorded that:

> *The Crafts are very depressed. It is certainly not a good look out for him poor chap – Agnew has not sold last year's picture, and of course will not buy this one if he cannot place it, ... I fear he has been living in a fool's paradise and thinking his position more assured than it really is. But he has lots of energy and will buckle to with a will.* (letter dated 7 April 1887)

Craft was a showman, as much in his painting as on the stage. He conceived the picture as a setting for an incident; the figures were dressed in costume, rehearsed and carefully placed for maximum dramatic effect. But they gestured woodenly, without the reality of light and colour that informs the best of Newlyn painting. Yet at a time when elaborate genre painting was well received, Craft maintained a reputation at the Academy and elsewhere with a succession of sentimental paintings. 'The Empty Chair' exhibited at the Royal Academy in 1889 shows a widower with his motherless family. Attached to the picture was a piece of verse which read 'What is a home without a mother. What are all the joys we meet, when her loving smile no longer greets the coming of our feet?' One local reporter protested, 'Sentiment looks not well when clothed in doggerel'.

With difficulties over his work, and to better accommodate his family Percy Craft decided to make St Ives his base. He moved there in June 1887, but continued to make frequent visits to Newlyn. From his St Ives studio on Bunkers Hill, Craft painted 'Heva, Heva' (1889), ('Heva' is the cry raised by the huer when he sighted a shoal of pilchards at sea; it brought every man, woman and child out of their houses, to help secure the fish). Frank Bourdillon, usually kind in his comments, noted: 'it is a good subject but a little beyond poor old Craft's technical ability. However he is coming out of it very well, but I am afraid he will not sell'. The painting displays an engaging attention to detail and portrays many of the St Ives seamen. But in spite of the labour that went into it the action is frozen and the gestures unconvincing. Nevertheless it was much admired and was later exhibited in Liverpool at The Walker Art Gallery, and in 1890 it was taken to Australia.

A sequel to 'Heva Heva', painted eight years later, was 'Tucking a School of Pilchards on the Cornish Coast' exhibited at the Academy in 1897. This is by far the most successful of Craft's Cornish paintings and one of the last. It was painted from a low perspective, as if from a boat at sea, as a circle of seine boats gather to draw in the great net around a shoal of pilchards. It is richly painted

PERCY ROBERT CRAFT

Tucking a School of Pilchards on the Cornish Coast, 1897.

oil on canvas, 1200 x 2050mm.

PENZANCE AND DISTRICT MUSEUM AND ART GALLERY.

and describes well the ordered bustle as the fishermen plunge baskets into the swirling fish to scoop bring them in their already heavily laden craft. Like 'Heva, Heva' it is a sustained effort of characterisation, an assembly of portraits of local men emphasising their strenghth of character and rugged appearance. It has an extra importance as a record of a fast disappearing activity, for soon the huge shoals of pilchards disappeared from the Cornish coast.

In November 1886 the *Cornishman* newspaper told its readers:

Mr Percy Craft (an entertainment in himself) visited the Central Hall at Penzance last Saturday night and, with his friends the artists and their fair partners, gave a most enjoyable entertainment. If Mr Craft can do so much for our friends in the neighbouring town, surely he might get one up for the central part of Newlyn to while away the dull hours of a Saturday night. What say you Mr Craft? (The *Cornishman,* 25 November 1886).

This encouragement persuaded Percy Craft to bring the artists of Newlyn together to form a dramatic society, with himself as manager, Dochie Garstin as secretary, and Forbes as treasurer. Craft's studio frequently doubled as a rehearsal room, and he organised many theatrical performances and concerts in which he also took part. He was a hard task master, yet most of the artists and their wives participated, and their shows were popular. In 1890 Forbes felt obliged to withdraw from the group temporarily because theatricals had begun to interfere with his painting. He was concerned that most of his friends were still addicted to acting because they were within two months of sending-in day, and some of the pictures for the Academy were hardly begun.

The antics of the artists sometimes attracted unwelcome attention from the press. In 1887 an unfriendly article in the *Cornishman* read:

Gent and lady artists with their sister, cousins and aunts going it as usual in Newlyn. Their ways are not our ways, they romp and flirt and spoon and sing at unearthly hours in the mornings, sketch and altogether carry on in what Mr Bolitho calls a 'Bahemian' [sic] way, and that the good people of Newlyn who see some of these naughty things don't like it. (The *Cornishman*, 5 October 1887).

The reports were not all bad, however. In December 1890 the *Illustrated London News* carried a full-page article on the Newlyn Artists' Dramatic Society's ambitious production of 'She Stoops to Conquer':

The arts are all sister and it is therefore not surprising to find that the wielders of the brush seem to be in touch with the stage... Small case for astonishment then to find that the little colony of painters who have taken up their quarters in Newlyn, (only some ten miles distant from the Land's End) should have established a dramatic society of their own and made a reputation for themselves that assures a good house whenever they appear on the boards. (*Illustrated London News,* December 1890).

The Crafts left Newlyn in 1899, for Herefordshire, and later moved to London. Percy became organising secretary of the Royal British Colonial Society of Artists, and helped to form the Imperial Arts League. He continued to perform, and during the First World War he took part in 'Patriotic Concerts' in aid of the wounded, reciting his own poems. He died in London at the age of seventy-six.

The presence of a large number of artists in the town also affected Newlyn's development. The rooms or cottages rented from the fisherfolk became insufficient for their needs, and purpose-built studios began to appear. In 1888

Theatricals.
The Newlyn Players.

Stanhope Forbes is standing in centre of the group dressed as a policeman; next to him is Mrs Garstin. Norman Garstin, dressed as an Arab, is sitting on the right.

Arthur Bateman, a painter and a member of the group with a sense of business, bought a field at the bottom of the lane known by the artists as 'Rue des Beaux Arts'. Here he built several studios, first for Stanhope Forbes, then for Frank Bramley. The latter's was as 'a lovely glass house... four sides and a roof of glass, a sort of dignified conservatory not lumbered up with plants and water pots'. (Bourdillon letters). Another, shared by Bourdillon and Garstin, gave each of them a fine studio with projecting bay windows to the south. Bourdillon found it luxurious compared with his cramped room in the town, but confessed that it was too pleasant to work in and attracted too many visitors.

Arthur Bateman (1847–1894) was described by Forbes as one of the best friends the artists ever had. They had met in Newlyn in 1885 and Forbes found him an agreeable companion with tastes similar to his own. ' He is one of the enthusiastic sort, fond of music and art and sport and ready to go in for anything' (30 November 1885). He was sociable, fond of boating, a frequent companion at dinner parties and theatricals, and at concerts where he played the flute. He was also a purchaser of paintings. Arthur Bateman came from a wealthy family from Clapham Park near London, with many overseas interests, including railways. As a young man he wished to study painting but it was not until the death of his father in 1881 that he was able to paint seriously, and enrol at the Slade. He was thirty-eight when he came to Newlyn and combined his skill as a painter with his undoubted business flair. In 1885 he exhibited a portrait at the Academy and two years later his painting 'Day Dreams' was hung 'just above the line'. He did not show again until 1894, the year of his death.

In 1889 the Batemans decided to emigrate to California, Bourdillon was doubtful about the wisdom of this:

It would serve Bateman a good deal if he had to forfeit his passage money at the last moment. He is such an enthusiast about everything he takes up, that just as likely as not he will plunge into some wild speculation when he gets to California and think all the time that he is investing in some solid farming and industry. (Bourdillon letters, 29 January 1890).

The Batemans left from Penzance on the *Dutchman* and were given a grand send off by their Newlyn friends. Bateman later bought land in California and planted it with vines, apricots and a flock of sheep. He became a naturalised American and a man of means, living at 'Newlyn Ranch', Hanford, Kings County, California, where he died aged forty-seven.

The area in Newlyn where the studios were grouped became known as 'Bateman's Meadow', or sometimes 'California' in memory of Bateman's emigration, and the studios became the focal point for an important annual event. This was the 'show day' or private view that took place in March, a few days before pictures were to be submitted to the Royal Academy. It became customary to issue invitations to friends to view the paintings in the studios: landladies and models were invited to come in the morning and the 'big wigs' in the afternoon:

from 5.30 till dusk the doors were opened to everybody who wanted to come in. There was a rush of dust and heat! Fearful to endure. How the ladies bore it I can't think, but I know I was tired enough! We must have had a thousand people here altogether. (Bourdillon letters, 1 April 1890)

The informal show days in the studios ceased when proper exhibition facilities were built. Newlyn Art Gallery, close to the water's edge, at the eastern

The Passmore Edwards Art Gallery Newlyn.

Photographs of the exterior and interior taken at the time of the inaugural exhibition in 1895.

ROYAL INSTITUTE OF CORNWALL.

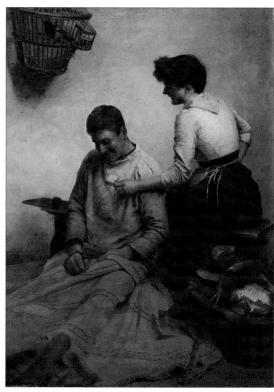

ARTHUR BATEMAN

Courtship and *Marriage*.

PRIVATE COLLECTION.

end of the town, opened in October 1895, through the generosity of the London newspaper proprietor J. Passmore Edwards, in recognition of the national respect earned by the Newlyn artists. Small but well arranged, the gallery was intended to give the artists a more satisfactory place to display their work before sending it to the Royal Academy.

John Passmore Edwards (1823–1911) was one of the great nineteenth century philanthropists. Born at Blackwater near Truro, the son of a carpenter, his village education was expanded by self-improvement and an absorbing interest in literature. He became a working journalist on the *Sentinel*, a failing newspaper in Manchester, where he was introduced to the teaching of Cobden and Bright, and became deeply involved in the Peace Movement and an ardent advocate of political and social reform. His first venture into publishing was a failure, but with true Victorian tenacity, he continued his adventures in journalism, and in the 1870s entered a period of great prosperity with his ownership of the *London Echo*, the first halfpenny evening paper in England. This provided him with the means to implement his radical and advanced views, and he embarked on a series of public buildings which he also endowed, stocked and equipped, as centres for education, healing and recreation. Within a period of about fifteen years he erected twenty buildings in his native Cornwall and nearly fifty in London and the south of England including libraries, hospitals, convalescent homes, even drinking troughs for horses.

The Newlyn Gallery was the first art gallery in the county. It was built of Cornish granite, and dedicated to John Opie, the first of the Cornish painters. On its facade are four large copper plaques, made by Philip Hodder and the students of the Newlyn Industrial Class. The gallery was built for the use of living artists, not as a museum, and the Newlyn Society of Artists was formed at the same time by leading painters of the group.

Norman Garstin, whose first articles appeared in *The Studio* at that time, was cautious in his welcome. He expressed reservations about 'A granite picture-gallery dumped down amongst us,... for it plunged the artists into discussions and differences of opinion and, an even greater horror, committee meetings!' He soon felt that his worst fears were realised:

> *It has all come too late, the colony in Newlyn is dispersing and some share of the blame must be taken by the new gallery... It has seemingly led to a disintegration of the Newlyners... This is only a coincidence, but certainly we cannot shut our eyes to the fact that Newlyn has thinned lately – leaner by many good men and good painters. Frank Bramley is near Droitwich, at Ombersley, in the heart of the Midlands, far from the sea and sea-folk that he loved to paint in times past. Chevallier Tayler, too, has folded his sketching umbrella and silently stolen up to Kensington. John da Costa is no more seen among us; Bourdillon has cleaned his palette for good and aye, has taken orders, and is a missionary amongst the mild but impenetrable Hindus. It is an Exodus, an Hegira. (The Studio VI. No.34 January 1897).*

Another venture which affected the artistic life of the area was the development of Newlyn metalwork. The fishing industry was notoriously uncertain; good catches might be followed by long periods of poor weather which prevented the boats from leaving the port, and there were times when the price of fish was abysmally low. The Newlyn Industrial Class, and its successor Newlyn Art Industries, was an unusual yet typically Victorian combination of instruction and practical Christianity, which brought together the artists and fisherfolk of Newlyn in an effort to provide alternative employment for young men of the town and to relieve them from the vagaries of the fishing trade.

Norman Garstin gave a romanticised account of the founding of the Newlyn Industrial Class:

> *In the beginning there was a fretwork class carried on over a fish cellar in Newlyn, but even that does not primarily express the case because it does not take into consideration the previous existence of a school master, a rich man and a telegraph clerk, all actuated by the desire to compete with the devil in finding work for idle hands to do. Then some artists were drawn into the competition who seemed to feel the inadequacy of fretwork or even of woodcarving to keep Satan at bay, so copper and brass were introduced, and little trays and candlesticks, and etc., were beaten by fisherlads in the winter nights in the loft above the fish curing yard by the sea. (The Studio 1896).*

Garstin was describing events that followed the arrival in Newlyn of John D. Mackenzie in 1888. Mackenzie had worked as an illustrator and painter in London before coming to Newlyn to continue his painting career. He took lodgings in the Rue des Beaux Arts, just above the Board School, and soon became friendly with other artists who had identified themselves with the plight of the poorer members of the fishing community. With them – especially Bourdillon and Craft – Mackenzie helped to run the Seamen's Rest, and performed many acts of help and kindness to local people. He was a committed Christian and an active member of Paul Church, where he regularly read the lesson and taught at Sunday school. Other artists who were involved were Thomas Gotch and Reginald Dick.

The 'rich man' of Garstin's description was T. B. Bolitho of Trewidden, Penzance, Liberal M.P. and a member of a leading Cornish family with interests in banking, tin mining, shipping and fishing. (His brother, Simon Bolitho, had been the moving spirit in financing the alterations to the port of Newlyn.). The financial support of the Bolithos made it possible to create a series of workshop classes in metalwork, enamelling and embroidery. The first teachers were local men, and Phillip Hodder the 'schoolmaster' referred to by Garstin, who made the copper plaques which decorate the Newlyn Art Gallery facade from designs by Mackenzie and Gotch. William Pezzack the 'telegraph clerk' was a skilled woodworker.

There was no shortage of artistic skills in Newlyn, but what was also needed was an experienced craftsman. John Pearson was the man who filled this gap. A founder member of C. R. Ashbee's 'Guild of Handicraft' in Whitechapel, London, and its senior metalworker, Pearson had a considerable reputation in repoussé metalwork, using designs and motifs – ships, fish, flowers, peacocks – which originated in the decorative tiles that he had studied in the Victoria and Albert Museum. Pearson spent six years in Newlyn, leaving probably in 1898. John Mackenzie continued as director of the workshop until his death in 1918.

The Newlyn venture in artistic craftwork made an important contribution to the Arts and Crafts Movement, which had grown in the 1890s from the teaching of John Ruskin and William Morris. A measure of its success was the inclusion of a group of work from Newlyn in each of the annual exhibitions staged by the 'Home Arts and Industries Association' in the Albert Hall. *The Studio* felt that 'The Newlyn School of Craftsmen may now quite creditably take their place beside the painters with whom we associate their name.' (*The Studio* 1900). Stanhope Forbes, who described Mackenzie as seriously minded but 'a bright and cheery comrade', was of the opinion that 'nothing was ever more conducive to the maintenance of really good relations between the village folk and us painters – the strangers within their gates – than the work of these my friends.'

By the end of the century, the London art world had formed an easy familiarity with the village of Newlyn. It was regularly pictured as a confusion of cob-walled cottages strongly lit against the horizon, the brown sailed luggers in the bay, and the shining sands had been portrayed often and by many hands. Also well known were the settings for well known paintings, the old foundry painted by Stanhope Forbes; the village schoolroom which Elizabeth Forbes so vividly brought to life and the harbour wall, a stage for so many scenes of high drama. Indeed:

> *no other place has received such complete and minute illustration at the hands of a group of artists... the most trivial aspects of its daily life have been the subjects of imposing canvasses We know its weddings and its funerals, its feasts and its festivals,... and almost expect to share in the hazardous life of those Cornishmen who go down to the sea in ships and occupy their business in great waters.* (Charles Hiatt 'Mr Frank Bramley ARA, and His Work', *Magazine of Art* 1903).

While some of the artists prospered, others failed to please the selectors of the Academy. Ralph Todd's work brought him little success, yet he persevered painting mainly in watercolour, using the stippled technique favoured by the Birmingham artists. His unpretentious scenes of working life in Newlyn have a freshness and authenticity, but they lack the invention of his more ambitious colleagues. In 1888 Todd married, and four years later he left Newlyn, settling first in St Keverne on the Lizard peninsula, and later in Helston. His son Arthur Ralph Middleton Todd became a distinguished Royal Academician and remained closely connected with Cornwall.

Todd's friend Fred Millard also had limited success with his work. His painting 'Walls Have Ears' (1888), which depicts two old men gossiping in a public house, brought him some attention when it was used by Alice Meynell to illustrate her major article on Newlyn in the *Art Journal* in 1889. But Millard also left Newlyn in the early 1890s. Little is known of his later life but in 1920 he was reportedly living in Falmouth.

Walter Langley was away from Newlyn from 1885 to 1887, living in Birmingham and painting in the Midland villages. In 1886 his major watercolours were shown at Birmingham Museum and Art Gallery, but it was evident that his clients preferred the heroic themes of fishing life. Langley returned to Newlyn, and Forbes reported, 'Things are not prospering with the little man. He has not sold his pictures at all lately. So he will try Newlyn again and see if old Tom Tiddler's ground will bring him luck again'. (26.5.1887)

During his early years in Newlyn Langley was consistently successful with his work, but he did not establish a major public reputation, chiefly because he painted almost entirely in watercolour, a difficult medium in which he acquired considerable fluency but which, in the public mind, remained secondary to oil painting. Watercolour had its own supporters however, and the Royal Watercolour Society – known as the 'Old Society' – had been created in the early nineteenth century by a group of painters who felt that their work was not taken seriously by the Royal Academy. In time they became increasingly conservative and in 1882 the 'Institute of Painters in Watercolour', the 'New' Society, was established. It drew together younger, more experimental artists and its exhibitions were innovatory, with members attempting complex figure subjects from classical or biblical themes. Walter Langley was elected to the 'New Society' in 1883 for his study of an old fisherwoman, entitled 'Time moveth not; our being 'tis that moves'.

Although there was a strongly serious aspect to Langley's work, he was not by any means a morose individual. He was generally cheerful and on good terms with his fellow artists, and on social occasions he could be very good company, as described earlier. He also became single bowls champion of Penzance. His annual submissions for the 'New' Society were generally scenes of high drama, but the greatest part of his work reflected quieter moments in the village of Newlyn and its people, in their domestic situation. The contrast between age and youth is a favourite subject. 'Wonderland' known as 'I think I'll be a sailor' painted in 1884, focuses upon the dreaming imagination of a young boy, lying in a meadow with a model boat – a Newlyn drifter – in his hands, anticipating the joys of a life at sea, with little thought for its attendant dangers.

Langley now had a considerable following, but some of his greatest successes were yet to come. In the early 1890s he returned to the use of oil colour, and produced a major painting which became one of the most popular of all late Victorian scenes of suffering. The title, '... Never Morning Wore to Evening but Some Heart did Break', are lines from Tennyson's *In Memoriam*. The painting is a further re-enactment of the drama of two lives blighted by loss. A young girl sits by her widowed mother, 'mourning for some sailor who has gone from Newlyn harbour never to return'. These pathetic figures exist in the enveloping shadow of

STANHOPE FORBES

*Young Apprentice,
Newlyn Copper Works,*
1908.

oil on canvas, 760 x 550mm.

PENZANCE AND DISTRICT MUSEUM
AND ART GALLERY.

Newlyn Copperware.

Photograph from the
Percy Craft Album.

WALTER LANGLEY

Never Morning Wore to Evening but Some Heart did Break, 1804.

oil on canvas, 1200 x 1500mm.

CITY OF BIRMINGHAM MUSEUM AND ART GALLERY.

death, enclosed by the horizontals of sea and pier and lit softly by the last rays of the sun reflected from a sea that is at last tranquil, the lighthouse glows dimly in the background. The painting made a considerable impact at the Royal Academy in 1894 and was reportedly selected for purchase by the Chantry Bequest. Unfortunately Langley had already sold the picture and in spite of his offer to buy it back at an increased price, the new owner refused to sell.

Langley did not only deal with tragedy and disaster at sea. In his quieter paintings he captures the more intimate details of Newlyn life, scenes in the homes of working people, children at play, gossiping villagers. However he usually points up his theme with an expression of emotion, or pathos, as in his study of a Newlyn cottage interior, 'The Orphan' (1889). The simple furnishings and few possessions – for example, the earthenware pitcher that Langley includes in many of his paintings – are subordinate to the pity and concern displayed in the faces of the two women as they watch the hungry child.

He attracted further attention with a large painting of a cottage interior where a young mother shares a simple meal, prepared for herself and her daughter, with a boy beggar. It is highly realistic in its treatment of the rough surfaces of white-washed walls, trodden earth floor and simple furniture. The few glowing coals of the fire give a soft radiance that contrasts with the gloom of the chimney corner. This painting was given a title from Pope's *Essay on Man*, 'In Faith and

Hope the World will Disagree, But all Mankinds concern is Charity' and was illustrated in *Royal Academy Pictures* of 1897. Upon the basis of the illustration Count Leon Tolstoy singled it out as:

> *an admirable and true work of art, and Langley's portrayal of the scene as evidently understanding for the first time, what poverty is, and what inequality is... one feels that the artist loves this girl, and that she too loves.* (Count Leon Tolstoy *What is Art*, London 1898, trans. and edited by Aylmer Maude 1929).

In his desire to share the burden of misery and pain that he found in Newlyn, Langley expressed depths of pathos dear to a section of Victorian England:

> *His interest... has always been with the workers and toilers, and although not to be termed a pessimist, he is for ever impressed with the signs of the struggle for existence which are so apparent throughout nature, and which entails here and there so much misery and pain.* (*Moseley and Kings Heath Journal*, July 1897. Vol.VI No.62.).

Langley spent the last thirty years of his life in Penzance. There is some falling off in the quality of his later work; he grew increasingly remote and painted less. However, he continued to show regularly with the Royal Birmingham Society of Artists until two years before his death and at the Royal Academy and the Royal Institute of Painters in Watercolour. Yet a childhood friend remembered him in his last years:

> *It was almost a shock to find how little joy his success had brought him and I think I caught a slight glimpse of what Jacques meant by 'the bubble reputation' and the settled gloom of the mature and successful artist, in contrast with his debonair youth, was a singular confirmation of Stevenson's aphorism "it is better to travel hopefully than to arrive."* ('The Art of Walter Langley' by Walter Turner, from *W. J. Wainwright RSW. RBSA*, Cornish Bros. Birmingham 1935).

Frank Bramley's last years in Newlyn led him into the Royal Academy and to a new reputation as a portraitist. The great popularity of 'A Hopeless Dawn' was not repeated, but he continued to exhibit major narrative paintings such as 'Saved', subtitled 'Oft in a Humble Home a Golden Room is Found' (1889), a complex story of the rescue of a Spanish girl snatched from the sea by a Cornish life-boat crew 'descendants of her forefathers bitterest foes'. The girl has been brought to a fisherman's cottage, where she is slowly recovering before a warm fire. While cottagers and children gaze in pity and curiosity, through the open door the lifeboat crew is seen preparing for another rescue. This was the last major picture to be painted in the cramped conditions of Bramley's cottage studio in Rue des Beaux Arts, for later that year he moved to the newly built 'glass house' studio in The Meadow. After a protracted love affair, which was followed with interest by the other artists in Newlyn, Bramley married Katherine Graham. They were married in 1891 and lived in Orchard Cottage, Newlyn.

Bramley was often criticised for the lack of colour in his pictures – 'undue attention to darkness, a chief drawback of the Newlyn school...' (*Magazine of Art*). His use of colour was restrained and strong contrasts of light and dark set the mood of his painting. Grief, in the ordinariness of a familiar setting is the subject of 'For Such is the Kingdom of Heaven' exhibited in the Royal Academy in 1891. In a chequer-board of black and white, it depicts the funeral of a Newlyn child. Children led the slow procession along the harbour road carrying flowers and prayer-books. They are dressed in white, as are the four maidens who support the tiny, flower-decked coffin. Other mourners surround this sad drama played against the grey background of the harbour, the pier and lighthouse in the background. The white-gowned, flower-bedecked figures at first appear joyful, as white is traditionally the colour of hope and happiness. It is only when the small coffin is perceived that the meaning of the painting becomes clear.

In 1894 Bramley was elected Associate of the Royal Academy the same year as Sargent and two years after Forbes. Portraiture now assumed a more important place in his work and he frequently required the use of a London studio. In 1895 the Bramleys left Newlyn for Droitwich in the Midlands, eventually settling in Grasmere, Katherine's family home. In later life Bramley's figure paintings were increasingly loaded with symbolism. He used the bright blooms of flowers and foliage to highlight his figure paintings and portraits and his style loosened, causing one reviewer to criticise his over-vigorous use of the palette knife:

> very clever no doubt, but even Rembrandt and Velasquez did not paint thus... here we have a sort of anatomical chart of faces that loudly cry out for the covering of skin that has been omitted for the display of naked muscle. (*Magazine of Art*, writing of the RA Exhibition of 1898).

Bramley was elected Royal Academician in 1911, but soon after he became seriously ill and in 1913 excused himself from duties at the Academy. After a number of years in Grasmere his health deteriorated further and he ended his days confined to a London flat and died after a long period of illness in 1915 at the age of fifty-eight.

For a number of the artists who remained in Newlyn the realistic treatment of nature became restricting. They felt the need to search for an inner world, to express in poetic terms that secret relationship between man and nature which had preoccupied the French Symbolist writers and painters. Such deep probing of the unconscious was not to English taste, but the extravagances of the Aesthetic movement and of Art Nouveau in England had drawn inspiration from France and a number of Newlyn artists came to prefer the symbolic rather than the real, choosing subjects from mythology or the medieval. The Arthurian legends, Grimm's Fairy Tales and the works of Shakespeare – especially *A Midsummer Night's Dream* – were of primary importance. They were also inspired by the work of the Pre-Raphaelites, many of whom were still alive and producing work of surprising richness.

The imagination of Thomas Gotch had not found full expression in his somewhat pedestrian efforts to describe the working life of Newlyn. He discovered a more spiritual wine on a visit to Italy in the winter of 1891–92 with his wife Caroline. In Florence they studied the work of the Quattrocento artists, an experience which greatly enhanced his sense of colour and design, 'My Crown and Sceptre' (1892), exhibited at the Royal Academy, a painting of studied formality in which a young girl, with fair pale hair and blue eyes – his daughter Phyllis – wears a richly embroidered robe and sits upright on a straight-backed chair, before a background decorated with fleur-de-lys. She carries a green reed in her hand as her sceptre and is crowned with a wreath of flowers. It was described as 'a curious tour de force' (*Art Journal*) and became

WALTER LANGLEY

The Orphan, 1889.

watercolour, 655 x 950mm.

THE TREHAYES COLLECTION.

one of the pictures of the year, and was awarded gold medals in the Paris Salon and in Berlin.

Gotch continued to produce landscapes of great delicacy but he had left behind the traditional subjects of the Newlyn painters. In the 1890s his work becomes a celebration of childhood and womanhood, as he watched his daughter Phyllis grow up with the Newlyn children. Paintings such as 'The Golden Dream' (1893) and 'Child Enthroned' (1894), are a vision of childhood within a setting of religious medievalism. They have a dream-like quality, although the detail is highly realistic.

Occasionally his work showed a darker side. In 'Death of the Bride' (1894–95), the smiling invitation of the young woman is made more enigmatic by the transparent black veil that she wears. She is a figure of fantasy, a 'Queen Mab' of the spirits, surrounded by scarlet and mauve poppies, symbolic of the sleep of death and also associated with opium, which removes the pain of death. Gotch explored his own thoughts of death in verse:

And as I move
Through an obscure and poppied world behold
a shrouded form that seems to question me!

Is this the dread destroyer, Death? is this
the end? ah no! The pallid arms are raised.
The veil divides, a faint sigh breathes my name,
and lo! Not night, but dawn; not death, but life,
or better, life through death, yea Death the Bride.

(Letter from Marquise de Verdieres Bodilly to Miss Pierce quoted in 'The Portrayal of Women and Children by Thomas Cooper Gotch' unpublished thesis by Cecile Bradshaw, the University College of Wales, Aberystwyth, 1987).

This painting aroused much speculation and led to a correspondence with an American who offered to purchase it for the substantial sum of £500. However Gotch was told that the would-be purchaser intended to commercialise the painting by displaying it as a curiosity in America with black velvet curtains and green lights. When Gotch refused the first offer it was immediately increased to £1000, but the showman was then told that the picture was not for sale. To Tom Gotch's satisfaction, the painting was later acquired by the Art Gallery in Kettering, his birthplace.

The high point of Gotch's career was his painting 'Alleluia' (1896) which was purchased by the Chantry Bequest. A Pre-Raphaelite choir of young girls stand in two rows before a gilded background upon which is inscribed the words of the ancient 'Alleluia'. In the centre, with clasped hands, 'she who was enthroned' is framed in a golden niche between companions in robes of rich

THOMAS GOTCH

Allelulia, c.1896.

oil on canvas, 1300 x 1800mm.

THE TATE GALLERY
(CHANTRY BEQUEST).

materials, who are singing from scrolls. The formal costumes of the older girls contrast with the simpler party frocks of the younger children in the front row. All of them have the fresh faces of country girls.

From 1887 until about 1900 Thomas and Caroline Gotch lived in the Malt House, an ancient house in Newlyn Hill, and their hospitality made Forbes describe it as the 'artistic centre' of the colony. In 1900 they left Cornwall and for several years were at Shottermill in Surrey, and in London. They returned to Newlyn in 1910 and for a time Gotch used the big studio in Trewarveneth, in succession to the Forbeses. They then settled at Wheal Betsy at the top of Newlyn Hill. Many of his earlier friends had now dispersed but Gotch remained a close friend of Tuke. His house now became a meeting place for some of the younger artists who had come to the colony, friends of their daughter Phyllis. Thomas Gotch died in Newlyn in 1931 'from overwork and a worn-out heart'.

Stanhope and Elizabeth Forbes remained true to Newlyn. After their marriage in 1889 they lived at Cliff Castle, overlooking the bay. With the birth of their son Alec, they moved to Trewarveneth (the House-on-the-Hill), on Paul Hill built by William Godolphin in the seventeenth century. Elizabeth retained her desire to work as far as possible out of doors. She built a studio on to the old farmhouse and in the orchard behind she had a hut for outdoor painting. The move to the country gave Elizabeth a new and enchanted setting for her work. In 'The Edge of the Wood' (1894), she places two young rustic lovers in this garden, whiling away a grey autumn afternoon among the feeding turkeys. Much of her later work is set in a medieval world of chivalry, inspired by Malory's *Le Morte Arthur* and Spenser's *Fairie Queen*. Portraits of her young son Alec and his childhood companions were her favourite subject. Working as far as possible out of doors, she used her considerable talent to create a world of fantasy and make-believe described within the known environment of her own garden.

She had two exhibitions of paintings and illustrations based on her love of children, often in a medieval setting. In 1900 at the Fine Art Society, her exhibition was entitled 'Children and Child Love' and in 1904 at the Leicester Galleries, 'Model Children and Other People'. She wrote:

> *The little sunburnt faces and the little calico frocks become as much a part of the bright landscapes as the patches of pink thrift in the clefts of the granite boulders. And one marks the flight of the years with their changing. The yellow haired baby of one summer is the sturdy brown-legged urchin of the next.* (Foreword to the catalogue of an exhibition at the Leicester Galleries, 1904).

Stanhope Forbes' continued dedication to outdoor work was demonstrated in the painting 'The Quarry Team' (1893), which Forbes described as his *magnum opus*. This large canvas was painted by the roadside, near to the Sheffield Quarry, where the huge blocks of granite were carried down to Forman's Granite Yard at Wherry Town for shipment to London for the building of the Victoria Embankment. Forbes made an arrangement with the quarry whereby the last load of each day would stop for a while so that he could continue with his painting. He later recounted the incident that happened one afternoon when the quarry team did not arrive as expected. Instead a herd of bullocks came rushing down the hill. Canvas, easel and artist were ignominiously evacuated quickly over the Cornish hedge to avoid being trampled on. This painting was later shown at the Royal Academy in 1894. During the exhibition the painting was attacked and seriously damaged by Suffragettes.

As many of their friends and contemporaries left Newlyn, Stanhope and Elizabeth Forbes were prompted to follow – to London, or perhaps back to France. To consider their future they took an extended painting trip to the Basque region of south-western France. After a long search on bicycles they found a village in the low Pyrenees 'where we might set up our easels and unfurl our sketching umbrellas'. Each day was spent in sketching and painting out of doors. The Basque peasants were fascinated by the artists who sketched them at work. One group of sunburnt girls, described by Elizabeth as 'lively as green lizards on a sunny wall, and apparently as poor', made particularly good models, and accompanied the Forbes on their expeditions into the high mountains overlooking the Bay of Biscay. ('On the Slope of a Southern Hill', by Mrs Stanhope Forbes. *The Studio*, vol. XVIII No.79 October 1899).

After this period of soul-searching Stanhope and Elizabeth Forbes made a positive decision to remain in Newlyn. In an effort to continue the community which they so much valued and to replace their departing friends they decided to open a school of painting and drawing 'following the example of many of those greater French artists, and to throw open a studio to all who would care to enrol themselves as his pupils.'

Stanhope and Elizabeth Forbes opened their school in Newlyn in 1899 and it was to have a considerable influence in the area. They offered a full curriculum, based on drawing and the study of nature. Teaching took place in three studios in The Meadow – a steeply sloping, half-wild garden overlooking the sea. One studio, filled with plaster casts that they drew from, housed a beginners class. Another was used for painting from the model. For clothed poses such as fishermen or dairymaids, or in the exotic medieval costumes Elizabeth had made for her historical paintings, models were found in the village; but for nude poses, professional models (often Italian) were brought from London. On three afternoons a week Lionel Birch led sketching expeditions in the village. For more advanced students a walled garden provided an outdoor studio where they could follow the change of light and shadow upon the model.

For Stanhope Forbes, teaching was a relaxation from painting and he spent much time in the school, often painting alongside the students. He was a natural teacher and particularly enjoyed the informal Saturday morning criticisms, when he led stimulating discussions of the students' work. The school attracted students from as far away as America, Australia, Canada and India. The costs were modest; bedroom and sitting room in a cottage 'approved by Mrs Forbes' was between nine shillings and one pound per week; meals, including Cornish cream, junket, milk, eggs and vegetables and, of course, fish, cost an extra nine or ten shillings a week. Fees for the summer term – June to mid September – were ten guineas; and for the winter term – October to March – twelve guineas.

In 1904 Stanhope and Elizabeth Forbes moved from Trewarveneth to Higher Faugan, a splendid new house at the top of Newlyn Hill, looking over the moors to the sea. It was designed by Forbes and built to his requirements, encircled by a rampart. Here he was able to develop his love of gardening and he assumed the character of a country squire, frequently entertaining students and artist friends at musical evenings.

THOMAS GOTCH

*Mount's Bay,
Autumn*, 1905.

oil on canvas, 305 x 455mm.

ALAN SHEARS FINE ART.

*Painted from the garden of
Wheal Betsy, on Newlyn Hill,
the home that Tom and Caroline
Gotch had built about a year
before this picture was painted.*

ELIZABETH FORBES

*Jean, Jeanne and
Jeanette,* c. 1822.

oil on canvas, 575 x 455mm.

MANCHESTER CITY ART GALLERY.

Photograph of Elizabeth
Forbes in her painting
hut for outdoor work
in the garden of
Trewarveneth.

REPRODUCED IN *THE STUDIO*,
VOL. 4 NO. 10, OCTOBER 1894.

THOMAS GOTCH

The Lantern Parade,
c. 1910.

oil on canvas

PRIVATE COLLECTION.

Inscribed on the reverse:
*This was painted by my
grandfather, T. C. Gotch. I am
one of the children holding the
lanterns. Daphne Mc Clellan,
grandaughter of the Artist.*

STANHOPE FORBES

The Quarry Team, 1894.

oil on canvas, 1500 x 2450mm.

PRIVATE COLLECTION.

8

A ROMANTIC VISION

Artists of St Ives.
DRAWINGS BY FITZ

above:
Louis Grier
Arthur Mead
Julius Olsson

right:
John H. Titcomb
Thomas Millie Dow
Moffat Lindner

Up to and beyond the end of the nineteenth century the London art world remained firmly resistant to the charms of Impressionism. It retained a special dislike of things French and preferred the home-grown products of the Royal Academy. In many respects Impressionism was unacceptable to an English audience. The paintings lacked a subject, certainly a story. French painters used simple themes, without historical or classical allusions, preferring the newly-built Parisian suburbs and those places of doubtful entertainment, the theatres and cabarets. The Impressionists' use of strong broken colour to produce the effects of sunlight was in total contrast to the even-modelled tones preferred by English painters. They also ignored the traditional harmonies of composition and proportion; that interplay of horizontals and verticals which served as a regulator of proportion, the use of a diagonal formed by an upraised hand or a sloping roof; an arc formed by branches or architectural features at whose centre the composition revolves:

> *All those devices which were brought to perfection by Poussin, were foreign to the impressionists, and may have seemed irreconcilable to their technique. As a result they could achieve neither the scale nor the air of permanence of their greatest predecessors.* (Kenneth Clark, *Landscape into Art*, 1949).

The rise and sudden fall of the aesthetic movement owed much to continental sources and offended national taste at that sensitive point where art came into contact with morality. In 1895 Aubrey Beardsley was forced to resign from the 'Yellow Book' because of charges of indency. Then came the sordid disclosures of Oscar Wilde's trial and imprisonment. In 1897, the year of Queen Victoria's Diamond Jubilee, chauvinism was triumphant. The might of an Empire 'on which the sun never sets' was paraded through the London streets, and every village and hamlet joined in the celebrations. Two years later patriotic fervour was again generated by the outbreak of the Boer War. In 1858 the *Magazine of Art* could say of the New English Art Club 'French influence of the worst sort is disappearing gradually from the walls, and the spirit of the old masters of England and the Continent is re-asserting itself...'. ('New English Art Club', *Magazine of Art* 1898).

In the search for more acceptable, more British, alternatives, many painters turned their attention to the great landscape painters of the early part of the century, particularly Constable and Turner, and towards the end of the nineteenth century much of English landscape painting was reminiscent of Constable's sketches; huge skies, wide vistas seen from great heights and low horizons. The Symbolist writer Arthur Symonds described it when he wrote of a view from a Cornish village:

> *further on towards the sky, the blue glitter of the sea, shining under sunlight, with great hills and palaces of white clouds, rising up from the water as from a solid foundation.* (Arthur Symonds, *London – A Book of Aspects*, 1909).

It was to this earlier romanticized view of nature that most of the sea and landscape painters working in Cornwall subscribed. In 1896 Norman Garstin took his readers through the 'labyrinths of St Ives', '...there appeared before us a procession of men, knickerbockered and guernseyed, bearing aloft pictured canvasses.' In Arthur Meade's Porthmeor studio he took part in a critical discussion of their work. The landscape painter Arnesby Brown showed large canvasses, 'whereon a warm sunset flooded a flat world with light'; one of Meade's most important pictures was 'a wide stretching perspective of landscape at evening, seen through a screen of trees, the moon rising ruddy into the sober greys of night'. John Noble Barlow and Julius Olsson both showed seascapes, the latter a canvas 'upon which a deeply purple sea was covered by a sky strained with clouds, hot and cold as the evening knows how to blend'. Millie Dow had two pictures that were going for exhibition with the Munich Secessionists in Stuttgart 'of which protestant body Mr Dow is a member'. (*The Studio* 1896).

A leader in this group was Julius Olsson, a romantic naturalist, powerfully built, blue eyed and fair haired. In his vigorous paintings he captured the many moods of the sea and the turbulent effects of weather, painted in fresh tonal colour and with clear brushwork. He was also a daring yachtsman who made many deep-sea voyages in his own boat, and at sea he would search for effects that he would later develop in the studio. He was described by Folliot Stokes as a 'A big man with a big heart, painting his pictures with a big brush in a big studio'.

Julius Olsson (1864–1942) was the son of a Swedish father and an English mother and was born and brought up in London. He showed an early talent, and after a short training in London and abroad came to St Ives at the age of twenty-six, and lived there for more than twenty years. In addition to being a founder member of the St Ives Arts Club and its President three times, Olsson took an active part in local affairs, becoming a town councillor of St Ives, a Justice of the Peace, and President of the Lelant Golf Club.

Olsson's painting depended upon directness of approach and a bravura technique. Sometimes he made quick studies in paint or with black and white chalk on paper to better understand the massing of light and shade and the movement of waves and foam. After carefully studying the structure of sea or rock, he would work on a toned canvas with large brushes. The main composition was swiftly painted in with the minimum of colour, working at top speed, aiming to convey a sense of movement and direction with the minimum of preliminary drawing. The restful line of the horizon gave strength and support to the masses of moving water below and sky above. Little detail was included in the earlier stages of painting, the foreground of rocks or shore would be touched in for completion later. He relied upon memory backed by keen observation. He wrote:

For one whose heart draws him to the sea must, in the first place, have an exceptionally retentive memory, and be able to grasp in a few moments the effect of the ever-changing movements of the sea and sky; he must have a delicate and subtle sense of colour, and have the ability to place the main features of his impression of the subject on the canvas with a few strokes of the brush, and, beside this, he must be prepared to fight the brave fight with the elements, which will be frequently against him. (Foreword by Julius Olsson to *The Technique of Seascape Painting* by Borlase Smart, London, 1946.)

In the 1890s Julius Olsson exhibited with the Newlyn painters and became a member of the New English Art Club. He also became a prolific exhibitor at the Royal Academy. His first painting exhibited there was 'Sea Breezes', in 1890. He was elected an Associate of the Royal Academy in 1914 and a full Academician in 1920. In all he exhibited one hundred and seventy-five paintings in the Summer Exhibitions. His romantic naturalism also made him a popular exhibitor with other societies in London. He became a leading member of the Royal Institute of Oil Painters, and their President in 1917. His work was equally well received abroad. He won two gold medals at the Paris 'Salon' and was declared *hors concours* and was twice elected to the International Jury of the Carnegie Institute in Pittsburgh.

He became known for his coastal scenes and for his seascapes by moonlight, painted with great restraint of colour, he also painted many views of St Ives from The Terrace overlooking the town. In some of his most popular paintings Olsson studied the effects of the moon rising in St Ives' Bay; the warm air from the dunes giving it a coppery tone, the sea ruddy with a golden reflection. These atmospheric paintings are frequently of considerable beauty, but he often exaggerated for dramatic effect, and he was taken to task for this; he never forgave the critic Konody for speaking of his marine paintings as 'Neapolitan ices'!

Olsson's best known work 'Moonlight Shore' (1911), painted at Carbis Bay, was exhibited at the Royal Academy in 1911 and purchased for the Chantry Bequest. It was because of this and other successes that Julius Olsson moved to London at about this time, and after 1913 he was only an occasional visitor to St Ives. He died in 1942 at Dalkey, County Dublin, after he had been forced to leave London when his home was damaged by an air raid.

In 1895, in partnership with Louis Grier, Olsson opened a School of Landscape and Marine Painting with the aim of giving students the opportunity to study outdoor effects. He ran this from his large studio overlooking Porthmeor beach. As a teacher he was respected rather than loved; his school

JULIUS OLSSON

Sunset at Land's End.

oil on canvas,
590 x 740mm.

ROCHDALE ART GALLERY.

Julius Olsson in his Porthmeor Studio.

PHOTOGRAPH BY PERMISSION OF ANDREW LANYON.

was spartan but his energy was stimulating and he inspired students by his own industry. The students worked out of doors in all weathers. Emily Carr, a talented young Canadian artist, was told when she first became his student in about 1901, 'He worked you to your last gasp!'. She also believed that he favoured the boy students, treating them as fellow workers and showing them the fine seascapes he worked on in his studio up the hill.

Olsson gave criticisms at the school three times a week, and on the other three days by these were given by Algernon Talmage, who succeeded Grier as a partner in the school. In the autumn Talmage took the students to France to work in the landscape. He was more sympathetic towards his students, but admitted that Olsson was the better artist: 'what I have has been got through grind, probably that helps me understand my students better.' If he lacked Olsson's genius, he made up for it by perseverence, and the pains he took to understand his students' problems. Olsson and Talmage did not always see eye to eye on the subject of their students' work, what one taught, the other untaught. Emily Carr found it baffling but broadening. She remembered that under Talmage's instruction she had painted some studies of the woods at Tregenna which he had later praised. She knew the work was good – 'happy, honest stuff' and was desolate when Olsson described it all as 'maudlin rubbish', and advised her to 'whiten down the low-toned daubs, obliterate 'em. Go out there' (he pointed to the glaring sands) 'Out to bright sunlight – PAINT'. (Emily Carr, Autobiography *Growing Pains*). After working in St Ives, Emily Carr continued her training at Herkomer's school at Bushey and later became one of the most notable women painters in Canada.

Algernon Talmage (1871–1939) came to St Ives as a young man, probably in 1894. He had spent the two previous years as a student at Herkomer's School, at the same time as Lucy Kemp Welsh, who showed extraordinary brilliance in her painting of horses, and who later ran the school. Like her, Talmage became well known as a painter of horses and a fine landscapist. In St Ives he formed a close friendship with a talented young painter, Hilda Fearon (1878–1919), and lived with her until her early death. She had come from the Slade to study at Julius Olsson's school. Her early landscapes gave way to portraits and figure groups of women and children, often set in her studio at Pendolver. She was

ALFRED BENTLEY

Drawing of Emily Carr at St Ives.

also a model for Talmage – she is probably the figure in his painting 'The Hammock' (1914) which was exhibited at the Royal Academy.

By contrast to the athletic, outgoing Olsson, Algernon Talmage was modest, reserved and physically frail, (a boyhood accident with a gun had crippled his right hand, and he painted with his left). In spite of his physical limitations, Talmage was a hard worker who painted his landscapes and cattle on the spot, working mostly in the woods around Tregenna. These landscapes, described as 'honest as Constable' are clearly stated, without exaggeration of form or colour. He looked for breadth of composition, broad skies subordinated to the overall colour of the day, and a strong instinct for weather. He became a regular exhibitor at the Royal Academy. Folliot Stokes, a fellow artist in St Ives, decribed his 'love of nature... deep and reverend, and he spares no paint to interpret her truly. At the same time he is careful to choose of her best and to see it under the most beautiful and often the most transient aspects.'

A painting done shortly before he left Cornwall 'The End of the Shower' (1907) was described by Stokes as:

> *The somewhat sombre beauty of Cornish moorland... one of the 'soft' days so common in western winter. The great seaborne clouds are charged with rain, and the gorse and bent grasses of the foreground are dripping with moisture from a shower which is seen passing over St Ives Bay and the country beyond.*
> ('The Landscape Paintings of Mr Algernon Talmage', by A. G. Folliot Stokes, *The Studio* vol.42, No.175, 1907).

In 1907, returning from a painting trip in Picardy, Talmage stopped in London for a few days. He became entranced by the city, particularly at dusk and in the early mornings, and he began to paint it with a poetic feeling inspired by Whistler. These pictures formed the basis of his successful first one man exhibition at the Goupil Gallery, London, in 1909, which established his reputation. He severed his connection with Cornwall, and went to live in Chelsea. In 1918 he became an official war artist to the Canadian Government, and with a Canadian Cavalry regiment made many portrayals of dead or wounded horses on the battlefields. After the war he returned to his main theme, the English countryside in all its unspoilt splendour. He was elected ARA in 1922 and RA seven years later. He died at Sherfield English, near Romsey in Hampshire.

Olsson's direct methods of teaching attracted a number young artists from overseas who later played an important part in the artistic development of their home countries. In the early years of the century several Australian artists came to St Ives, for example Arthur Burgess, Will Ashton and George Bell. The young Arthur Burgess (1879–1957) was on the verge of returning home to Australia after a particularly severe 'crit' from Olsson, but on learning that others had similarly suffered – Olsson had a painful toothache on that day – he decided to stay. He later became a leading marine painter, and an official war artist for the Australian Government. He captured on canvas a number of the important sea actions of the Great War and in the Second World War he produced many fine paintings of the Atlantic convoys as well as the famous incident of the sinking of the *Bismark*. Will Ashton (1891–1963), the son of an English drawing master, was educated in Australia and then studied with Olsson in St Ives before going to Julian's atelier in Paris. In 1905 he returned to Australia and became well known for his Impressionist seascapes. He had a distinguished career in Sydney and Adelaide, with frequent visits to London and Paris, and became Director of the Art Gallery of New South Wales and was knighted. George Bell had studied at the Melbourne Gallery School under McCubbin and in Paris before working in St Ives for a year in 1909. After some years in Chelsea he also became a war artist and was strongly influenced by post-Impressionism. In Australia he became an influential critic and teacher and a leader of the modern movement in Australian painting. (*Australian Painting from 1788 to 1970* by Bernard Smith, Oxford University Press, Melbourne and Oxford 1971; and the *Australian Dictionary of National Biography*).

An Australian painter who had a long connection with St Ives was Richard Haley Lever (1876–1958). He had left his home in Adelaide, South Australia, at the age of seventeen to train as an artist in Europe, and his work soon began to attract attention in London and Paris. In 1900 he was introduced to the St Ives Arts Club by his fellow Australian Louis Grier (Whybrow, *op.cit.*, p.213) and in that same year he married Aida Gale in St Ives. From this time he was one of the group working with Olsson and Grier, with a studio above Langhams Gallery. With St Ives as a base, in the following years he explored sea subjects in Brittany and along the south coast of England. In 1912 he moved to New York and took American citizenship. His paintings of the Hudson Valley, Nantucket and Vermont brought him an international reputation, but he regarded the work that he had done in St Ives as some of his best.

Many of Olsson's students later settled in St Ives, among them John Park and Borlase Smart, and a number of distinguished women artists including Mary McCrossan (1863–1934), who later ran her own painting school in St Ives.

The teaching of the Hungarian born Hubert von Herkomer had a powerful effect upon a number of painters who were students at his celebrated school in Bushey, and who later came to St Ives. At the height of his fame as a Royal Academician, Herkomer was asked to give instruction in drawing and painting to the niece of a wealthy neighbour. He refused, but indicated that he would be prepared to teach a group of students. The neighbour, Mr Gibb, agreed to erect a suitable building and to cover the costs. Applications poured in from prospective students, and the school, built beside his opulent home Lululand, opened on 23 November 1883 with seventeen men and fifteen women as the first students.

Algernon Talmage was one of several early Herkomer students who later came to St Ives, others included the landscape painter Arnesby Brown and his wife-to-be, Mia Edwards, and also W. H. Y. Titcomb and Arthur Meade. Another student was William Nicholson who came to Bushey at the age of sixteen, and met the talented Mabel Pryde. They later married and their son Ben Nicholson was to have a profound effect upon a later generation of artists in St Ives.

Teaching at the school was centred upon the highly personal views of its principal, Hubert von Herkomer, who was strongly opposed to the academies. He insisted that each student possessed unique personal abilities, and that these should be individually brought out and developed. He defined his school as 'An art school for the supression of the student', and hoped thus to avoid the plodding conformist who lacked anything but the capacity to win prizes. Direct work from the figure was at the heart of his method of teaching and admission to the life class was the aspiration of every student:

we open for him all the possibilities of the painter in form and colour, in manipulation, in strength and delicacy. In that study he becomes the 'painter'

SIR J. A. ARNESBY BROWN
(opposite).

The Raincloud.

oil on canvas, 580 x 800mm.

Royal Academy Diploma work, 1915.

ROYAL ACADEMY OF ART.

proper; he learns to grasp the difficulties of reality, of actuality, he becomes master of his artistic language, of technique... He learns, in the exercise, to love nature for nature's sake. (A. Lys Baldry 'The Herkomer School', *The Studio*, October 1898 vol. VI No.31).

There was no Bushey style and the artists who emerged showed diversity and benefitted from his broad outlook. When they came to St Ives they also brought something of the community spirit of Bushey; light-hearted, yet optimistic and adventurous.

The paintings of John Alfred Arnesby Brown (1866–1955) epitomise the tranquility and slow pace of the English countryside in the years before the First World War. Brown painted the moors of West Penwith – dark ragged clouds overhead, swept by rising currents of warm air and gilded by the evening sun. His subjects were atmosphere and weather; the end of a warm day with the suspicion of a storm approaching, huddled groups of cattle in the foreground. His work had an easy naturalism which captured the poetry of landscape, and he was able to treat the subjects that moved him simply. He was concerned to discover the broadest graduations of tone, and to describe the openness and scale of the country, the place and time of day. He also painted a number of memorable sea pictures. His paintings are innovative, within a tradition which included the early French and Dutch landscapists, and a special reverence for Constable. His essentially English quality was characterised by his love of the country and his love of animals. He was described as 'a townsman by birth, a countryman by inclination'. (*The Studio* Vol.20 Sept. 1900).

Arnesby Brown was born into a well-respected Nottingham family. His father was a wine merchant and a part-time painter and author. He studied at

ALGERNON TALMAGE

Evening in St Ives.

oil on canvas, 400 x 450mm.

DAVID MESSUM FINE ART.

MIA EDWARDS
Morning Sunshine.
oil on canvas, 380 x 330mm.
DAVID MESSUM FINE ART.

MARY MCCROSSAN
Wind and Surf.
oil on canvas, 310 x 430mm.
DAVID MESSUM FINE ART.

the local school of art and at the age of nineteen he became a pupil of the Nottingham painter Andrew McCallum, whose detailed realism was lost on Brown, but who introduced him to the discipline of working out of doors. While still in Nottingham he began to make an income from portraiture, which continued for a large part of his life. The most creative part of his training, however, was the fresh and vigorous teaching he received at Herkomer's School. Brown made his first visit to St Ives while still a student at Bushey, and while there he painted one of his first exhibits at the Royal Academy – 'St Ives, Cornwall.'

Soon after his student days, in 1894, Brown came to stay in St Ives, and two years later married Mia Edwards, a fellow student from Bushey. She frequently showed her paintings of children at the Royal Academy and was included in many exhibitions with Elizabeth Forbes and Marianne Stokes. Shortly after their marriage the Browns bought a house in Norfolk, and for many years spent the summer and autumn there and the winter and spring in St Ives. Arnesby Brown was a well known winter resident of St Ives and in 1900 he became President of the St Ives Arts Club. In his later life he was described as 'a big, slow moving man, suggesting a country squire, exceedingly quiet in manner and scant of speech, though he was a good companion and universally liked'. (*The Times*, Obituary, November 1955). He would start a painting out of doors, working from the subject and finish it in the studio, where he could draw on his total experience of the scene. 'I know the effect on nature that I am working for, and I can remember my first impression of the scene vividly for a long time, which is a decided asset'. (*The Artist*, August 1933). In pursuit of his first idea he abstracted the elements of landscape, and allowed his imagination to enter into the mood of the composition. He possessed the skill of knowing what to leave out, what to refine and modify, without losing the essentials of his subject. 'If an artist has felt a scene sharply, he ought to be able to pass on that feeling to the spectator', he said. ('The Changing Hours', exhibition catalogue, London Leicester Galleries 1909.)

Arnesby Brown was in tune with his time and success came to him. In 1901 his painting 'Morning' was bought from the Royal Academy for the Chantry Bequest. Two years later he became an Associate of the Academy, and in the same year held a successful exhibition at the Leicester Galleries in London. The critic of the *Art Journal* admired the freedom of handling, the effect of light in his paintings and his lack of sentiment. 'He feels the rhyme and not the blank verse of Nature, and measures and composes with an eye to form and balance.' (*Art Journal*, 'The Royal Academy' by A. C. R. Carter 1905, p.169).

Towards the end of his time in Cornwall Brown's work developed a greater freedom. The dramatic contrasts of light and shade gave way to more subtle colouring and atmospheric effects. In 1910 Brown bought a house in Cheyne Row, Chelsea and from this time ceased to visit Cornwall. In 1918 he was elected to full membership of the Royal Academy, and his work was bought for many provincial collections as far afield as New Zealand. In 1934 his work was chosen to represent Britain at the Venice Bienniale, and four years later he was knighted for his services to painting. In the last years of his life failing eyesight made him unable to paint, and for a number of years he became totally blind. He died at Haddiscoe in Norfolk at the age of ninety.

In St Ives the cottages of Downalong tumble along the quayside, a confusion of whitewashed cob walls and green-grey slated roofs. The names of its narrow streets – 'Bible Christian Street', 'Bethesda Hill', 'Teetotal Street' and

'Salubrious Place' – reflect the reforming zeal of Methodism, for John Wesley made twenty-seven visits to St Ives and described it as 'the first place in Cornwall where we preached, and where Satan fought fiercely for his kingdom, but now all is at peace'.

The religious fervour of the fishing community, centred upon the Primitive Methodist Chapel, captured the imagination of one of St Ives' few figure painters, William Holt Yates Titcomb (1858–1930). The Chapel, in Fore Street, St Ives, was an important power for good in the community, to whom it brought the direct message of the Bible. For Titcomb, who came from a strong religious background, it offered a subject for several of his most successful paintings. The first of these was 'Primitive Methodists at Prayer' (1889). In the bare chapel, lit by bluish light from a high window, the small congregation sit in attitudes of prayer and contemplation. In sympathetic detail Titcomb describes the sorrowful reflections of the aged, the furtive play of the young boys, and the efforts of the Minister to arouse spiritual understanding in an unresponsive congregation. He used mostly local people as models; Captain Dick Harry is the main figure in the composition, who kneels facing the artist, faced by Captain Veal. As the model for the Minister he used the painter and founder of the Arts Club, Louis Grier (better known as an ambitious drinker, and more likely to be found in the Sloop Inn than the Methodist Chapel). When the painting was exhibited at the Royal Academy in 1889 the *Art Journal* admired the characterisation of the figures: 'In their quietness is a strenuous sentiment, with that sincerity which is rare in art as it is happily frequent in life'. (Review of the 'Work by Herkomer's Students' at the Fine Art Society, *Art Journal* 1892).

WILLIAM HOLT YATES TITCOMB

Primitive Methodists, 1889.

oil on canvas

DUDLEY ART GALLERY.

Titcomb was the son of a renowned Anglican clergyman, and was brought up in Lambeth, London. After an undistinguished school career at Westminster School, but with an apitude for drawing, he was offered a place at the South Kensington Schools. At a time of family crisis, following the death of his wife, the Reverend Titcomb accepted the appointment as the first Bishop of Rangoon, and in 1880–81 took his son William to spend eight months in British Burma, a visit the young artist found greatly stimulating. He was entranced by the relaxed and happy character of the Burmese, and their love of colour and decoration in dress and religious celebrations. He settled to a period of painting and drawing in the city of Rangoon and in the country districts. He made friends among the Burmese, and was given the title 'The Royal Artist'. On his return to Europe he continued his studies in Paris at Julian's Academy; in England at Herkomer's newly formed School, and then in Antwerp at Verlat's Academy.

In 1887 Titcomb moved to St Ives. Five years later, on a painting trip to Etaples in France, he met another student, Jessie Ada Morison, and they were later married. Jessie Titcomb continued to paint – mostly children's portraits – and exhibited at the Royal Academy in 1895 and 1897. She probably gave up painting seriously in 1898 when her first child was born.

As a figure painter Titcomb had more in common with his Newlyn colleagues, particularly Forbes and Bramley, than with the sea and landscape painters in St Ives. One of his best known character studies was 'Old Sea Dogs' (1891), which depicts three old fishermen reminiscing on Smeaton's Pier in St Ives. If there is a stiffness about the posed conviviality of the figures, there is also a feeling of colour in the sparkling view of St Ives' Bay which distances this painting from those of his Newlyn contemporaries. A later painting 'A Pilot' (1905) celebrates the St Ives custom of holding an outdoor service of the Passion on Good Friday, on the wharf. In the picture the harbour is packed with boats brought in for Easter. The young priest

WILLIAM HOLT YATES
TITCOMB

Old Sea Dogs, 1891.

oil on canvas, 1550 x 1200mm.

NOTTINGHAM CASTLE MUSEUM.

addressing the fishermen was Father Bernard Walke, who later became a notable figure in the area, and a good friend of the artists. The altar boy holding aloft the crucifix was Titcomb's son Frank.

Titcomb was a man of some means, as his travels testify. In 1889 he inherited property in Yorkshire, in the village of Wickersley, an industrial town near Sheffield. On his frequent visits he found subjects in the factories where hand processes were still competing with machines. Then after eighteen years in St Ives, Titcomb and his family moved to Dusseldorf in Germany, as Ada Titcomb insisted upon a German education for her two children. In 1909 the family returned to England, to Bristol where he painted the poor and the deprived in the city's orphanages, blind asylums, alms houses and schools. The last ten years of his life were mostly spent travelling abroad.

St Ives was the home for a number of painters whose work described the incidentals of Cornish life; spring in the valleys, the coast and the sea. In their tonal and atmospheric painting, many of them owed a debt to Whistler.

Moffat Lindner (1852–1949) was an early visitor to St Ives in the late nineteenth century, and an important contact with the London art world. He was the son of a wealthy Birmingham merchant. For a short time he worked in his father's business, but left with a small allowance to study art, and was a student at the Slade and Heatherley's. His work was widely exhibited in London. He was elected to membership of the Royal Society of British Artists in 1888 during Whistler's turbulent Presidency and to the New English Art Club in the following year. He became a friend of Philip Wilson Steer, and in 1890, when Steer was painting some of his finest impressionist beach scenes, Lindner, Steer, and Fred Brown painted at Swanage for the summer. The magazine *The Whirlwind* reported 'Mr Steer has I understand owing to a rumour of our threatened reproduction of one of his pictures, left town hurriedly. He is said to be hiding at Swanage as company with Mr Moffat P. Lindner who is known in artistic circles as "the moonlighter"'. (*The Whirlwind,* 5 July 1890).

In 1900 Lindner entertained Steer and Brown in St Ives, and on that visit Wilson Steer painted a portrait of Lindner's wife Augusta (née Baird Smith), herself a painter. The portrait was exhibited at the New English Art Club in the following year. In 1902 Lindner moved into a new studio in St Ives, one of five newly converted from fish lofts overlooking Porthmeor Beach, and described as 'very commodious, with good aspect and splendid sea views' (Whybrow, *op.cit.,* p.30). He later acquired ownership of the group of studios, and established a trust for them to be in permanent use by painters, a gesture of lasting benefit to later generations of artists in the town.

Although he was often in London, Lindner became President of the St Ives Arts Club in 1899, in 1911 and again during the wartime period from 1914 to 1917. His exhibits at the Royal Academy included many St Ives subjects, alternating with views of Venice and other continental centres. He romanticised St Ives and made many comparisons in his painting between water-based subjects and the effects of light on the waters of St Ives and Venice, painted in soft transparent colour. His work was harmonious and finely coloured and whether he was painting in Venice, on the Spanish coast, in Holland or St Ives, there is the same feeling for atmosphere, light and the reflections upon water. Lindner was a respected figure in St Ives, and a staunch champion of the colony. His Porthmeor studio later became the St Ives School of Painting. He died in St Ives in 1949 at the age of ninety-six.

' ...St Ives was in its heyday at the turn of the century, a complete artists' colony. It was still an unspoilt fishing village, and most picturesque...' (Norman Wilkinson in *St Ives: A Brush with Life*, Seeley Service 1969). The resident group included a number of well established artists who had a high local reputation but who failed to attract major national attention, but they formed a friendly community as much of the social life revolved around the St Ives Arts Club.

Arthur 'Bluebell' Meade (1852–1948), arrived in about 1890 and lived there until his death. He had trained in Paris, and at Herkomer's School in Bushey. He had a preference for country subjects, often combined with figures, and found his subjects on the coast and inland areas of West Penwith. He also made occasional visits abroad to such distant and exotic places as Morocco and India. His studio overlooking Porthmeor Beach (now the St Ives School of Painting) was a popular venue for visitors on show days. Meade was a staunch supporter of the St Ives Arts Club, and its President on a number of occasions; he was a regular exhibitor at the Royal Academy from 1888 onwards.

Edmund G. Fuller (c.1860–1930) was also an early resident and was living in Barnoon in 1892. Dressed in a green tweed suit, cap and stick, he was a well known and well liked figure in St Ives. His paintings of sea and coast were rendered in Impressionist colour, influenced by Whistler. Such paintings as 'Clear Shining after Rain' exhibited at the Royal Society of British Artists in 1896, 'Sun Kissed Foam' and 'Cornwall's Ironbound Coast' exhibited at the Royal Academy in 1899 and 1902 respectively, dramatized the effects of the weather. His close friend Fred Milner (d.1936) also arrived in St Ives in the 1890s and painted the harbour and the effects of morning and evening light along the coast. He exhibited at the Royal Academy from 1898.

MOFFAT LINDNER
A Foreign Town.
watercolour, 230 x 290mm.
PRIVATE COLLECTION.

EDMUND FULLER
White Water.
oil on canvas, 510 x 765mm.
THE TREHAYES COLLECTION.

A painter of landscape, who kept well within the romantic tradition, was John Noble Barlow (1861–1917). Manchester born, he spent most of his life in St Ives. He painted the coast and evocative studies of landscape, seen at dawn or dusk, and his work was admired for its sound craftsmanship. He was a regular exhibitor at the Royal Academy from 1893 to 1916. He found many of his subjects in the wooded valleys of Lamorna, and taught a number of the younger artists there, including Charles Simpson. However his own work is constructed on older principles, inspired by his training in Paris under Lefebre and Delance, and his reverence for the Barbizon painters, particularly Corot.

Many regular visitors to St Ives also became closely identified with the town. One of these was Terrick John Williams (1860–1937), born in Liverpool and trained in Antwerp and Paris. He came to St Ives frequently from about 1890 onwards, and painted sea and landscape subjects. These are strongly painted studies but they lack colour, and are more in the manner of the Barbizon painters than the Impressionists. Williams was a drawing master at the Royal Military Academy in Woolwich until 1902, when he became a full-time painter, and he was able to spend more time working abroad, in Brittany, Holland and Italy – particularly Venice, interspersed with frequent visits to St Ives. He was a prolific worker and was elected an Associate of the Royal Academy in 1924. In 1933 he became President of the Royal Institute of Painters in Watercolour, and in 1936 a Royal Academician.

One of the larger-than-life visitors to St Ives was the American, Walter Elmer Schofield (1867–1944), from Philadelphia, a man of the out-of-doors. 'He is for the wind on the heath, free limbs of life, a big movement and the big line in nature, vast views and vaster spaces, the outlook of Walt Whitman and Adam Lindsey Gordon.' (C. Lewis Hind in 'Landscape Painting, W. Elmer Schofield', *The Studio*, vol.LVII 1912–13). Schofield could properly be called one of the founders of American landscape painting, his work was spacious, broad and simple. After training at the Pennsylvania Academy of Fine Arts he was in Paris in 1892 at Julian's Academy, and with many visits to Fontainebleau and Brittany. In 1903 he came to St Ives, where he was resident for four years. After this he saw England as his adopted home and moved between Cornwall and his own land. One of his better known paintings 'Sand Dunes near Lelant, Cornwall' in the Metropolitan Museum of Art, New York, is a study from high ground of the perspective of the flat land bordering the Hayle river, boldly executed in strong colour. His was an art without mystery, carried through out of doors with enthusiasm. 'Zero weather, rain, falling snow, wind – all these things to contend with only make the open-air painter love the fight.' (C.Lewis Hind *op.cit.*).

Although Schofield retained his American citizenship, he remained a close friend of many of the Cornish artists. He painted in Dieppe with Julius Olsson and in 1905 he served with Alfred East on the International Jury of the Carnegie Institute in Pittsburgh.

In 1915 he joined the British Army as a private and with Julius Olsson's help he obtained a commission. In the artillery he took part in the Battle of the Somme and he left the army with the rank of Major. Towards the end of his life he and his family moved to Godolphin Manor, near Breage, one of the great historic houses of Cornwall, that had been purchased by his son Sydney. Here Elmer Schofield lived until his death.

Between the artists of Newlyn and St Ives there were close connections and many friendships. There was perhaps more lightheartedness and sociability among the St Ives group for a number had private means and were able to enjoy a social life of some quality; painting was part of this life, but not all of it. By comparison the Newlyners were thought to be dedicated but humourless. According to one writer the Newlyners were looked on as 'ivory necked mourners following on the wake of a funeral', by the painters of St Ives, 'because we work so hard in the week, and rest on Sundays, and are all teetotallers and go to bed at 10 pm occasionally... but our work is our sorrow.' (Frank Richards, 'Newlyn as a Sketching Ground', *The Studio*, Vol. V 1895).

WALTER ELMER SCHOFIELD
A Cornish Cove, 1912.

The tradition of 'show days' – such a feature of Newlyn, before the Passmore Edwards Art Gallery was built – was continued in St Ives. A lively annual pilgrimage of art lovers, and the merely curious, wended their way up and down staircases and alleyways, from studio to studio, to see the pictures intended for the Royal Academy and other spring exhibitions. Each year between two hundred and three hundred paintings were sent from St Ives to the Academy Summer Exhibitions alone. The Sloop Inn on the old harbour became a gathering place for artists, and held a permanent, changing exhibition of the work of some of its more distinguished regulars who had made St Ives their home; Olsson, Barlow and Grier gathered in its round bar. Herbert Lanyon painter, photographer and father of the abstract artist Peter Lanyon, held regular Sunday soirées, and arranged exhibitions in his studio.

More serious commercial activity took place at the premises of James Lanham, whose long-established business in the High Street offered a variety of goods and services including furnishing, china and glass, wines, spirits and house agency. Lanham also sold a range of artist's materials by leading manufacturers, and made weekly trips by pony and trap to Newlyn with a selection for the artists there. On the return journey he brought Newlyn copperware to sell in St Ives. In 1887 Lanham opened a gallery in his two large first floor rooms, and arranged exhibitions of work by the leading painters of St Ives and Newlyn. He also acted as agent and picture framer for a number of them. A small committee composed of members of the Arts Club advised on the selection and presentation. Norman Garstin described the gallery in *The Studio*:

> *Here, under an awning that softens the strong glare of the sky-light, you find a very charming little show, always fresh and interesting. Every month it is rearranged, and new blood infused; the fearful gaps made by that ruthless devastator of exhibitions, the buyer, are filled up; and so from year's end to year's end this gallery flourishes like a tropical forest dropping now and then a leaf though knowing no season but one.* ('Studio Talk' by N.G. *The Studio* Vol.VIII No.42 September 1896).

Despite the generally good relationships between the artists of Newlyn and St Ives there was one important matter on which they were opposed. Stanhope Forbes wrote of '...a rather bitter rivalry... Oh, it was nothing to do with painting or art of any kind; it was much more serious, for it concerned cricket!' (Forbes, paper of 1939, p.9). Matches between opposing teams of artists had taken place in Brittany in 1885, when the British and American artists of Concarneau received a challenge from their colleagues in Pont-Aven to play them at

Lanham's Art Gallery, St Ives, with the cellarman standing in the doorway.

Newlyn Cricket Team
*c.*1890.

Stanhope Forbes is seated on the left, next to him, standing, is William Wainwright. Edwin Harris is second from the right, standing. The captain, Frank Bramley, is seated in the centre in a striped cap; to his right is Fred Millard.

baseball. By the following year, several of the Concarneau players were in St Ives and the game was cricket. The first annual cricket match between Newlyn and St Ives took place in 1886, Adrian Stokes and the three Americans, Butler, Simmons and Chadwick were among the St Ives team, and the Americans acquitted themselves well, Chadwick from Boston, making the best score. The game was marred by an unfortunate accident, when two of the Newlyn players, Millard and Scully, accidently collided in midfield whilst running for the ball. Both were seriously injured and for a time it looked as if Millard's life was in danger. Newlyners were doubly upset by having lost the match, and Butler wrote 'The Englishers are very much cut up over their defeat and we have agreed to play a return match tomorrow. We will probably let them win.' (letters from Howard Butler to his family, quoted in *The Good and Simple Life, op.cit.*).

Each year the first match was played in Newlyn and a return match at St Ives. The Newlyn team had Frank Bramley as its captain, a keen cricketer who became considerably more animated on the cricket field. His team included Forbes, Langley, Tayler, Harris, Rheam (a notable cricketer 'imported', as Forbes explained, 'at vast expense from Polperrow'[sic]), Blackburne and da Costa, Frank Richards and Fred Hall; Gotch and Mackenzie were umpire and scorer respectively. Chevallier Tayler had prowess as a batsman. The St Ives team included Adrian Stokes – considered to be the most formidable of the St Ives players, with the Australian Louis Grier, W. H. Titcomb, a fine bowler and Edward Simmons, 'all of whom were most energetic and good cricketers, and more often than not did all the work for their side.' (Frank Richards *op.cit.*). In later years these matches became eagerly awaited annual events, as Frank Richards reported:

> *for lighter enjoyment on a hot summer's day we indulge in cricket. Newlyn versus St Ives is the match of the year, generally terminating in a victory for the home team over their friendly opponents.* (Frank Richards, *op.cit.*).

9

THE LAMORNA VALLEY

W est Cornwall was far removed from the London art world, yet its artists were not unaffected by the radical changes taking place there in the first years of the twentieth century. The most momentous confrontation with entrenched English taste came in 1905, with the exhibition of French Impressionist paintings arranged by Durand Ruel at the Grafton Galleries. Here were displayed some of the finest paintings produced in France over the previous thirty years – ten or fifteeen masterpieces by each of the leaders of the movement, Monet, Manet, Renoir, Pissaro, Degas and Cezanne.

Frank Rutter was one of the leading critics of the day. As he explained:

The effect was overwhelming. It was a revelation to London of a new world of colour. Never before, so it seemed to us – and it was true – had we seen nature painted in all of the prismatic radiance of summer sunshine. These pictures sparkled, they scintillated with light, not with the 'golden glow' of academic convention, but with the dancing pin-points of myriad hues. Here were masters who appeared to paint not with dull pigments extracted from tubes, but with all the colours of the rainbow. (Frank Rutter, *Art in My Time*, Rich and Cowan 1933, p.101–2).

LAMORNA BIRCH

Spring Morning.

oil on panel, 260 x 175mm.

PENZANCE AND DISTRICT MUSEUM AND ART GALLERY.

Support for Impressionism grew, and although the painters in Cornwall were not radical, their work soon responded to the new freedom of colour and the more expressive arrangements that were the product of Impressionism. Many artists settled in and around the deeply wooded Lamorna Valley some six miles from Newlyn, on the south coast. Lamorna Birch came to live there in 1902, after visiting Newlyn a number of times. Harold and Laura Knight came in 1908 and were resident until after the First World War. Alfred Munnings was an enlivening visitor as was Augustus John. Younger artists also came – Dod and Ernest Proctor, Charles and Ella Naper, Robert and Eleanor Hughes, and others who gave the Lamorna colony its own particular character.

Lamorna Birch (1869–1955), born Samuel John Birch in Egremont near Birkenhead, Cheshire, was the eldest of nine children. His father, a painter and decorator, died when he was a boy and the family moved to Manchester. John left school at twelve, and became an office boy. Later he worked at a mill near Lancaster, lodging with a gamekeeper who taught him the ways of the country – particularly the art of fly-fishing, which became a life-long passion. He also worked in a linoleum factory and attributed his physical strength to carrying heavy rolls of lino between departments. Despite the long, tedious hours of work, the young Birch taught himself to draw, and encouraged by his mother, began to paint. His paintings became known locally, and with savings and sacrifice, and the proceeds of sales from an exhibition at the Lancaster Art Gallery, he decided to become an artist.

Birch was already aware of Newlyn's reputation as an artists' colony, and in 1889 he came for an extended visit, with £25 and his belongings in a tin trunk. He found lodgings at Boleigh Farm at the head of the Lamorna Valley, and began to work from the landscape. Up to that time he had no training in art and on the advice of Stanhope Forbes he went to Paris in 1895 where he painted from the figure at the Atelier Colorossi. He also spent a considerable part of that year painting by the Seine and sold the pictures in Lancaster on his return. After Paris, Birch returned to Cornwall and until 1902 he lived at St Buryan, near Land's End. That year he was asked by a local girl, Emily Houghton Vivian (known as 'Mouse') if he would give her painting lessons. He agreed, and their acquaintance soon deepened. Four months later they were married, and bought Flagstaff Cottage, formerly the Harbour Master's house, at the seaward end of Lamorna Valley, on a narrow twisting road overlooking the cove. Two daughters, Lamorna (1904) and Joan (1909), were born to them.

The Lamorna Valley, brilliant in summer, deserted and unwelcoming in winter, is an unspoiled beauty spot, best reached by walking, three miles along the coastal footpath from Mousehole, six miles from Penzance. Small irregular fields with Cornish walling, topped with gorse, descend to the stream in the thickly wooded valley bottom, abundant with wild daffodils and bluebells in the spring. At Lamorna Cove, where the stream meets the sea, there is the sudden opening of the wide, rough beach, deeply cut into the granite cliffs with clearly defined vertical strata. There is no easy landing for boats, only a steep slipway gives limited shelter behind the few cottages. Laura Knight recalled her first visit to the Lamorna Valley through the mud and puddles from Newlyn:

> we had suddenly entered Paradise; a densely wooded valley filled with lichen-covered trees of a greenish grey; whose branches threw a bluish tracery of shadow over the rich tufts of grass already speckled with the yellow of early primrose and white anemone. Violet-tinted grey granite boulders bordered a stream that found its way to Lamorna Cove – beauty pictured best by John himself in his many watercolours and oil canvasses. (Dame Laura Knight 'S. J. Lamorna Birch as I knew him', reprinted in the catalogue to the exhibition 'Samuel John Lamorna Birch R.A.' Galerie George, London, 1986.)

Birch was a romantic naturalist, and worked at all times of the year out of doors, often in difficult conditions. In his early years he cycled around the countryside to find paintable spots, storing unfinished pictures in local barns for his return. His best known subjects were Lamorna Valley and it's boulder strewn cove – hence the name 'Lamorna', which is said to have been suggested by Stanhope Forbes to distinguish him from Lionel Birch who lived in Newlyn. Lamorna Birch had the appearance of a countryman and a fisherman. Again to quote from Laura Knight:

> I remember the brownish tweeds he wore – and a rather battered hat, a tweed homburg with a host of artificial fishing flies stuck in it. He was slender of build and tallish of height; his beard and hair were dark brown; his face was tanned, his cheeks were rosy; his skin was smooth and fine; and a full generous mouth showed beneath his moustache. His knickerbockers, strapped and buckled just below the knee, allowed the display, as he came down the hill, of

his splendidly developed legs, the calves of which could have been the envy of any man. (Dame Laura Knight 'S. J. Lamorna Birch as I knew him' *op.cit.*)

Birch was an intense, likeable and lively man and a hard worker. He painted each day from breakfast until evening of doors in the valley or in a small wooden studio buried in the wood. Water held a particular fascination for him, both as a subject for painting and also as an enthusiastic and skilled fisherman. Charles Marriot remembered. 'Birch taught me all I know about trout fishing. I have seen him cast a fly against the wind through a hole in a blackberry bush and drop it exactly over the rising trout.' (Charles Marriot 'Memories of Cornwall's Art Colonies',

LAURA KNIGHT

Lamorna Birch and his Daughters, begun 1913, completed 1934.

oil on canvas, 2300 x 2550mm.
NOTTINGHAM UNIVERSITY.

Cornish Review, Autumn, 1949.) Alfred Munnings wrote 'When he was not painting he was fishing. When he was not fishing he was painting'. (Alfred Munnings, *An Artist's Life.* Museum Press, 1950.).

In 1893 Birch had his first work accepted by the Royal Academy, he later became one of its most prolific exhibitors. Soon his work was regularly seen with the Royal Institute of Painters in Watercolours, and in Birmingham, Liverpool and Manchester. In his earliest landscapes there is little colour, and a tonal arrangement that shows the influence of his Barbizon training, studies of clear skies, fresh woodland scenes with farm animals at pasture. He closely observed the effects of weather, Charles Marriot remembers meeting him in 1901 when Cornwall had one of its rare falls of heavy snow. 'I shall never forget Birch's delight at the novel effects created by the deep drifts on the Lamorna Valley and on the surrounding gorse-clad moors'. His work noticeably brightened and strengthened in colour after 1900, but he did not use the many-hued palette of the Impressionists, preferring more pastel tones, the colour tinted with white for the lighter shades, black or brown for the darker ones. In about 1911 he developed a method of drawing in pencil overlaid by a light wash of watercolour, which helped him to capture the fleeting effects of sunlight and changes of weather. From many such drawings and oil sketches made on the spot, large canvases would be painted in his studio by the stream.

Laura (née Johnson) and Harold Knight came to Newlyn in 1908. Harold was thirty-four and Laura three years younger. Both were from Nottingham, where they had met at the School of Art. Laura Knight (1877–1970), had an unsettled childhood. She was the youngest of three sisters whose father had left the family when she was born. Her mother, Charlotte Johnson, struggled to bring up her daughters and pursue her own career as an artist and a teacher of art. By the age of twelve Laura had formed the ambition to attend one of the 'ateliers' in Paris, and through a family connection she was able to spend some time in St Quentin in France, but the precarious family finances failed and she was forced to return to England. She became a part-time student at Nottingham School of Art at the age of thirteen. Charlotte Johnson died two years later, and Laura's eldest sister, still only seventeen, became responsible for her younger sister's education. Despite severe poverty Laura continued her studies and was awarded a scholarship to the value of twenty pounds for two years.

LAMORNA BIRCH

Tregiffian Cliff.

oil on canvas

CITY OF BRISTOL
MUSEUM AND ART GALLERY.

Harold Knight (1874–1961) was the star student at the School of Art. His painstaking studies from the model and his dedicated hard work had a powerful effect upon Laura. Her own temperament was in sharp contrast, she was by nature impulsive, attracted to the exotic and bizarre, capable of great bursts of energy, but lacking Harold's stamina. Through these difficult years, parentless and in real poverty, she was sustained by his friendship, and they drew increasingly together. After leaving the Art School, Laura set up in a rented studio with the intention of earning a living as an artist: Harold studied for several months at Laurens' Academy in Paris. In 1903 Laura had her first picture 'Mother and Child' accepted by the Royal Academy, and it was bought by no less an artist than Edward Stott R.A. who had influenced many of the Newlyn painters.

This success, and a good portrait commission for Harold, decided them upon marriage. On their honeymoon in London they were both impressed by the work of the Dutch landscape painter, Matthew Marais, and in the summer of 1904 they spent six weeks at Laren in northern Holland. On their return they joined the small colony of artists who had settled in Staithes, a fishing village near Whitby on the Yorkshire coast. The Yorkshire winters were harsh, little outdoor work could take place, and the grinding poverty of many of the fishing folk was a constant reminder to Laura of her own lack of means, but she loved the austerity and the wild coast, and admired the resilience of the people. In these early years, her subjects were sombre, drawn from the working life of the fishing village. She painted in a rich impasto of greys, and the imaginative arrangement of the figures gives these low-toned paintings their animation. One of her most ambitious paintings from her last year at Staithes reveals her ability to identify with her subject. 'Dressing the Children' (1906) is set in a cottage kitchen, warmed by a glowing range, where a young mother prepares her children for school.

LAURA KNIGHT

Self Portrait, c.1902.

chalk drawing, 385 x 290mm.

LAURA KNIGHT

The Beach, 1908.

oil on canvas, 1250 x 1500mm.

LAING ART GALLERY, TYNE & WEAR MUSEUM SERVICE.

HAROLD KNIGHT

In the Spring, 1908.

oil on canvas, 1350 x 1550mm.

LAING ART GALLERY, TYNE & WEAR MUSEUM SERVICE.

LAURA KNIGHT

Cornwall, 1912.

chalk and watercolour,
540 x 760mm.

EDITIONS GRAPHIQUE GALLERY,
LONDON.

A second and longer visit to Holland enlarged the Knights' knowledge of the Dutch masters and excited their interest in landscape. Laura saw paintings by Van Gogh in Amsterdam, but found them hard to understand – she said that she had no eyes for the intensity of his vision. Harold was particularly impressed by the interiors of Vermeer, which were then unknown in England. After a further year in Staithes he had his own success when his large painting 'A Cup of Tea' (1905) was purchased from the Royal Academy for Brisbane Art Gallery, for the grand sum of £100. The sale enabled them to go back to Laren for a third successive year.

Soon after their return to England, and in search of new places to paint, the Knights left Staithes for Cornwall. Laura's first impressions were mixed. On their arrival in Newlyn they were warmly welcomed by Stanhope Forbes, to whom they had an introduction. However:

Newlyn itself was at first a disappointment and Cornwall seemed so pale. After Staithes' cobbled streets the mud was distressing in the harbour roads. The women were not so magnificently upright, they carried no weights on their heads nor did they work among the fishing. In some cases a man's cap was fastened on to an untidy pile of hair with a long hat pin. Slippers slopped from house to house... (Laura Knight, *Oil Paint and Grease Paint,* Autobiography, London 1936).

Soon the Knights came to love Cornwall dearly. At first they lived in a cottage in the shadow of Paul Hill, Newlyn; two sheds with skylights served as studios. Later they moved to Penzer House, in the centre of Newlyn – known as 'Beer House', after the landlady 'Granny Beer', who offered 'French cooking'.

For Laura, Cornwall was a revelation, colour was everywhere and the climate noticeably milder. She found a particular joy in the quality of light and the swift changes of weather. Her quick brush caught the sparkle of sea and sand, the movement of water and the enjoyment of children at play. The cares of the North East had been left behind, and she found a new freedom, the ecstasy

HAROLD KNIGHT

The Sonnet,

Reproduced in The Studio,
Vol. 57, No. 237, 1912.

of direct expression in paint. 'Great is the joy of attempting to paint the impossible', she wrote, '...let the pencil or brush speak of its own accord to tell the little one can ever know'. (Laura Knight, *op.cit.*). In a succession of paintings between 1908 and 1912 she captured the holiday mood of Cornwall. Her first major painting 'The Beach' (1908) depicts groups of children in patterned smocks and straw hats playing happily on Penzance beach, exploring the rock pools left by the receding tide. From her high viewpoint, the sea moves through a spectrum of light blues, strong cobalts and ultramarines, offset by the yellow sand, the coloured dresses of the prancing children with the deep purple and violet shadows. When it was shown at the Academy in 1908 it attracted considerable attention, as did her smaller painting of the following year, 'Flying a Kite'. These enjoyable paintings are not built on theory, they are the product of her exuberance and vitality. The essentials of Impressionism emerge naturally on to her canvas. 'How glorious it was to be young and strong and able to splash with paint on canvas any old thing one saw, without stint of materials or oneself,' she wrote. (Laura Knight *op.cit.*).

Laura was unable to find female models in Newlyn willing to be painted in the nude, so she brought professionals from London, posing them on the rocks and making study after study in sunlight. Amongst her young friends, nudity was acceptable, and the artists and the models swam and dived in the deep pools at low tide or basked in the sun 'How holy is the human body when bare of other than sun.' she wrote. (Laura Knight *op.cit.*). The locals were shocked, but when 'Daughters of the Sun' (1911) – painted on the rocks beyond Lamorna Cove – was shown at the Royal Academy, it attracted much favourable attention and the critics were silenced. The painting was later toured around the provincial galleries, but was greatly damaged in store and later destroyed. Laura also made copious drawings and notebook studies in line and colour, but

LAURA KNIGHT

Daughters of the Sun,
c.1912.

oil on canvas

FROM *THE STUDIO*, VOL. 57,
NO. 237, 1912.

this celebration of the human body, thousands of notes and a pile of sketch books four feet high, was also irretrievably damaged by being stored in a damp cupboard for months and the mildewed remains were burnt. There is therefore little remaining evidence of her intensive study of the nude figure in its natural surroundings.

One of the most wholly satisfying of Harold Knight's paintings was also one of his first in Cornwall 'In the Spring' (1908–9), is a conversation piece in which two young people sit at tea in a Cornish orchard; the girl in sunlight, the man *contrejour*. It is solidly drawn and there is evident pleasure in the carefully constructed masses of foliage and blossom and the patterning of sun and shade. Yet Harold Knight lacks the spontaneity of Laura, he is more reluctant to leave his tried methods of academic drawing, and his work lacks her response to light and colour. Laura found her subjects out of doors, on beach or hillside. Harold preferred indoor subjects, in which he could observe the controlled effects of light, with models posed against the window, carefully composed and full of detail. He is at his best in group portraits – the quiet enjoyment of a summer afternoon, when poetry is read to a group of well-dressed ladies and gentlemen picnicking in a wooded garden. Laura Knight, Phyllis Gotch and other friends often acted as his models, their costumes improvised from their own or Laura's wardrobe. He would also picture them in some simple domestic task – arranging flowers, reading or sewing in a chintz-filled drawing room. Harold describes the ordered world of the middle class, servants out of sight, free from all care or struggle, but the lack of incident in his paintings too frequently produced dull conformity.

In the years leading up to the First World War Laura portrayed Cornwall's beaches as an idyllic pleasure ground, with young people in holiday mood basking in the sun, or bathing in a caressing blue sea. She found that she was capable of extraordinary concentrated feats of painting that allowed her hand and eye to work without conscious intervention of thought:

LAURA KNIGHT

On the Cliffs, 1917.

oil on canvas,
635 x 760mm.

Private collection.

With a blank canvas or paper in front of me, I could put myself in an attitude of mind to work straight from the sub conscious, and achieve new compositions. Unfortunately that state of mind will not always come at my bidding, but when it will I still glory in giving reign to something that knows better than I. (Laura Knight *op.cit.*)

One of her best large portraits – of the professional model Doby Small – was painted out of doors in the space of one day. The model turned as the sun moved across the sky and the painter followed changes in weather from an overcast sky to strong sunlight, her canvas roped down and bellying in the wind. At the end of this exhausting day she had used nearly three pounds of flake white, but the portrait required little further alteration and she knew it was good. The painting, known as 'The Green Feather' (1911) was exhibited at the Royal Academy and bought by the National Gallery of Canada, Ottawa. In its pose and general character it is very close to the smaller painting of Dorelia, by Augustus John of the same year, called 'The Red Feather'.

Harold and Laura Knight were fiercely committed to their life as artists. They had little money and for some years continued to live sparingly, financing their next period of painting with sales made at their last exhibition. Their successes at the Royal Academy had attracted attention and soon both Laura and Harold could sell nearly everything they painted. By 1910 life was going with a swing. As Laura Knight said 'we had health and strength for hard work and for play', she could 'go abust' on canvasses and paints, new tubes and boxes were stacked high in the studio and sometimes she had as many as three London models posing at the same time. Until 1912 the Knights were able to rent the old farmhouse Trewarveneth with the big studio where Stanhope Forbes and Tom Gotch had worked. They also had a painting hut on the coast at Lamorna. Then they moved to Oakhill, a house in Lamorna converted from three cottages by Colonel Paynter who built each of them a studio hut on the

LAURA KNIGHT

Self Portrait, 1913.

National Portrait Gallery, London.

LAURA KNIGHT

The Green Feather, 1911.

oil on canvas, 2100 x 1550mm.

THE NATIONAL ART GALLERY
OF CANADA, OTTAWA.

beach under the towering cliffs of Carn Bargis. With enough money to buy a small car, they made painting trips to Mousehole, Sennen Cove and St Ives.

Laura Knight and others in Newlyn were fascinated by a newcomer, Alfred Munnings. He was unconventional, even by the standards of the art colony. He had a raffish air, and an unshakeable confidence in his own abilities. He dressed like a horse-coper in a black and white check suit set off by a yellow scarf, and judging by his tap room manners and his extremely free conversation, apparently had no idea that conventions of any kind existed. He possessed great vitality and magnetism, and in Newlyn it was said that he organised more parties, picnics, outings and Christmas festivies than anyone in the county. He was also short tempered and outspoken, quick to take offence, and on occasions he could be vindictive. Munnings brought scandal to the village, and he was at the centre of scenes of riotous behaviour with some of Stanhope Forbes' younger students.

Alfred Munnings (1878–1959) was of East Anglian farming stock and brought up in Suffolk, the second of four sons of a prosperous miller at Mendham. After boarding school at Framlingham College, he was apprenticed as a lithographic artist to Page Bros in Norwich, with evening instruction at Norwich School of Art. At weekends he explored the unspoilt Norfolk countryside, cycling, or walking with a sketchbook and visiting many of the glorious old churches. At his father's mill and on the nearby farms there were always horses and other farm animals and he had a genius for their representation. In the six years he spent with Page Bros he became a highly skilled lithographic artist, designing posters, catalogues and decorative wrappings, and with his employer he made several business trips to Europe. He had also begun to paint and two of his pictures were shown at the Royal Academy by the time he was twenty.

After his apprenticeship he returned to Mendham, and in a studio converted from the local carpenter's shop, he began to paint with enthusiasm. He also made a detailed study of Stubbs' *Anatomy of the Horse*. During this period he lost the sight of his right eye, resulting from a wound from a briar when lifting a dog over a fence. He was required to spend months in hospital, followed by a long period of convalescence. He wrote:

I wasn't allowed to use my remaining eye for months afterwards, and when I began to do so I could not judge distances, and poured water on the cloth, missing the glass. I went to paint, and my brush either hit the canvas before I knew it was there, or was not touching it... What I wouldn't give to see with two eyes again. (A. J. Munnings, *An Artist's Life*. Museum Press 1950).

Two short periods of study in Paris in 1902 and 1903 were spent mainly at Julian's Academy, followed by several years painting country subjects in East Anglia. Munnings lived at Swanisthorpe, south of Norwich, where he rented a farm and created a studio. His work was regularly exhibited at the Royal Academy and in Norwich, and he built a reputation as a 'native painter'. He would set off for weeks at a time in a blue painted caravan, with a string of nondescript horses and a donkey, on painting expeditions to the Ringland Hills in Norfolk and the Waverney valley in Suffolk. His man Bob was in charge of the procession together with a gypsy boy, called Shrimp, who was his principal model.

Munnings had made short holiday visits to Cornwall in 1908, and two years later he appeared in Newlyn, lodging at Chywoone Farm opposite Tom Gotch's house at Trewarveneth. A few days after his arrival he made the acquaintance of Laura and Harold Knight at a musical party in Gotch's studio. Munnings had admired Laura's large painting 'The Beach' (1908) at the Academy in 1909, and praised her talent. Laura was immediately attracted to him. She described him as a fine figure of a young man, with a pale face and light brown hair, combed forward:

who might have sat for a portrait of Robbie Burns, standing straddled there, strung upright, small head, wide shoulders, narrow hips... Never had I come across such overwhelming vitality. I could not take my eyes off him, he was the stable, the artist, the poet, the very land itself... I adored everything about him. Harold, not so impulsive as I, stood aloof, withholding judgement, fighting our friend's irresistable charm. (Laura Knight *op.cit.*).

Munnings was equally in awe of Laura Knight. He wrote, 'She possesses the energy of six, the studies for her larger pictures were wonderful... Laura Knight could paint anything be it a small water-colour or a nine foot canvas. Seeing is believing'. (A.J.Munnings, *An Artist's Life, op.cit.*).

Their personal relationship was more complex, Laura's marriage to Harold appeared to be a sterile affair. Harold Knight did not find Munnings amusing; he was affronted by his high spirits and earthy humour and most especially his love of blood sports and tales of the hunting field. Harold resented Laura's fascination with Munnings' extrovert behaviour, and observed that at times she could be as rowdy and vulgar herself. His feeling of inadequacy was deepened when, for several weeks, Munnings moved into the same lodgings as the Knights, sharing their dining and sitting room in Beer House. The boisterous conversations between Alfred and Laura and the coarseness that Laura demonstrated on occasion, clearly upset Harold. Laura possessed the same vigour and exuberance as Munnings and her two volumes of autobiography are full of their shared tomboyish enthusiams. There is no doubt that they were strongly attracted to each other, but it is unlikely that the were drawn together sexually. All of Laura's energies were absorbed by her painting, even to the exclusion of children from her life, and within the accepted morality of the time it is probable that she shied away from extra-marital affairs.

In 1911 Munnings established himself at Lamorna Cove, at the inn, known as 'The Wink', run by the jovial Mr Jory. His wife, Jessie Jory, who was not on speaking terms with her husband, ran the rival establishment in Lamorna, the Cliff House Temperence Hotel. Munnings made a studio in the stables of 'The Wink', where he also kept his horses which served as models for his painting,

ALFRED MUNNINGS

The Lamorna Inn.

oil on canvas

SIR ALFRED MUNNINGS ART MUSEUM, DEDHAM.

Mr. Jory, the landlord of the 'Lamorna Wink' holds two of Alfred Munnings's horses. Munnings is seen in the background.

and which provided accommodation for his groom Ned. His mother wrote in 1911, 'Alfred's mare and Taffy his dog gone to Cornwall. Now I feel I have lost Alfred. The mare and his dog were the last links between us'.

The artistic life of the area was further enlivened by the students of Stanhope Forbes' School in Newlyn, many of whom were becoming considerable artists in their own right. Many locals regarded the students as 'a godless though profitable nuisance... they brought a lot of money into the place but also brought frivolity and rebellion'. (C. E. Vulliamy an ex student.). Within a very short time the school became the centre for a group of talented and decorative young people, students and ex-students. Foremost among them were Ernest Proctor, then a gangling youth, and Charles Walter Simpson who had a passion for painting horses almost life-size. The girls included Dod Shaw (who later married Ernest Proctor), charming, well read and precisely spoken, and 'swift and active as a gazelle', Winifred Tennyson Jesse (known as Friniwed), who later became a writer, and her sister Cissi. The group lived at Myrtle Cottage, a substantial Georgian house in the centre of Newlyn, surrounded by a garden and myrtle trees and known by its occupants as the 'Myrtage'. Dod's mother, Mrs Shaw, presided over this select group, they talked literature, they wrote poems, they did woodcuts, some painted. They dressed in tussore silks, browns and art colours. Men's parties took place at Chywoone, the farm opposite Trewarveneth, and it was said that some of the young men, encouraged by Alfred Munnings became very drunk!

There was an easy social life among the young artists and they were warmly received by the older residents. They joined in dances and took part in the country walks. Dod Shaw and Alfred Munnings would jump the Cornish hedges, Dod displaying her fine legs. 'Just look at Dod's legs; she's got the best legs any gal ever had', Munnings would exclaim (Laura Knight *op.cit.*). There was dancing in the Knight's studio to a wind-up gramophone; evening coffee and paper games with the Forbeses at Higher Faugan; high-minded conversation took place under the benign eye of Mrs Shaw at Myrtle Cottage. There were uproarious parties at the Gotches, with crazy games and crazier solo acrobatic turns, much noise, singing and laughter. Caroline Gotch enjoyed acting as hostess and although Tom stayed in the background, he was equally hospitable – except for the not infrequent occasions when his studio was turned into a room for dancing by his daughter Phyllis. Laura Knight recalled one of the parties:

> *I can see him now among a mess of parcels of food piled on tables and chairs in the dining room, beating a mayonnaise with violence, his blue eyes snapping with rage, no one taking any notice as he repeated 'Phyllis, I will have no such party in my house!' The angrier he got, the thicker and smoother the mayonnaise became. The unconventional dinner that Phyllis had planned took place just the same. When at about two o'clock the guests started to leave, Harold asked Mr Gotch how he felt. His answer was 'My spirits are starting to rise.'* (Laura Knight *op.cit.*).

In the autumn of 1913 two new and splendid visitors came to Newlyn. These were Augustus John (1878–1961), whose prodigious talent and outrageous bohemian behaviour at the centre of the avant-garde in London and Paris had made him a subject of endless fascination, and his beautiful wife and principal model, Dorelia.

FRED PEGRAM

'Osses': portrait of Alfred Munnings.

The black eye and the bandaged hand are the result of celebrations at the Chelsea Arts Club, following the Armistice of 1918.

CHELSEA ARTS CLUB.

ALFRED MUNNINGS

Dame Laura Knight Painting.

oil on canvas, 500 x 610mm.

SIR ALFRED MUNNINGS ART MUSEUM, DEDHAM.

Augustus John

Photographed by John Hope-
Johnstone, 1922.

THE NATIONAL PORTRAIT
GALLERY.

Laura Knight recalled their arrival:

there was a stir in the village. Someone had seen Augustus and Mrs John driving down the lane, news came that they had settled at Mrs Jory's Temperance Hotel on the Hill. A. J. Munnings was living at that hotel at the time. He invited us to dinner to meet the Johns. John was powerful and broad-shouldered, his beard was tawny, his hair long, and he wore a tweed suit that had a thread of colour in it running both ways into a check; his shoes were cut dead square at the toes, had long vamps and wide laces. Mrs John wore the same kind of footwear. Her looks were startling in their rarity; it was easy to see the inspiration she might be to a painter. Her skin was ivory, her hair black; as she sat that evening with her hands folded like the 'Mona Lisa' portrait, her long, tapering, white fingers and beautifully kept nails impressed me profoundly. It was impossible to take your eyes off her for long. Her clothes were of her own particular style, and it was she who set the fashion for jumpers and short hair; out of doors she wore a long black cape. (Laura Knight *op.cit.*).

The Knights, Munnings and the other artists were stimulated by this larger-than-life personality, with great physical presence and an aura of internationalism. Augustus John then occupied a unique position in British art. He had a reputation as an anarchic independent, and had angered the art institutions: but he was a master of portraiture, and his large, symbolic figure groups captured the romantic spirit of the gipsies that he had lived with. He had travelled and painted in many parts of Europe; in Paris he had met the young Picasso as an equal, and he had an intuitive rapport with the spirit of Post-Impressionist painting. His 1910 exhibition 'Provencal Studies' at the Chenil Galleries held the light and colour of the Mediterranean in a series of powerful and swiftly executed landscapes peopled with his wife, his children and his Romany friends. It took place at the same time as Roger Fry's Post-Impressionist Exhibition. His work displayed the same outrageous evidence of modernism and attracted the same furious attention from the critics.

The years 1910 to 1913 saw a decline in John's artistic fortune. It was a restless period, spent wandering, gipsy style, in North Wales with a fated younger companion, John Dixon Innes, and an eccentric Australian artist Derwent Lees. Innes had become enchanted with a stretch of mountainous country near Lake Bala, centred upon the village and mountain of Arennig. In a burst of intense creative energy, John and Innes produced a group of lyrical paintings that captured the magic of the Welsh mountains. As Innes burnt himself up with frantic work, interrupted with periods of dissipation, his health deteriorated alarmingly and he was soon in the terminal stages of consumption. Derwent Lees, the lesser artist, was exhibiting the first signs of an illness that confined him to a mental hospital from 1918 onwards. In self-protection, Augustus John left his ill-fated companions in Wales and came to Cornwall.

Newlyn was, by comparison, a peaceful retreat and his fellow artists were sane, if a little dull. For a short time Augustus and Dorelia John became part of the Newlyn colony:

John would perform all manner of amazing tricks,...opening bottles of wine tenderly, without a corkscrew; flicking, from a great distance, pats of butter into people's mouths; dancing, on point in his hand-made shoes, upon the rickety table, and other astonishing feats, until dawn. Then, while the others collapsed into exhausted sleep, out he would go in search of Dorelia, and do little studies of her in various poses on the rocks. (Jean Goodman, *What a Go. The Life of Alfred Mullins.* Collins, London 1988).

He also painted a portrait of Lamorna Birch, but his work in Cornwall was of minor consequence. John later made other visits, but Cornwall could not replace the romantic intensity that he had found in the Welsh Mountains.

Harold Harvey (1874–1941) was one of the very few Cornish-born artists to make a major reputation. His father was a bank manager in Penzance and apart from a short period of study abroad, he lived his whole life in or near Newlyn. He received his early art training from Norman Garstin, and in the 1890s continued his studies at the Atelier Julian under Constant and Laurens. On his return he married a Penzance girl, Gertrude Bodinar, who was also an artist, and they took Maen Cottage, in Newlyn, overlooking Mount's Bay, with a studio nearby.

Harold Harvey did not seek to raise Cornwall or its people to heroic proportions, as did the earlier Newlyn painters, yet his numerous paintings form a fascinating record of the changing face of Newlyn in the early twentieth century. He describes the harmony of village life, the unspoilt countryside and its inhabitants from the viewpoint of one who had grown up there and knew it intimately. His paintings are direct, untheatrical, worked entirely from the object, and were frequently completed within the day. Much of his work is small and his prolific output is partly explained by his need to make a living from his art. In subject and treatment his earliest work owes a great deal to Stanhope Forbes, whom he greatly admired. Many of the evening scenes set in the port of Newlyn are strongly reminiscent of Forbes. 'The Pedlar' (1902) by Harvey has a similar setting to Forbes's 'The Letter' (1898): both describe the visit of a stranger to a cottage door – an object of curiosity to the women and children who come to meet him – and both paintings make use of strong contrasts of directional lighting. 'The Drinking Place' (1908), is in many ways similar to the more ambitious painting of the same title by Stanhope Forbes, painted eight years earlier.

As with other younger artists, colour soon enters his work in a more positive manner and some of his outdoor studies are close to Impressionism. 'Sport on the Shore' (c.1890), also called 'Boys on the Beach, A Crab Race', is a sparkling beach scene which might have been painted by Monet in northern France. Sunshine also pervades in the scene of apple picking in 'Apples' (1912). Although his work lacks the spirited vitality of Laura Knight it is evidence of a very considerable home-grown talent which responded to the world that Harvey knew well. He painted the country and the coast of Cornwall, men and women at work on the farms, the boats, and engaged in simple domestic tasks all with the same honesty and sincerity. Harvey first showed at the Royal Academy in 1907 and became a frequent exhibitor showing one or two, occasionally three paintings, each year, but he was never invited to membership.

In the years leading up to the First World War, more artists were drawn to the Lamorna Valley and it became

HAROLD HARVEY
The Blue Gown, 1917.
oil on canvas

DOROTHEA SHARP

The Patchwork Quilt.

THE PRIOR GALLERY,
CHELTENHAM.

an artists community in its own right. Many of Forbes' former students were now very evident among the younger group. These included Robert Morson Hughes and his wife Eleanor (née Waymouth). Eleanor Hughes (1882–1959) had been born in Christchurch, New Zealand and after a period in London, at the famous 'Yellow Door' studio of Frank Spenlove, she came to Newlyn to study under Stanhope Forbes in 1907. Two years later she met Robert Hughes (1873–1953), a fellow pupil who had been born in Kent and had previously studied at the Lambeth School of Art and the South London Technical College. Early in 1910 they were married at St Buryan Church, near Penzance. After a period of travel in Italy they settled in Lamorna in 1912 at Chyangweal with studios nearby, and became well liked and active in the area.

HAROLD HARVEY

Sport on the Shore.

CITY OF PLYMOUTH MUSEUM AND
ART GALLERY.

Both were landscape painters and much of their work was done within walking distance of their home. Robert made strong tonal paintings of the cliffs and the wooded valley, but by lunchtime, it was said, he could usually be found in 'The Wink' in Lamorna, a favourite haunt of the artists, smoking his pipe and playing euchre. (Caroline Fox, *Painting in Newlyn, 1900–1930, op.cit.*). Eleanor was the more sensitive draughtsman and a fine watercolourist. Although they remained committed to Lamorna they also made a number of painting visits to France, and from 1910 exhibited at the Royal Academy and the Royal Institute of Painters in Watercolour, and elsewhere.

Charles and Ella Naper (née Champion) were close friends of the Knights and the Harveys. Devon-born Charles Naper (1882–1968) had been an architectural student before turning to painting at the Royal Academy Schools. He met his future wife Ella (1886–1972) at Branscombe, Devon, whilst she was still a student at Camberwell School of Art. They were married in 1910 and came to Looe in Cornwall for two years before moving to Lamorna, where they built a house at Trewoofe. They became wholly identified with the area, and apart from service in France during the First World War, he seldom left Cornwall. Charles Naper worked from landscape, and became known for his detailed studies of the rock formations around Land's End. A number of these were exhibited at the Royal Academy between 1910 and 1933. Ella was more diverse in her work. She produced decorative enamel and horn-work jewellery and for a time ran a pottery in Lamorna with the potter Kate Westrop.

The figure painter Frank Gascoigne Heath (1873–1936), set his compositions in his sun-filled house with his three pretty daughters as models. He was born in Purley, London and studied at the South Kensington Schools and in Antwerp. He also spent some time with Herkomer in Bushey and painted in Brittany. In 1905 he was in Cornwall at Treveneth Farm, near Paul, and exhibited at the Royal Academy for the first time a painting with a Cornish setting, called 'Homeward' (1905). Still a student, he attended Forbes' school in Newlyn in 1908 where he met his future wife Jessica; they were married in 1910. After a short period in Polperro they returned to St Buryan in West Penwith, where they built a house, Menwinnion. During the First World War Heath served with the 2nd Sportsman's Battalion of the Royal Fusiliers and his Academy painting of 1914 was an army group 'Stories of the Gun'. He continued to exhibit at the Royal Academy up to 1935, the year before his death.

Dorothea Sharp (1874–1955) was a friend of Laura Knight's and their work has much in common. They shared an ability to capture in paint a feeling for light and swift movement. It is said that a legacy of one hundred pounds enabled Dorothea to become an artist, despite her parents' disapproval. With this she trained at the Regent Street Polytechnic in London, under George Clausen and David Murray, and continued her studies in Paris. Here she was particularly impressed by the paintings of Monet, an influence which she carried back to Cornwall and which is reflected in her beach scenes with children at St Ives, capturing the mood of holiday Cornwall in free, Impressionist colour.

The life of these young artists in the years before the First World War has an idyllic quality. They lived simply, valuing each others companionship. Gertrude and Harold Harvey became close friends of the Knights, the Napers and the Hughes. They shared similar interests and enjoyed many social occasions together. As a group they spent a long summer camping at Dozmary Pool, near Bodmin, where Charles and Ella Naper had built a hut for summer holidays. The others slept at the nearby farm which burnt peat fires, baked its own bread and provided scalded cream for the artists. Lamorna Birch was also part of this friendly group. His hospitality, and the Cornish pasties prepared by his wife 'Mouse', and the trout caught in the stream, provided picnics on the cliffs. The two Birch girls were frequently painted by the artists as they raced around the rocks and into the water. In 1913, in the clearing in front of her studio Laura Knight painted 'Lamorna Birch and his Two Daughters', one of her largest paintings, executed in strong vibrant colour slashed in with the brush and the knife, it was not completed until it was hung in the Academy in 1934.

CHARLES NAPER

The Coast near Land's End.

oil on panel, 875 x 1125mm.

PRIVATE COLLECTION.

This blissful period was brutally ended with the outbreak of war in August 1914. The Knights last years in Cornwall were disturbed and unhappy. Within a few months the effects of war began to be felt. There was lack of some foodstuffs and rationing. Above all the market for their work was reduced. They gave up Oakhill, and their car, and moved to lodgings in St Ives. Harold, a convinced pacifist, became increasingly withdrawn and nervous. He was called up in 1915, and faced a tribunal, who finally decided that he was a genuine conscientious objector and that he must work on the land. For Laura, Lamorna was no longer 'the happy valley'. She was incapacitated by a broken ankle for several months; her early enchantment had left her, and she was aware of the need to find fresh stimuli for work. 'Cornwall is beauty so fancified it is an easy place to go to sleep in', she wrote. (Laura Knight *op.cit.*). Her marriage was threatened by Harold's attachment for Ella Naper; in addition he was unable to paint for the duration of the war, and worked in the fields of North Cornwall in a state near to physical and emotional collapse.

The very act of painting became unpatriotic. In 1915 there were restrictions on painting any part of the coastline; even to draw the straight line of the horizon could be interpreted as a sinister act. Everyone was suspected as a spy and soon all out of door sketching was forbidden. Father Bernard Walke recalled how, on one occasion, he went with Laura Knight to the Corpus Christi Fair at Penzance, and

FRANK GASCOINE HEATH

Gulls in Newlyn Harbour, 1909.

oil on canvas, 700 x 900mm.

ROYAL CORNWALL MUSEUM, TRURO.

kept look-out for the police while she sketched in a notebook. (*Twenty Years in St Hilary* by Bernard Walke). In spite of the prohibition, Laura Knight was filled with a desire to paint a large landscape, and crouching among the brambles and gorse behind her Lamorna studio, she made quick sketches, knowing that to be seen through the telescope of a coast-watcher would have meant prison. From these rough notes and from memory, she combined her feelings of affection and despair for Cornwall, into a six foot painting 'Spring' (1916), in which a rainbow arches over a Cornish landscape. Ella and Charles Naper, with rod and basket, are the two figures in the foreground accompanied by a magpie. Many years later, in 1935, the painting was purchased by the Chantry Bequest for the Tate Gallery.

Alfred Munnings' love of Cornwall was later combined with personal tragedy. He wrote:

> *to lie on the sweet smelling turf, watching sea pinks trembling in light winds, and listening to the unceasing sound of the surf and the cry of gulls... nothing quite like this coast exists anywhere, gives peace and rest to body and soul...* (Jean Goodman, *op.cit.*).

For him Cornwall was a backcloth against which he placed his horses, his grooms and their accoutrements. He mostly avoided the sea and the coast that other Cornish artists painted, but loved a pub full of dealers and jobbers, 'drinking, singing and smoking.' Above all, he was moved by a hunt, and wrote, 'there is something about a crowd at a meet or in the hunting field that as yet has never been touched on; a winter sun on it all, too, is beyond words.'

Munnings was fascinated by the primitive and unspoilt village of Zennor near St Ives. Here granite was near to the surface, every field had its walls of boulders, and split granite lined each lane. He took his entourage there, his two mares, Grey Tick and Duchess, and his faithful groom Ned, and for five weeks he painted in and around the village – pigs lying in mud in the street, cows being milked and stock yards, and above all horses and hunting scenes. One of the best known of these pictures is ' Ned on the Grey Horse' (1913). It was painted looking towards Morvah where the heather-clad slopes run down to the sea. Ned rides Grey Tick on a boulder-strewn hill under a grey sky, silhouetted in his scarlet hunting coat; the hounds leap straight out of the picture. It was shown at the Royal Academy in 1919, the year in which Munnings was elected A.R.A.

In Newlyn Munnings had made the acquaintance of a beautiful and elegant girl, Florence Carter Wood, the sister to one of Forbes' students, Joey Carter Wood. Florence – always referred to as 'The Bloat' – was a frequent visitor to Newlyn and began to attend Forbes' school. She appears in Harold Knight's painting 'Afternoon Tea', exhibited at the Academy in 1910, in which a tail-coated waiter serves tea to two ladies in a tranquil upper-class drawing room. It was painted in the drawing room of the artist Garnet Wolseley, who modelled for the butler and the two ladies are portraits of Florence Carter Wood (in silhouette) and Laura Knight.

Florence Carter Wood came from a wealthy and devoutly religious family, and her childhood had been privileged and protected. Alfred Munnings determined to marry this desirable young girl, ten years his junior. When refused permission by her father, he set out to earn one thousand pounds in one year from the sale of paintings in order to prove his financial stability. Alfred Munnings and Florence Wood were married in January 1912 in Westminster, and spent

ALFRED MUNNINGS

Going to the Meet of the Western Foxhounds.

oil on canvas

Laing Art Gallery, Tyne & Wear Museum Service.

AUGUSTUS JOHN

The Red Feather, 1911.

oil on canvas

PRIVATE COLLECTION.

their honeymoon in London. During the honeymoon Florence tried to commit suicide by taking cyanide, but her life was saved. The circumstances of Florence's attempt upon her life were not fully explained, but it seems that there was a deep incompatibility between her and her husband. She returned with Munnings to Newlyn, and settled into a strained but independent arrangement with him. During Alfred's frequent absences, Florence began to paint; two of her pictures, 'China Bay' and 'Water' were shown at the Royal Academy in 1914.

War threatened, and in the last uneasy days of peace she and Alfred attended a party at Trewarveneth, by then occupied by Geoffrey Garnier, an etcher and engraver. As Garnier later reported:

> *At about midnight 'The Bloat' called to Munnings that she was tired and wanted to go home. ('Home' being the Cliff House, or Jory's Hotel, Lamorna). Munnings' answer, shouted across the studio, was 'All right, you bloody whore, buzz off!' Florence left in tears. The following morning, after breakfasting with her husband, she returned to her room, and half an hour later was found unconscious. She had again taken cyanide, and this time the dose was fatal. At the inquest she was described as suffering from depression, and Colonel Paynter, foreman of the jury, decided that the deceased's death was due to poisoning, self administered, during temporary insanity.* (Goodman *op.cit.*).

Laura Knight's grief was real and long lasting. 'The sight of this lovely young body is unforgettable. Aloof from all was her form as she lay still as the Botticelli Venus she so closely resembled'. (Laura Knight *The Magic of Life*, William Kimber, London, 1965). Many years later, in a letter to Munnings second wife Violet, written after Alfred's death, Laura referred to the episode:

> *I could absolve him (Munnings) from all blame on the tragedy he endured in his unfortunate association with 'Bloat', whose dramatic sense was apt to pass*

LAURA KNIGHT

Spring, 1916.

oil on canvas

THE TATE GALLERY, LONDON.

ALFRED MUNNINGS

The Setting Sun, c.1910.

*a study of Florence Munnings,
known as the 'Bloat'.*

oil on canvas, 510 x 610mm.

PRIVATE COLLECTION.

HAROLD KNIGHT

Afternoon Tea, 1910.

*The painting features portraits of
Laura Knight, Florence Carter
Wood (later Mrs Florence
Munnings, in silhouette) and
Garnet Wolseley.*

oil on canvas

DAVID MESSUM FINE ART.

*the bounds of true sanity, when she would stop at nothing, either to save herself
or others. That he retained his own sanity is astounding, for the refinement of
her cruelty, which I personally observed, was bound to meet with disaster.*
(Letter to Violet Munnings, 27 August 1961, Royal Academy Archives.)

Munnings left Lamorna in 1917 to join the army as a remount aide. Early in
1918 he was sent to France an an official war artist attached to the Canadian
Cavalry Brigade, where under the most difficult, and at times highly dangerous
conditions, he drew and painted the horses, close to enemy lines. A portrait of
General Seely, commander of the Brigade, painted less than two miles from
German lines, attracted great attention in London because of the circumstances
in which it was painted and also because of its fine execution. It set a pattern for
a type of equestrian portrait that assured Munnings a flow of commissions and a
ready source of income, taking him into the great houses of the rich. In January
1919 an exhibition of paintings by British and Canadian artists, telling the story

of Canada at war, was held in London and later in New York, Montreal and Toronto. It was dominated by forty-five pictures by Munnings which told of the war-time partnership between horse and man. Within a few weeks of the first showing Munnings was elected an Associate of the Royal Academy.

Painting trips to Cornwall came to an end when, in 1920, Munnings re-married. His second wife was a divorcée, Mrs Violet MacBride, a plain woman who, like Munnings, regarded dogs and horses as her only true friends. They settled near Dedham on the Suffolk border, where Munnings took his small stud of horses. Violet approached her second marriage with a businesslike air, believing that her function was to relieve Munnings from his domestic and financial worries so that he could devote himself entirely to art, which meant portraiture of famous people and their horses. 'It meant painting for money' she admitted.

As Munnings' fortunes grew so did his influence at the Royal Academy, and during the Second World War his name was put forward for the Presidency. At an election on New Year's day 1944 Munnings beat Augustus John into second place by twenty-four votes to seventeen. Other contenders included Harold Knight and (now) Dame Laura Knight. Munnings' Presidency in the first years of peace saw a tremendous expansion of interest in the arts. But his public criticisms of contemporary art did great damage to the Academy and to the course of art in Britain. Laura Knight however retained her high regard for Munnings. She wrote:

> His extraordinary vitality, his joy in his work, none of us could forget him. He was a fighter. He fought the wind that shivered his easel and canvas. He fought the heat and cold. He fought the shifting sun and the changing shadows.

Munnings died in July 1959. At his memorial service, a conspicuous mourner was Augustus John, wearing a wide-brimmed straw hat, daubed with black paint for the occasion. After the service he said 'I think Munnings was greater than Stubbs. He made it move, had greater narrative quality and his groupings are better.'

10

MODERNISM

In the early twentieth century the great problem for artists, and for the bewildered public interested in art, was the speed with which artistic movements appeared, and were replaced by other, more extreme, alternatives. The acceptance of Impressionism by an English audience had been much delayed, but no sooner had a measure of understanding been achieved than it was overturned by the more radical message of Post-Impressionism. Before long a flood of advanced continental ideas were absorbed into the mainstream of art, polarising artists into clearly defined groups, the 'modern' and 'traditional'.

The most decisive move towards modernism had been Roger Fry's London exhibition 'Manet and the Post-Impressionists', at the Grafton Galleries, in 1910. The work of Cezanne, Gauguin, Van Gogh, Matisse and other modern masters shown here created a scandalous sense of outrage among the public. To quote Frank Rutter:

> *they could hardly contain themselves for indignation. The angrier they got, the louder and more volubly they talked, the more and more people paid shillings at the turnstile, to see if the pictures were as abominable as they had heard. When they came out, they protested that the paintings were worse than they could have believed without seeing them. They said it loudly and often, and this sent more crowds into the Grafton Galleries to share their sensations and just indignation.* (Frank Rutter, *Art in My Time,* Rich and Cowan, 1933).

Art lovers witnessed an overturning of accepted values for which they were totally unprepared: the old and tried methods of recording nature were replaced by a burst of inventiveness which found expression in hitherto unexplored areas of heightened colour and exaggerated form. A new phrase 'significant form', invented by the critic Clive Bell, described that elusive quality of refinement that he found common to the work of Cezanne, Van Gogh and Gauguin. Critical response was slow and partial. C. Lewis Hind, who had frequently supported the artists of Newlyn and St Ives, wrote patronisingly:

> *it is amusing to find how just about everybody that one likes, and whose opinions one esteems, unites in disliking the work of the Post-Impressionists and has ridicule and amusement for the work of Matisse.* (C. Lewis Hind 'The New Impressionism', *The English Review*, December 1910).

Walter Sickert, who had a uniquely close acquaintance with the French painters, continued to pursue a more independent line. A nucleus of advanced artists led by Harold Gilman, formed a protective group around Sickert in his Fitzroy Street studio, and in 1911, Sickert, Spencer Gore, Robert Bevan and Charles Ginner formed the Camden Town Group. Spencer Gore was the first President, others who were drawn in included Lucien Pissaro, who had settled in London and who, through his father, had first-hand experience of French

Impressionism. Only three exhibitions were held – two in 1911, one 1912 – but they brought an expressive intensity into their descriptions of contemporary London.

In 1912 Clive Bell arranged the second of his Post-Impressionist exhibitions which introduced Cubism, with recent work by Picasso and Braque, and included the most advanced British painters – Spencer Gore, Vanessa Bell, Duncan Grant, Wyndham Lewis and Stanley Spencer. The radical forces of Futurism and Vorticism – represented in England by Wyndham Lewis, David Bomberg, Jacob Epstein, C. R. W. Nevison, William Roberts and Edward Wadsworth – joined for a time, leading to the formation of the London Group in 1914, which for many years provided a platform for the most advanced and varied ideas about art in England. In the same year the Rebel Art Centre was formed, which carried the diverse talents of some of its members to the furthest limits of abstraction.

The catastrophe of war curtailed these forward-looking movements, and in the 1920s revolutionary ideas of the pre-war years appeared to be a spent force, although Bloomsbury remained influential and Roger Fry and Clive Bell were still vocal. With the break-up of the Camden Town Group, Sickert was again an isolated figure. The explosive energies of Wyndham Lewis, previously so effective, were now spent largely in aggressive railing.

Artists in Cornwall did not play a central part in these dramatic events. Yet for a few brief years following the First World War, Cornwall became an important point of contact for a number of artists who were to be part of the avant-garde. The presence of Cedric Morris, Lett-Haines and Frank Dobson were a stimulating influence in Newlyn. Frances Hodgkins and Matthew Smith spent periods in other parts of Cornwall and a number of the most advanced of the London artists including Edward Wadsworth, Charles Ginner, Wyndham Lewis and Augustus John were occasional visitors.

Cedric Morris (1889–1982), the son of a wealthy iron founder in Sketty near Swansea, later became a Baronet. He had a broad interest in art and music, and from Charterhouse School he first went to the Royal College of Music, and for a time he did farm work in Canada. In 1914 he was studying art in Paris, when he was called for military service. He was discharged on medical grounds, but being a keen horseman he volunteered to train army horses for the front. He worked at Lord Rosslyn's stables near Reading where he met Alfred Munnings, who advised him to spend some time in Cornwall. In 1916–1917 Morris was at Zennor where he began to teach himself to paint in watercolour, making many studies of plants and insects. In London in the following year he made the acquaintance of a number of painters, dancers and actors, many of whom had been in Paris.

Soon after the Armistice, Morris met Arthur Lett-Haines (1894–1978), and the two formed a close friendship which was to last the rest of their lives. Lett-Haines had been educated at St Paul's School in London and the Royal Military Academy, Woolwich, and was a professional soldier before the outbreak of war. He had married at seventeen, but within a year his wife had died and he married again in 1916.

Morris and Lett-Haines came to Newlyn in 1919. Both had decided upon a career in art, but neither had received formal training; this was a time of experiment which led them towards the more avant-garde directions in painting and sculpture. They lived first by the bridge in the middle of the town, then in a sail loft, and finally in lodgings at Vine Cottage with Mrs Tregurtha, the mother

CEDRIC MORRIS

Portrait of Frances Hodgkins, c.1917

gouache on paper, 240 x 160mm.

THE TATE GALLERY.

179

of two handsome daughters, Cordelia and Mary to whom Cedric gave painting lessons. Morris and Lett-Haines converted a row of old cottages overlooking the harbour – The Bowgie – into a studio, and their lively lifestyle soon attracted considerable attention. Even Alfred Munnings, a considerable hell-raiser himself, found this new group alarming:

> *This rather warm element gave parties and set the pace in the Art Colony. Imagine a long, low, top-lit sail-loft, converted into a studio... a vast white damask tablecloth spread on the floor-boards, its centre piece a great pile of fruit – gilded melons, gilded pineapples, gilded grapes and vine leaves. There were dishes of food and troops of wine bottles, full and empty. In a blue haze of cigarette smoke, Roman revellers reclined on cushions around the feast on the floor. Japanese lanterns swung from the rafters and lit up the scene. Lovely, voluptuous reclining women smoking cigarettes in long holders. Amateurs and students, they were rather more competent in the art of seductive make up than in the art of painting. Their own attractive figures were totally unlike the strange shapes they put on canvas.* (Alfred Munnings, *An Artist's Life, op.cit.*).

These newcomers were much younger than the artists who had settled in Lamorna before the war and were highly unconventional. Not only did they give lively parties, but they invited to Newlyn some of the most radical young artists of the day, including Wyndham Lewis and Edward Wadsworth, whose acquaintance Cedric Morris had made in London. In the pre-war years Lewis and Wadsworth had been at the centre of that pre-war burst of energy Vorticism, the first blazing manifestation of abstract art in Britain. As a movement it had been extinguished by the war and did not survive into the post-war period. Their visits to Newlyn were brief and no work is known to have resulted from them.

Cedric Morris, who had previously worked only in watercolour, now began to paint in oils. His early paintings are comparatively unformed, but they possess an innate sense of style and strength of colour that showed his sympathy for the Post-Impressionists. Lett-Haines was a sculptor who frequently worked on a

A Newlyn 'drenchie', probably 1919.

The figures are:
1. *Harold Harvey.*
2. *Dickie Holmes. (decollete).*
3. *Sheelah Hayes.*
4. *Frank Dobson.*
5. *Cordelia Dobson.*
6. *Gertrude Harvey.*
7. *Gladys Hynes.*
8. *Dod Procter*
9. *Arthur Lett-Haines*
10. *Cedric Morris.*

PHOTOGRAPH BY PERMISSION OF PHOEBE PROCTER.

small scale. He was drawn to the world of the unconscious and of dreams and his sculpture moved increasingly towards the assembly of found objects and fetish figures.

Morris and Lett-Haines left Newlyn in 1920, and continued their interrupted studies at various ateliers in Paris – the Grande Chaumiere, Colorossi and the newly formed Académie Moderne under Othon Friesz, André l'Hote and Fernand Léger. From Paris they made extended visits to the countryside and to the Mediterranean coast. Towards the end of the 1920s they were mainly in London, exhibiting with the London Group and with the Seven and Five Society in company with Christopher Wood and Ben Nicholson. During these years they maintained their Newlyn connections, and returned frequently. Lett-Haines claimed that he and Cedric Morris knew Alfred Wallis before he was 'discovered' by Nicholson and Wood in 1928.

In 1936 Morris and Lett-Haines moved together to Suffolk and established The East Anglian School of Painting and Drawing at Benton End, an ancient house at Hadleigh with a fine garden overlooking the Brett valley. This school became a well-known centre for Modernism, and housed their collection of objects from many parts of the world. It is ironic that Alfred Munnings, who had been a friend of Cedric Morris in earlier days, was in Dedham on the night of the 26 July 1939 when the school was gutted by fire. Munnings had been outraged by the Modernism of Morris's work and teaching, and as the fire raged Munnings was driven up and down the village street waving his stick, shouting 'hurray'. He poured invective against modern art and rejoiced that the school would have to paint out of doors, for a time at least. (Jean Goodman, *op.cit.*).

Cedric Morris inherited the Baronetcy in 1947 and died in 1982. Two years later a major retrospective exhibition of his work was mounted by the Tate Gallery.

The sculptor Frank Dobson (1888–1963) was to became one of the most celebrated modern artists in Britain. He was the son of a London illustrator, and at the age of eleven he won a scholarship to Leyton School of Art. Following the death of his father he lived for a time in Hastings and for two years worked as an apprentice in the studio of the sculptor Sir William Reynolds-Stevens. But it was as a painter that he came to Cornwall in 1904, and for two years worked in watercolour from the landscape. He then won a scholarship to the Scottish Art School at Hospitalfield, Arbroath, followed by a period of study at the City and Guilds School, London. This long and varied training made him receptive to forward-looking ideas in art and he was deeply impressed by the second of Clive Bell's Post-Impressionist exhibitions in 1912.

Dobson had not yet formed a style of his own, nor did he have a secure income, nevertheless he found the means to return to Cornwall, and for a while he was a student at the Forbes School, but Forbes' attitude to direct painting meant little to him. He earned a precarious living by painting pot-boilers for the furnishing trade – highland cattle at a £1 a piece:

> *To economise on time he would set up six canvasses in a row and move rapidly along the line putting in first a mountain, then a cloud, then the setting sun, then a cow... and so on until all six pictures were completed.* (Sir Charles Tennyson quoted in *Painting in Newlyn 1900 to 1930*).

In Cornwall, Frank Dobson made his first carving – an oak figure about fourteen inches high. He showed his work to Augustus John, who was staying in Lamorna, and John arranged for him to show some work at the Chenil Gallery, Chelsea.

FRANK DOBSON

Portrait drawing of the Artist's wife, c.1920.

Frank Dobson's presence in Newlyn attracted other artists whose work was considered modern. Through his friendship with Augustus John, and on visits to London, he met other artists including John Currie (c.1884–1914), the greatly talented ex Slade student. Currie had left London in 1911 after an unhappy marriage and in the following year was working in Newlyn. He rapidly established a reputation, exhibiting with the New English Art Club from 1912, and becoming a member in 1914, but his brief career was extinguished when he shot himself and his mistress in a fit of jealousy in October 1914. Dobson also became a friend of Mark Gertler, Harold Gilman and other early members of the London Group, whose views affected the direction of his work. During the war he received a commission in the Artists' Rifles and in 1916 he saw two months active service in France, but he developed a duodenal ulcer and spent much of the remainder of the war recovering in hospital.

In 1919 Dobson returned to Newlyn and took lodgings with the Tregurtha family at Vine Cottage, later that year he married Cordelia the eldest daughter of the house. Dobson also became friends of Cedric Morris and Lett-Haines, and Morris became his assistant in a small studio at the back of Vine Cottage and posed for a torso which was included in Dobson's first one-man exhibition of sculpture at the Leicester Galleries in 1921.

In 1920 Frank Dobson was the only sculptor member of 'Group X', a radical group of artists formed by Wyndham Lewis to recover the ground that had been lost during the war by the Vorticists. The group held only one exhibition and its lack of success showed how the revolutionary ideals of pre-war movements that had seemed so important now appeared to be irrelevant. Nevertheless, in the early 1920s Dobson's reputation began to climb and he and Cordelia spent an increasing amount of time in London. Their Chelsea studio was a meeting place for distinguished figures of the art world and of London society, including T. E. Lawrence, Gilbert Murray, Bertrand Russell and the group around Duncan Grant. They were neighbours of the Sitwells, and knew the young Ben Nicholson before his marriage to Winifred Roberts. Cordelia became hostess, mentor and friend to many of the artists of the Chelsea and Bloomsbury set.

FRANK DOBSON

Kneeling female figure, c.1920.

sandstone, height 430mm.

Frank Dobson's work was greatly admired and he was fêted for his curtain design for 'Facade', a piece for theatre with music by William Walton, with a remarkable commentary spoken by Dame Edith Sitwell through a megaphone. His sculptures at this time included busts of the ballerina Lydia Lopokova and of Osbert Sitwell. The latter, now in the Tate Gallery, was described by T. E. Lawrence as 'his finest piece of portraiture, and in addition it's as loud as the massed bands of the Guards' (letter of 5 February 1923: T. E. Lawrence writing under the name of J. H. Ross). In the mid-1920s Dobson was seen as one of the most forward-looking sculptors working in Britain, but his position was soon to be overtaken by the more radical talents of Henry Moore and Barbara Hepworth. From 1933 Dobson was a regular exhibitor at the Royal Academy, showing portraits in bronze and statues in Portland stone and terracotta. He also worked on a number of architectural subjects. In 1942 he became an A.R.A. and later an R.A. For seven years he was Professor of Sculpture at the Royal College of Art. He died in London in 1963.

In 1923 Cordelia and Frank Dobson were divorced and she returned to Newlyn. Her younger sister Mary had married Albert Owen Jewels in 1918, but he was killed in the war shortly afterwards. Mary Jewels (1886–1977) became a painter of landscape and fishing scenes, thickly encrusted and worked with a naive passion. She had begun painting in 1915 'when Sir Cedric Morris gave me a canvas with four tubes of paint and one brush and told me to cover the canvas by the evening.' She was encouraged by her sister and by Augustus John who bought a number of her works. Her paintings were also admired by Christopher Wood. Nevertheless she wrote:

I am influenced by nobody and entirely self-taught, a true Celt, loving my Cornwall, its lovely stone hedges and the beautiful blue sea with puff-ball clouds and little fishing coves and corn in stukes, what could one wish for more.

The short period that Matthew Smith (1879–1959) spent in Cornwall was a time of physical and artistic recovery, after the trauma of the First World War. A shy and reticent man, he was the son of a Yorkshire manufacturer. He had left school in Halifax at the age of seventeen to work in a woollen mill and then for four years in the family wire works, before persuading his father to allow him to attend Manchester School of Art. At first he was only permitted to follow a

MATTHEW SMITH

Cornish Landscape, c.1920.

course in industrial design, but his main passion was painting and with reluctance his father allowed him to attend the Slade School in London for two years. Henry Tonks, the Slade Professor, had little regard for this self-questioning boy and was openly critical, threatening expulsion. This lack of understanding affected Matthew's health and he withdrew from the School under his doctor's care.

His real training was in France from 1908, where he worked mostly on his own, painting at Pont-Aven, as so many British artists had done, and at Etaples in the Pas-de-Calais. He enrolled at Matisse's school in Paris but attended only three criticisms of work by the master before the school closed. However Matisse's example made a lasting impression. At the outbreak of war in 1914 Matthew Smith returned to London. He was at first rejected for war service on health grounds, and continued with his painting. He found a studio in Fitzroy Street and in 1916 painted the first of the great paintings of the figure called 'The Fitzroy Street Nudes' – powerful designs in strong contrasts of colour, acid greens and yellows, flame red and deep blue. This blaze of creative energy was interrupted later that year by the call to army service, he was commissioned and later wounded. On demobilisation he returned to London. His health collapsed, anxious and depressed, he became highly critical of all the work he had done before.

In 1920, Matthew Smith came to the north coast of Cornwall with his wife and two children to try to recover the thread of painting broken by the years of war. Here, in the opulence of the Cornish countryside, he discovered a link with the Fauvism of his early years which later gave his work such glowing authority. He had visited Cornwall briefly in 1912, the year of his marriage to Gwen Salmond, herself a gifted painter, and one of that brilliant group of women students of the Slade School that surrounded Augustus John. Now, after the war, he found painting difficult and produced little, but as his health improved he worked more easily. From June to December in the village of St Columb Major, near Newquay, he painted in dark glowing colours; purples, greens and dark reds. His subjects were simple – views of the parish church from the upstairs window of the house in which he stayed, landscapes and flower pieces. These are disturbing paintings; strong horizontal bands of reverberating colour that flatten the forms of the landscape, glowing canvases which reveal his own sense of despair and desperation, yet in their creation he found a way through his personal distress.

In Cornwall, and later in France, Matthew Smith discovered a new freedom in direct painting, with a greatly extended range of incandescent colour which was to make him unique among British artists. But it was at the expense of considerable intellectual exertion. Shortly afterwards in Brittany, he had another breakdown, and it was some years before he fully regained his health, but his painting was soon recognised as wonderfully fluid creations of a talented draughtsman who is at the same time a great colourist. His first one man exhibition was held at the Mayor Gallery, London in 1926, and Augustus John lavishly praised the work in which the Cornish experience formed an important beginning:

With a cataract of emotional sensibility, he casts upon the canvas a pageant of grandiose and voluptuous form and sumptuous colour which are none the less controlled by an ordered design and a thoroughly learned command of technique. (Catalogue to the Exhibition at the Mayor Gallery 1926).

Charles Ginner (1878–1952) had been associated with Matthew Smith in the Fitzroy Street Group, and was similarly touched by the spell of Modernism.

CHARLES GINNER

Porthleven, 1922.
oil on canvas,
500 x 690mm.

THE TATE GALLERY, LONDON.

Ginner was born in France – the son of an English doctor – and his youth and early training in Paris, first as an architectural student and then as a painter, had made him receptive to advanced ideas of Post-Impressionist paintings, particularly the energy of colour in Van Gogh. In 1910 Ginner settled in London where he became closely associated with Spencer Gore and Harold Gilman and with them he was a founder member of the Camden Town Group and later of the London Group.

Ginner made a number of painting visits to Cornwall in the 1920s and 1930s. His landscapes of the Penwith and Lizard peninsulas are strongly patterned, boldly painted but with a clearly structured composition that draws on his architectural training.

Frances Hodgkins (1869–1947) was the daughter of an amateur painter in Dunedin, New Zealand. Her early work was in watercolour – Edwardian ladies reading or playing the piano – and bears little relationship to her later work, when familiarity with new developments in painting ripened a sensitive, personal vision. She was thirty when she first came to Europe and attended sketching classes in Brittany. For some years before the First World War, she taught watercolour painting at Colorossi's Academy in Paris, and made painting visits to Holland, Morocco and Italy. This work was exhibited successfully in Australia and New Zealand.

From 1914 to 1920 Frances Hodgkins lived in Cornwall, mostly in St Ives, where she occupied No.7 Porthmeor Studios and taught drawing and painting. Her studio was next to Moffat Lindner's and it was here that she painted the conversation piece 'Mr and Mrs Moffat Lindner and Hope' (1916), and was encouraged by Lett-Haines and Cedric Morris to paint in oils. In Cornwall she began to find the full evidence of her talent, painting freely composed landscapes and still lifes. Her work showed a strong contemporary influence – vivid colour boldly applied, in descriptions of sea, mountains, farm and country scenes. Her subjects were chosen for their associations; the places and people she loved, with farm implements and domestic objects. Distortion and improvisation play a part, and her spirited orchestration of the picture is close to Surrealism.

Frances Hodgkins believed strongly in her personal freedom and independence. She did not marry and had few friends, she was dedicated to her painting, had few possessions and moved frequently from studio to studio in England and France. After leaving Cornwall she lived in Manchester for a number of years. It was not until 1927, after a visit to Treboul in France, that she sought opportunities to exhibit her work in London, and her mature work dates from this time. She had an astonishing burst of creative experiment in the last part of the 1930s which undoubtedly drew on her Cornish experience, and when she was nearly sixty her work demonstrated a vigour and spirit similar to that of younger painters such as Ben Nicholson (who was twenty-four years her junior), and Ivon Hitchens, who were then leading the Seven and Five Society. She began to exhibit regularly with this group, and to show her work at the St George's Gallery in London, and when it closed in 1931, at the Lefevre Gallery. She returned to Cornwall in 1931, and stayed at Bodinnick near Fowey. Here her work entered its final and greatest period which was to last for a further sixteen years. (*Four Vital Years,* Arthur L. Howell, Rockcliff Publishing Corp. London 1981).

FRANCES HODGKINS

Mr and Mrs Moffat Lindner and Hope.

tempera

Dunedin Public Art Gallery, New Zealand.

LAMORNA BIRCH

*Our Little Stream
Lamorna,* 1934.

oil on canvas, 620 x 765mm.

ROYAL ACADEMY OF ART.

A number of the artists who had settled in Newlyn and the Lamorna Valley in the pre-war years came to maturity as artists in the 1920s, and produced their finest work. Excluded by temperament from the ranks of the radical avant-garde, they nevertheless responded to the use of heightened colour and informal arrangements of composition that was characteristic of Post-Impressionism. Lamorna Birch frequently painted on a large scale; paintings of five or six feet were not uncommon, and in these he achieved a measure of majesty and simplification that made them prominent in group exhibitions. In 1926 he became an Associate of the Royal Academy, and his work was shown widely in Britain, Europe, Australia and New Zealand. He was elected Royal Academician in 1934, and from then until the end of his long life he generally exhibited six works in the annual Summer Exhibition, and his views of the Lamorna Valley were highlights of the show. His diploma work for the Academy, 'Our Little Stream Lamorna' (1934), was one of his best and most typical paintings of this wooded valley. In 1947 two of his paintings were sent as a wedding present from the people of Cornwall to the Queen and Duke of Edinburgh.

Harold and Laura Knight left Cornwall for London in 1919. They returned for summer visits, but their close attachment to the county now ceased. Laura Knight became the personification of the Royal Academy artist, regularly putting impressive, large scale work before a welcoming audience. In addition to her Cornish pictures, she emphasised the exotic in her paintings of the Diaghilev Ballet, clowns and acrobats of Bertram Mills Circus, and idealised figure groups. She was described by the poet and essayist, E. V. Lucas as: 'being free to divide her time... in summer among the rocks and pools and moorlands of the Delectable Duchy, and in winter in the dressing room of Lydia Lopokova!' (E. V. Lucas, Introduction to the Exhibition by Laura Knight at the Alpine Gallery, London, 1922). Harold Knight, a recluse by nature, suffered from the popularity

Members Varnishing
Day, 1934.

*Photograph of Dame Laura
Knight showing fellow
academicians her portrait of
Lamorna Birch and his children.*

THE ROYAL ACADEMY OF ART.

that accompanied his wife's success, but his work continued to command much
respect in the Academy, where he exhibited numerous conventionalised
portraits, well observed and good likenesses. He also painted a large number of
interior scenes – country drawing-rooms with posed figures standing in half
open doorways, lit by warm afternoon sunshine. Both artists became Royal
Academicians; Laura was made Associate in 1927, Harold a year later. Laura
became a Royal Academician in 1936, again followed by Harold a year later.
Laura Knight was only the second women to be elected in modern times (the
other being Annie Swynnerton who became A.R.A. in 1922 but who did not
achieve R.A. status). She and Harold were the first married couple to become
members. Laura was appointed Dame Commander of the Order of the British
Empire in 1929, and received honour and respect for her work until the end of
her life. She died in 1970 at the age of ninety-three, outliving her husband by
twenty-nine years.

The engraver and printmaker Geoffrey Garnier (1889–1970) and his wife Jill
were also part of that group of friends that included the Birches, the Knights
and the Harveys. After training as an engineer, in 1910 Geoffrey Garnier went to
Herkomer's school in Bushey and then to Stanhope Forbes' school in Newlyn.
During the Great War Garnier first served in the Army – the Oxford and
Buckinghamshire Light Infantry – from which he was invalided out after
pneumonia, and in 1915 joined the Royal Navy with the rank of Lieutenant. He
had meanwhile retained his studio at Trewarvenenth in Newlyn shared with R.
C. (Seal) Whetherby, and it was at one of his weekly parties that the incident in
which Munnings was inexcusably rude to his wife occurred.

In 1917 Geoffrey Garnier married Jill Blythe, who had been a fellow student
at the Forbes' School, and they took up residence at Orchard Cottage, Newlyn,
where they were to live for the remainder of their lives. After the war, for a time

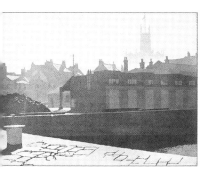

GEOFFREY GARNIER

St Mary's Penzance.

aquatint, 230 x 305mm.

PRIVATE COLLECTION.

Garnier set up as an engineer in Birmingham, as part of the firm Horton and Garnier, but in 1922 he returned to Newlyn. He extended the accommodation of Orchard Cottage by acquiring the next door property and an acre of land in the middle of the town. Studios were built, an intaglio press was set up and husband and wife continued as an artistic team. Geoffrey Garnier worked principally as an engraver and etcher and was generally active in Newlyn affairs, and a supporter of the Society of Graphic Artists and the Royal West of England Academy.

The Forbes' School of Painting continued until the Second World War, surviving Elizabeth Forbes' death in 1912 and Stanhope Forbes' subsequent re-marriage in 1915 to Maudie Palmer, also a painter. In 1916 Forbes' only son, Alec Stanhope Forbes, was killed on the Somme. Forbes became a prime mover in proposals for a war memorial in Newlyn, and his painting 'News from the Front' (c.1917), in which an elderly man and his grandson read through casuality lists in the *Evening News*, is a touching recollection of his loss. The painting was donated by the artist to raise money for the War Fund.

Stanhope Forbes remained a staunch supporter of the Academy. After his election as Royal Academician in 1910, he continued to send his best work to the annual summer exhibition usually showing six works, the maximum permitted. When he died in 1947 he had exhibited a total of 286 works there. In Newlyn, Forbes was a much respected leader in the arts, but as the town changed he found that the modern fishing port meant less to him, and he increasingly found his subjects in the lanes and farms near his home. His studies of figures and landscape seen in brilliant sunshine form an intimate record of the working people of Newlyn and Penzance. The dark tones of his early work were replaced by a brighter, more highly coloured palette. Water is a recurrent feature – sea, ponds, river or glistening sand – serving to bring the reflected light of the sky into the lower part of many of his compositions.

Forbes' principle of direct painting from nature continued to influence Harold Harvey. During the first war Harvey remained in Newlyn and because of wartime restrictions many of his paintings at this time were set indoors: studies of his wife Gertrude in their cottage, the sun pouring through the windows, with titles such as 'Winding Wool' (1914), 'The Green Gown' (1916), 'The Blue Gown' (1917). Although he remained bound to his native Cornwall, the free Impressionist treatment of the pre-war years gradually gave way to a greater simplification and bolder use of colour. In the 1920s Harvey became a Roman Catholic and increasingly used symbolism and religious subjects in his work. 'The Flight' (1926), set against a wild Cornish moor, is his version of the Flight into Egypt. A later painting 'Ancilla Domini' (1928), also with a Cornish background, describes the Annunciation. Harvey became a good friend of Father Bernard Walke of St Hilary, near Penzance, and with other artists helped to decorate the interior of the church there. He remained a productive artist and showed regularly in London at the Mendosa Galleries, the Leicester Galleries and Barbizon House. He continued to be a regular exhibitor at the Royal Academy, where his work attracted favourable attention but he was not invited to membership. Gertrude Harvey began to show her work more frequently in the 1930s and from 1930 onwards she regularly exhibited flower studies at the Academy. She also had several joint exhibitions with her husband.

As a popular student at Forbe's School, and with friends and family in Newlyn, Dod Procter's early years had been a happy beginning to her career, and she later became one of the most successful artists in Newlyn. Dod Procter (1892–1972) was born Doris Shaw, the daughter of a ship's doctor who died when she was very young. Dod and her brother were brought up in Tavistock by their mother, Eunice Shaw (née Richards), an artist trained at the Slade. When Dod was fifteen her mother decided to enrol her two children as students at Stanhope Forbes' School and to accompany them to Newlyn. Already established at the school was a young painter, Ernest Procter (1886–1935), a dedicated disciple of open-air painting, and equally talented. Whereas Ernest was earnest and serious, Dod was outgoing, light-hearted with a keen sense of adventure. Ernest Procter was four years older than Dod. He was born in Tynemouth, Northumberland, the son of a scientist who became a Professor at the University of Leeds. Ernest attended Bootham, the Quaker School in York, and Leeds School of Art. In 1910, after three years study in Newlyn, and on Stanhope Forbes' advice, he went to Paris, to the Atelier Colorossi. Dod persuaded her mother to accompany her to Paris so she could attend the same school, and in the following year she and Ernest were married in Newlyn. They returned immediately to France in order that Ernest could continue with a group of landscape paintings that he had been working on, one of which 'The Terrace, Versailles', was shown at the Royal Academy in 1914.

On their return to Newlyn Dod and Ernest Procter lived at Dunton House at the top of the hill, where their only son, Bill, was born in 1913. Painting was a priority for each of them but Dod was ill for several months and their work was soon overtaken by the outbreak of war. As a Quaker and a committed pacifist, Ernest worked for the Friends' Ambulance Unit in France. He managed to make a number of small watercolours and drawings of the life of the serving men, and towards the end of the war he produced watercolours of the work of the Red Cross, some of which were later bought by the Imperial War Museum. Dod Procter remained in Newlyn, finding life with a small child in wartime trying and difficult. Her depression at being unable to paint was complicated by financial problems. Her one consolation was that their rented house had a large garden which she cultivated with care. Growing flowers, their arrangement, and the paintings that she made from them, were for her all part of the same creative act. In 1916 three of her works were shown at the Royal Academy, all paintings of flowers from her garden.

After the end of the war Ernest Procter returned to Newlyn, and in 1919 he and Dod were invited to decorate the Kokine Palace in Rangoon, which belonged to a Chinese millionaire. They designed and supervised the execution of ornate decorations for this oriental palace, working with a team of Burmese, Indian and Chinese decorators, including skilled plasterers, carvers and gilders. This commission lasted for a year but financially it was not rewarding and they were poorly treated by their wealthy client. They were able to spend four months travelling in Burma, however, and their introducion to the principles of oriental design had a considerable effect upon their later work. When they returned to Newlyn, Ernest opened a painting school in partnership with Harold Harvey, in a large studio near the harbour, which ran until the mid 1920s. In 1923 the

Dod Procter painting in her garden at North Corner, Newlyn.

By permission of Phoebe Procter.

189

HAROLD HARVEY

Gertrude Harvey with Parrot in the Artist's House, 1916.

oil on canvas

THE PORTHSCATHO ART SOCIETY.

Ernest Procter.

BY PERMISSION OF
PHOEBE PROCTER.

Procters purchased a small house at North Corner backing on to The Meadow in Newlyn. This gave them a shared studio and a steeply-sloping garden. They took great pride in both house and garden, carefully renovating what was to become their home and workplace for the rest of their lives.

In the 1920s Ernest Procter painted the coasts and inlets of West Penwith, which he explored vigorously on foot. Much of his work was in watercolour and was readily saleable. Increasingly he shares with Harold Harvey a pronounced sense of flattened design and bold colour, which is particularly effective in large decorative paintings, such as 'The Merry-Go-Round', exhibited at the Royal Academy in 1924. This is a light-hearted spectacle of the fair on Newlyn slip. The curve of the harbour and the houses of Newlyn Town are expressed as a great vortex, centred upon the merry-go-round which attracts hundreds of Bruegel-like figures, hurrying to join in the excitement.

Ernest Procter exhibited frequently in London, with the International Society from 1916 and at the Royal Academy from 1921. He became an A.R.A. in 1932. At a joint exhibition by with Dod Procter at the Leicester Galleries in 1925, he showed one of his most important symbolist paintings 'The Zodiac', painted in the style of an early Italian allegory, and about which he had written several poems. This was purchased by the Chantry Bequest soon after his death. He also painted a number of large scale classical subjects, with such titles as 'Cupid and Psyche', and 'The Judgement of Paris' (both of 1926), in

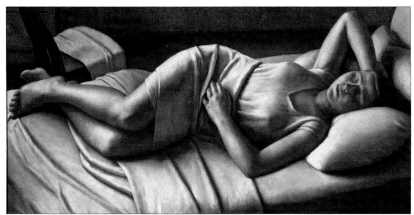

ERNEST PROCTER
The Zodiac, 1925.
oil on canvas, 1924 x 1676mm.
THE TATE GALLERY, LONDON.

DOD PROCTER
Morning, 1926.
oil on canvas, 262 x 1524mm.
THE TATE GALLERY, LONDON.

Dod Procter with other artists on the beach at Sennen.

Standing on the left is Ernest Procter and Charles Simpson. Seated on the left is Dod Procter, next to Ruth Simpson and Ella Naper.

which he used the naked figure as an emotional vehicle. He received considerable publicity when the latter painting, depicting three nude goddesses and the shepherd Paris, was withdrawn from exhibition at the Northampton Art Gallery on grounds of indecency. Ernest Procter wrote indignantly to the *Daily Mail* 'The question at issue is, therefore, not of the individual indecency of these pictures, but of the intrinsic indecency of the human figure'.

Earlier Ernest Procter had worked on commission for Fry's Omega Workshops, and he made a number of decorations for houses and public buildings including works on layers of glass, called 'Diaphaenicons', which he described as 'a new art'. The first of these were exhibited in 1931 at the Leicester Galleries, and it was announced that they had the additional advantage of serving 'as a minor sources of light, rendering a lamp unneccessary... all movable but can be built into the fabric of the house, on walls, floors, ceiling, etc '. (Introduction to the Exhibition of Recent Work by Ernest Procter, December 1931, Leicester Galleries).

Ernest Procter was deeply Christian and towards the end of his life he worked on several church interiors, including a number in Cornwall. For Bernard Walke, he painted a Visitation 'Of great simplicity and highly stylised', and two years later a Deposition and a series of panels around the base of the pulpit at St Hilary, celebrating the saints connected with Cornwall. For St Mary's Church in Penzance, he produced a complex decoration over the high altar: a choir of celebrating angels drawing back a curtain to reveal a reredos with the Madonna and Child with St John and the Holy Ghost – an unusual combination of modern decorative elements with a strongly oriental feeling, reminiscent of his early work in Burma. In 1934 he was appointed Director of Studies in Design and Craft at the Glasgow School of Art, but the pressure of work here and from his many commissions, contributed to his early death in 1935.

Dod Procter had begun to exhibit her portraits and figure studies of women soon after the First World War. They were to make her one of the most famous women painters of her time. The best known, 'Morning' (1926), is of a girl reclining on a bed. Sixteen year old Cissie Barnes, daughter of a Newlyn fish merchant, frequently modelled for her. Here she wears a nightdress, and the flickering light falling across her body emphasises its solidity and contour. As Dod Procter recalled 'the picture developed rapidly in my mind whilst I was arranging the model and came to its full growth as a design while I was drawing it. Every line and mass of the picture was definitely fixed before I started to paint... I did it straight off without thinking of or touching anything else in the way of work – as I always do. I can never do more than one thing at a time'. ('Painting the

Picture of the Year' quoted in *Painting in Newlyn, op.cit.*). Although the idea of the painting came quickly, its execution required some eight weeks of painstaking effort. The picture was exhibited in Newlyn before being sent to the Royal Academy, and was bought by a journalist for the *Daily Mail*. At the opening of the Royal Academy exhibition in 1927 it was highly praised by the critics, and acclaimed 'the picture of the year'. The *Daily Mail* presented it to the nation, with great publicity. A similar sensation occurred two years later when 'Virginal', a sensual study of a nude woman of Florentine fullness, with a dove, was rejected by the Academy. It was immediately exhibited at the Leicester Galleries, again accompanied by great attention from the press.

The paintings that Dod Procter did in the 1920s display an evident, if sublimated, sexuality in the languorous poses of models clothed and unclothed, and in the direct gaze with which they look from the canvas. The figures are sculptural, restrained in colour and heavily modelled, with simplifications of form used by Frank Dobson in his sculpture, or Picasso in his classical paintings. She felt a natural sympathy for the modern movement in Paris, and is reported as saying of Picasso 'You would never have suspected THAT influence, would you? I digested him well'. (Caroline Fox, *Painting in Newlyn 1900–1930*.). In the 1930s the weight of her earlier figure paintings is replaced by more thinly painted studies, full of light and colour. She continued to reveal mood and expression, and by the close scrutiny of every fold of material and detail of pose, she manages to extract from her sitters, many of whom were children, a super-real quality, close to the dream-world of surrealism.

Dod Procter was elected A.R.A. in 1934, two years after her husband. After Ernest's early death she continued to exhibit her work and to travel, visiting Africa and the West Indies, and she frequently painted from African or West Indian models. She became a Royal Academician in 1942, and she lived in Newlyn until her death in 1972.

A close friend of Dod Procter's over many years was the painter Harriet Gluckstein (1895–1978), known as 'Gluck', who came to Lamorna in 1916 at the suggestion of Alfred Munnings. She was at this time only twenty-one years old and on the point of committing herself to a career in art. She was encouraged to paint by the Knights and the Procters and became a portrait painter. Harriet came from a wealthy background, she was the only daughter of Joseph Gluckstein, a Jewish businessman and one of the founders of J. Lyons. Stylised, perceptive, sometimes inclined towards the grotesque, her work has much in common with that of Dod Procter. She saw her time in Cornwall as the dramatic gesture of her youth, and her association with these 'real artists' represented a break with her privileged background and a dedication to art. 'I ran away with 2s/6d in my pocket, and no food card, a necessity during the war,' she wrote. Her portraiture and flower studies had a poised character, an ability to deal with the sophisticated society in which she moved, on its own terms. Although she later returned to London she retained a long connection with Lamorna and made use of a cottage there for many years. She remembered Dod Procter as:

> *being like a nymph. She had great charm, a keen sense of humour and was always ready for any adventure. If she made a remark she would cock her head and watch for the effect on the listener, a trait she never lost... and she certainly never gave the impression of becoming the serious hard-working artist she became...* (Fine Art Society 1972 Introduction, quoted in *Painters in Newlyn 1900–1930, op.cit.*).

ALETHEA GARSTIN

Village Band, Newlyn.

oil on panel,
490 x 370mm.

CITY OF PLYMOUTH MUSEUM AND
ART GALLERY.

Another close friend of Dod Procter and a companion on many expeditions abroad, was Alethea Garstin (1894–1978). She was born in Penzance, the daughter of Norman Garstin. She was also his pupil and accompanied her father on many of his sketching tours, and remembers as a young girl being carried around France on the handlebars of his bicycle. In a long painting life she travelled to many colourful parts of the world including Morocco and the West Indies. Her painting of these exotic subjects have a Fauve intensity of colour, yet there is no forced exaggeration and she retained the strongly disciplined tonal sense that she derived from her father's teaching.

Alethea Garstin first exhibited at the Royal Academy when she was eighteen. Her painting 'The Chair Makers' (1912) was praised by the President, Sir Edward Poynter, who asked to meet her. She became a regular exhibitor at the Academy throughout the 1920s and 1930s, portraying incidents of village life and character from her trips abroad. But it is for her many paintings of the homely corners of Penzance and West Penwith that she is best remembered, small in scale, glowing with colour on a tinted ground and with a strong sense of design. These light-hearted and inventive paintings are a patchwork of light and colour, reflecting from the sparkle of granite and sea, whitewashed houses and green turf. In 1978, the year of her death, Patrick Heron described her as 'England's leading Impressionist painter'. ('Norman and Alethea Garstin, Two Impressionists, Father and Daughter', exhibition at the Penwith Gallery, St Ives, arranged by Michael Canney. Catalogue introduction by Patrick Heron).

11

A HOLIDAY PARADISE

The annual 'show days' in St Ives, which had been such a popular event, were revived after the war. In 1920 more than fifteen studios were open in Downalong, the old Piazza studios, the Porthmeor studios and those along the Wharf. Some five hundred visitors came to see 'the great pictures of this year' intended for the Summer Exhibition of the Royal Academy, and other institutions. Soon visitors came in larger numbers, as they had done before the war, and the Great Western Railway arranged special excursion trains.

These were years of rapid social change, characterised by economic depression, high unemployment and sharp contrasts in the distribution of wealth. For artists, sales were few, and the buying public was unsettled. But Cornwall appeared to be a land bathed in summer sunshine, and its artists

Fishing boats at St Ives in the 1920s.

PHOTOGRAPH BY PERMISSION OF ROGER SLACK.

Charles Simpson's
studio on Show Day at
the Piazza Studios,
St Ives, 1920

PHOTOGRAPH BY PERMISSION OF
LEONORA SIMPSON.

relished this relaxed, protective environment. Many had a modicum of financial independence; others sold their work as best they could, or worked as designers for industry. They exhibited in London, at the Royal Academy and with the artist societies such as the Royal Watercolour Society and the Royal Society of Portrait Painters. The landscape and sea painters, such as Olsson, Talmage and others, made a conscious effort to purify their subjects, and to distance themselves from the catastrophe of war by describing those aspects of nature such as beauty and permanence.

Some of the more prominent painters had left St Ives, but it still had a large resident group. In 1921, the *St Ives Times* reported that 'Art, as far as St Ives is concerned seems to have recovered in a most marked manner from the depressing effect produced by the aftermath of the war'.[*]

No less than forty-four artists were showing their work to the public, but the economic climate was far from good:

Although the picture market at the present time is most discouraging to the selling of pictures, and works of art in general, yet thanks to the annual spirit of occasion, the existence of the Royal Academy and other kindred art institutions in London and the Provinces, art workers seem to bury the hatchet over past rejections... and rise to a point of inspired determination to at least be represented by one picture if not the three allowed by the rules... Every artist has a distinct style, and after all the St Ives Colony is the most unique of its kind in the world. (St Ives Times, 1921).

The character of St Ives slowly changed during the inter-war years. It had ceased to be a fishing port when the great shoals of pilchard were no longer seen from its headlands, and in 1922 the remains of the fleet of seine boats were burnt on St Ives' beach, outdated by larger, sea-going boats from Newlyn and other deep water ports. The decay of the tin and copper mining industry reflected the general depression that affected Britain. But there was financial

---

[*]A full list of the studios and their artists was given in the *St Ives Times*, March 1921: 'The Shore Studio had work by C. W. Simpson and Miss Fenell. Miss F. A. Williams showed at the studio in Norway House. In the Porthmeor Studios, (called the New Porthmeor Gallery) were Clare Day, Beale Adams, Moffat Lindner, Borlase Smart, Arthur Meade and Miss Euan. The St Eia studio had work by Mrs F. Lloyd, Mr Lowell Dyer, Mrs J. Douglas. The Red House studio showed Mr W. Herbert Lanyon (photographer) and Mr E. Smithells. The Malakoff Studio showed Mr W. B. Fortescue. The Tregenna Hill Studio had work by Mr Claude Berry, Mr G. F. Gossey and Arthur White Esq. The Attick Studio showed Mr Arthur White. Messrs Lanhams Galleries showed work by Mrs Harley, Miss Cohen, Mrs Alexander, Miss Burne, Mr J. Titcomb, Mr W. S. Parkin and the late Mr Louis Grier. The Balcony Studio had work by Borlase Smart, Mrs Hewitt and Mrs Cuneo. The Blue Studio showed Miss Tysoe Smith, Mr Moffat Lindner, and the Harbour Studio Miss Knapping and Mrs Grills. The Green Studio had work by Mr Francis Raymond.

In the following year some new names were noted at the High Street galleries, including Bernard Leach, who exhibited a superb collection of etchings; the Island studios had work by John Park and Dr McVie, the Piazza studios had work by Ruth Simpson, Miss Ballence and Mr Ballence. The Beach studio showed Captain Moore and Miss Fortune and the Den Studio Miss Bliss Smith'. (*St Ives Times*, 18 March 1922).

compensation for Cornwall in the new industry of tourism. The rise of a middle-class of salaried workers, for the first time entitled to paid holidays, brought a dramatic invasion to Cornwall. The beginning of tourist traffic by private car began a year or two after the Armistice and this pressure continued steadily. That champion of the Cornish, Sir Arthur Quiller Couch noted 'how rapidly the strain has come upon us; an ancient people, with its in-rush of motors and the descent of the ready-made bungalow builder, the hotel investor, the holiday maker who thinks no cove complete without a minstrel (negro) and a gramophone, the pater familias who brings his youngster to Tintagel with spade and bucket.' (*Cornwall, a Survey* prepared by Hardy Thompson. Preface by Sir Arthur Quiller Couch. University of London Press 1930).

The railway companies were quick to see St Ives as a holiday venue. Norman Wilkinson, who later became President of the Royal Institute of Painters in Watercolour, had visited St Ives at the start of his career as a marine and landscape painter. In 1923 he was commissioned by the London Midland and Scottish Railway Group to make posters for the railway. To seek out other interested artists, he wrote to a large number of members of the Royal Academy, including Arnesby Brown, Algernon Talmage, Julius Olsson, Adrian Stokes and Stanhope Forbes, asking if they would provide a design for a fee of £100, plus a commission on sales to the public. Most of those approached did provide posters. Their work gave character to 'holiday Cornwall' and aroused great public interest. (Norman Wilkinson, *A Brush with Life*. Seeley Service, London 1969).

As in earlier times, artists from abroad continued to visit St Ives. The American Impressionist painter Wilson Irvine (1869–1936) spent four months there in 1923. He was part of an adventurous art colony in Lyne Connecticut and a well known painter of marine subjects. On his arrival in February he recorded that he '...left the car in a garage and headed for the dock. Great! In two hours I had a studio. Col. James' place on the wharf, hardly more than a barn but roomy, airy (very) and good northern light for work.' He found the fishermen civil and kind 'as all people seem to be who follow the sea'. But he noted that 'they are desperately poor and many are being helped'. The weather was trying with almost continuous rain in February, but 'when the sun shines in St Ives, as it did last night, nothing could be handsomer'.

There were many links between Newlyn and St Ives. One of Forbes' most talented pupils was Hope Joseph (working 1907–1930) who moved to St Ives about 1907, and then to Paul, near Newlyn in the following year. Her principal subject was the harbour and the boats in St Ives, which she portrayed in clear Impressionist colour. Her treatment of water and its reflections owes much to Forbes, but her work has a remarkable strength of colour. She exhibited her work at the Goupil Galleries in London, and with the Society of Women Artists and the Royal Academy. Her later work developed a more pointillist style as she sought to enhance the strength of light and colour.

Another connection was provided by Charles Simpson (1885–1971) who moved from Newlyn to St Ives. He was born in Camberley, and came from a military family, but a riding accident prevented him from pursuing an army career. He grew up with a love of animals. and for a short period attended the School of Painting at Bushey, then run by Lucy Kemp-Welch. Simpson's paintings of horses developed during this time and he formed a close friendship with Alfred Munnings, painting with him in Norfolk during the early 1900s. It may have been Simpson who encouraged Munnings to visit Cornwall. Simpson

STANHOPE FORBES

The Permanent Way, 1924.

Poster for the
Great Western Railway

ALAN SHEARS FINE ART.

HOPE JOSEPH

Moorings St Ives, 1924.

oil on panel

DAVID MESSUM FINE ART.

CHARLES SIMPSON
*Newlyn Harbour, c.*1924.
oil on canvas, 1020 x 510mm.
PRIVATE COLLECTION.

CHARLES SIMPSON
The Sand Castle, 1924.
tempera on board, 535 x 750mm.
ON LOAN TO PENZANCE AND
DISTRICT MUSEUM AND ART
GALLERY.

Charles and Ruth Simpson teaching on the beach in St Ives.

came in 1905, and took lessons from the St Ives artist, J. Noble Barlow. A year later he was in Newlyn. Laura Knight admired the scale of Simpson's early work, he painted horses nearly life-size, and she remembered, 'He was so prodigal with paint, he could be traced by the colour left on the bushes' (Laura Knight *Oil Paint and Grease Paint,* Nicholson & Watson, 1936, p.162). Simpson later studied in Paris at Julian's Atelier and became a proficient portrait artist. In 1911, back in Newlyn, he met Ruth Alison, a student at Forbes' school, and they were married two years later. After three more years in Newlyn they moved to St Ives and opened a substantial school at the Piazza Studios overlooking Porthmeor Beach, which taught 'All branches of painting and drawing and especially the modern methods of handling oils, tempera, watercolour, etc. and illustration work with a view to reproduction'. (Prospectus, the St Ives School of Painting 1916). Simpson became a well-known painter of birds and animals and a regular exhibitor at the Royal Academy. His work was reproduced frequently in *Country Life* and he illustrated a number of books and articles. Because of the success of this aspect of his work the Simpsons left St Ives in 1924 for London. He returned to Lamorna in 1931 and continued to paint landscape and hunting scenes. He died in Penzance in 1971.

Many of the older painters remained true to the broad, tonal treatment which characterised much of the early sea and landscape paintings of St Ives. But others had modified their work in relation to Impressionism. Of these John Park was the most prominent. Park was a friendly and popular figure and one of that small group of thoroughly professional artists that carried on the painting tradition of St Ives in the years between the wars.

John Park (1880–1962) first came to St Ives in 1899 as a youth of nineteen, one of a large working-class family from Preston in Lancashire. He had worked in the cotton mills from the age of eight and later as a decorator's assistant to his father. Before coming to Cornwall he had received no training, except that which he gave himself, mostly drawing and painting family likenesses. In St Ives he attracted the attention of Julius Olsson, who found him an apt and willing pupil and gave him free tuition. Park soon began to improve considerably in portraiture, which brought him commissions, and he exhibited at the Royal Academy for the first time in 1905 when he was still only twenty-five, three harbour scenes of St Ives. On the advice of Olsson he went to Paris in 1906, at a time when the work of the Impressionists and the Post-Impressionists were capturing a wider public, and he studied at the Atelier Colorossi under Delaclause at the same time as Modigliani. The experience of modern French painting, seen at first hand, was to have a lasting effect upon his work.

For a short time before the First World War, John Park painted in Polperro and in Plymouth. At the end of the war he returned briefly to his native Preston, and came to St Ives permanently in 1921. He had developed a direct way of painting in full colour which captured the sparkle of sunlight on water,and he found an abundance of subjects in the old fishing port, where the white sands and multi-coloured hulls of working boats gave endless movement and reflections. Equally evocative is his description of a pearly morning, as the small fishing fleet prepares to leave harbour, the water radiant in the early light, the hulls and sails dark scattered shapes.

In most of his work John Park describes St Ives welcoming the summer visitor, and it was the limitation of this exuberant colourist that he remains within the range of such gentle pleasures. However the work that he produced in the 1920s and 1930s – with frequent painting trips to Exmoor, France, Spain and Italy – brought him considerable success and many of his paintings were reproduced as prints or postcards. He exhibited at the Royal Academy each year, and in many of the London societies, becoming a member of the Royal Society of Oil Painters in 1923 and the Royal Society of British Artists in 1932. He was a regular exhibitor at the Paris Salon, and was awarded their Gold medal in 1934. One of his most important paintings 'Snow Falls on Exmoor' (1939), was bought for the Tate Gallery under the terms of the Chantry Bequest in 1940.

John Park was founder member of the St Ives Society of Artists, and in St Ives a roomful of his pictures was usually on exhibition in his favourite pub and frequent resting place, the Sloop Inn, and he worked from a studio nearby. These successful years led him to move to London in the early 1930s but he remained attached to the West Country for subjects, and he soon returned. He finally left St Ives in 1957 at the age of seventy-seven and returned to his native Preston where he died five years later.

Julius Olsson's teaching had made St Ives an internationally known centre for marine painters. The most notable of these in the post-war period was Robert Borlase Smart (1881–1947) who had been brought up in Kingsbridge, Devon, where his parents were schoolteachers. The family later moved to Plymouth, where he attended Plymouth Public School and then the Art College, before training as a teacher at the Schools of South Kensington. For a number of years, whilst living in Plymouth, he was art critic for the *Western Morning News*. He came to St Ives in 1913 as a student of Julius Olsson, who introduced him to marine painting and was converted to Olsson's message of direct painting from nature. The large seascape 'Clear After Rain, St Ives Bay' (c.1913), painted soon after his apprenticeship with Olsson, shows an already

John Park.

PHOTOGRAPH BY PERMISSION OF THE MONTPELIER STUDIO.

JOHN PARK

By the Harbour St Ives.

oil on canvas, 600 x 750mm.

THE MONTPELIER STUDIO,
LONDON.

mature artist capturing the slow movements of heavy seas and the weight and thrust of great mountains of water.

During the First World War Borlase Smart served in France as a subaltern in the Queen's Regiment and with the Artists' Rifles. In 1916, with the newly formed Machine Gun Corps, he saw action in France, and in spite of his duties, he was able to make a number of powerful sketches at the Front. From these he made a series of paintings and drawings of the battlefields which were shown in his first public exhibition – 'From Vimy Ridge to the Somme' – at the Harris Galleries in Plymouth in 1917, and later at the Fine Art Society in London. The drawings are freely executed in pastel and chalk, a delicate medium that contrasted with the drama and devastation portrayed. The reviewer of the *Western Morning News* wrote that 'He lifts the veil on the illimitable power of modern explosives'.

It was as a result of the war Borlase Smart met, and in 1917 married, Irene Godson. She was the young sister of Smart's platoon sergeant, and Captain Smart had the unpleasant duty of visiting the family to report the death of her brother, killed in action.

His experiences of the harsh realities of war reinforced his determination to continue his interrupted career as an artist. Whist being re-grouped, after action on the battlefields of France he met Leonard Fuller, the portrait painter. They each decided that on demobilisation they would join the art colony in St Ives.

BORLASE SMART

*St Ives from
Penolver Rock,* 1924.

ink and gouache, 450 x 635mm.

PRIVATE COLLECTION.

Because of his teaching commitments Leonard Fuller did not move to St Ives until 1938. He later became a very prominent member of the art community and founded the St Ives School of Painting which he ran until his death in 1973, when it was taken over by his widow Marjorie Mostyn.

Borlase and Irene Smart settled in St Ives in 1919, he worked at Ocean Wave Studio, converted from old fish lofts overlooking Porthmeor Beach. Vigorous and articulate, Smart retained the military air of a gentleman. A photograph in the Picture Post of 1939 shows him completing a large painting of a rocky headland out of doors, in his trilby hat, well cut shirt and tie, St Ives Bay in the background

His painting was direct, based on observation interpreted through sound draughtsmanship and a vigorous and bold use of paint. He was fascinated by the structure of landscape, the weight and mass of rock and the change of weather; but the sea was his principal subject, the effects of light on water, the formation of the waves and the parade of boats and shipping. As a teacher he was capable of clear and invigorating explanation. In 1929 he published 'The Technique of Seascape Painting', a manual illustrated with some of his best paintings and drawings, which remained a useful guide for many years. It showed his imaginative response to the motion of water, the wrath and boiling of the sea and the organic construction of rock forms. In his later work he found a greater freedom and a more substantial use of colour – strong blues of sky and sea against the lighter hues of rock, expressed in bravura painting.

BORLASE SMART

Cornish Cliffs, Zennor, 1923.

oil on canvas, 1000 x 1260mm.

ROYAL CORNWALL MUSEUM, TRURO.

Smart travelled a good deal, recording H.M.S. 'Implacable' and Nelson's 'Victory' in Plymouth Harbour and the buildings of the old town of Plymouth, fast disappearing in the 1920s, and totally destroyed during the Second World War. He also undertook a considerable amount of commercial work, including railway posters, cigarette cards and calendars, and during the second war he designed propaganda posters for the Royal Navy. He exhibited at the Royal Academy and was a member of the Royal Institute of Oil Painters, the Royal Society of Watercolour Artists, the Royal Society of Marine Painters and other associations.

Borlase Smart had a breadth of view that gave him a unifying role in St Ives. In the late 1920s he spent three years in Salcombe, Devon, and for that reason he was not among the founders of the St Ives Art Society in 1927. On his return to St Ives however he became closely associated with the new group, acting as their secretary, and later, president. His sympathy for the aims of younger artists was particularly evident immediately after the Second War, when artists were deeply divided in their loyalties. After his untimely death in 1947, he was remembered with great affection by his younger friends. Peter Lanyon paid public tribute to him. 'If it hadn't been for Borlase Smart', he said, 'I should never have started painting at all. If it hadn't been for him there would be very few artists in St Ives today'. (Peter Lanyon speaking at the opening of an exhibition of his work in Plymouth 1955). As a measure of the respect and affection felt for him, the Penwith Society of Artists, formed in 1949 and soon to become the most prominent exhibiting society in Cornwall, declared that it was founded as 'A Tribute to Borlase Smart'.

The potter Bernard Leach (1887–1979), one of the great innovative artist-craftsmen of the century, made St Ives his home from 1920 onwards. He had recently returned from Japan and in his first years in St Ives he struggled to make a living. By an extraordinary display of courage and by work of the highest quality, and later by his highly influential writings, he launched a national movement that raised the work of the craftsman-potter to an accepted art form. Leach was born in Hong Kong, where his father was a judge. His mother died at his birth and he lived for his first four years with his grandparents in Japan. When his father re-married he returned to live with him in China and spent his childhood mostly in Singapore and Penang, before coming to school in England.

Although his family had planned a career in banking, Leach managed to gain entry to the Slade School where he became a proficient draughtsman, and to the London School of Art, where he learnt etching under Frank Brangwyn. It was as an etcher and engraver that Leach returned to Japan at the age of twenty-one, fascinated by the memories of the country areas, and inspired by the writings of Lafcadio Hern. He was greatly moved by the living traditions of the great potters and became a student of the master potter Ogata Kenzan. He was soon able to start his own pottery in Japan, and over a period of eleven years he absorbed Oriental attitudes to the making of fine pottery, which he tempered with his European training. While in Japan, he married his cousin Edith Hoyle. Their children David, Michael and Eleanor were born there, but at the end of the First World War they returned to England so that their children could be educated there.

Bernard Leach came to St Ives at the invitation of Margery Horne, a textile worker who had settled in St Ives at the beginning of the war. She started a Handicraft Guild in Hazelbury House, selling woven items, embroidery and baskets, all made on the premises. In order to extend the range of crafts, she agreed to give financial assistance to the pottery that Leach started with his

Japanese colleague Shoji Hamada. Their large wood-fired kiln was the first Oriental climbing kiln to be built in the western hemisphere – arranged so that the heat travelled up a series of steps in order to produce different temperatures at different levels. Their methods were a considerable technical innovation, for at that time stoneware and thrown porcelain were not made in England, nor was wood ash and other organic material used for glazes. However St Ives was a poor location for a pottery, as wood was not readily available to fire the large kiln and the local clay was unsuitable for stoneware.

After three years at the pottery, Shoji Hamada returned unexpectedly to Japan because of a major earthquake in Tokyo, which Bernard Leach described as the 'greatest earthquake disaster in modern times'. (*St Ives Times*, 28 December 1923, p.5). The scale of the tragedy was truly enormous, a total death roll of about 250,000. Yokohama was wiped out and two thirds of Tokyo was burnt down. All Hamada's relations lived in Tokyo and for nearly three months he anxiously awaited news of their fate. Letters were lost and cables undelivered, but finally he heard that his family had escaped death by the narrowest margin. At Bernard Leach's instigation St Ives played its small part in raising funds to alleviate this disaster by presenting a Cornish morality play, *The Kite in the Castle* by R. Morton Nance, a dialect tale of old Cornwall set in the Lamorna valley.

Bernard Leach determined to demonstrate that making pottery was part of a continuous creative activity in which the artist's eye and the craftsman's hand are of equal importance. His greatest achievements were to educate a public unfamiliar with this medium and to find a market for it. In the early days sales were infrequent, and it was only by the continued popularity of his work in Japan that the pottery was able to continue. As the pottery became well known, Leach began to take students, the most notable of whom was Michael Cardew, who also came to St Ives in 1923. Others who worked in the pottery in the 1920s included Katherine Pleydell-Bouverie and Norah Braden. At this time Leach was clarifying his views about the way in which Oriental purity of form and simplicity of decoration could combine with the more robust forms of early English slip decoration. He found an international audience with his pamphlet 'A Potter's Outlook', published in 1928.

At the invitation of Dorothy and Leonard Elmhurst, in the early 1930s, Bernard Leach set up a pottery for Dartington Hall in Devon, to develop rural crafts within the community, and there were serious discussions as to whether the Leach pottery should be moved from St Ives to Dartington, to take advantage of the better commercial opportunities. Bernard's son David had joined the St Ives workshop as an apprentice in 1930 and he realised the serious difficulties faced by the pottery, and in spite of his father's opposition, took a course in industrial production at Stoke-on-Trent. He later became manager of the Leach Pottery and greatly improved the methods of manufacture and control, and his participation allowed Bernard Leach greater freedom to travel, to teach and to write. It was Dorothy Elmhurst who sponsored him to return to Japan in the early 1930s in order to lecture and study. Leach's researches were published in 1940 as 'A Potter's Book', the most influential study of Oriental techniques in pottery to appear in this country. It successfully advanced the position of 'the artist turned craftsman' and was largely responsible for a revival of the art of pottery in England.

Bernard Leach was undeviating in his zeal to combine the traditions and philosophies of Eastern art with Western skills. In his writings he brought an authority and conviction to his drive to bridge East and West. Through his

BERNARD LEACH

Stoneware Jug with mottled olive glaze, 1930.

PHOTOGRAPH BY PERMISSION OF THE HOLBURNE MUSEUM AND CRAFT STUDY CENTRE, BATH.

Bernard Leach at his kiln, 1957.

TATE GALLERY ACHIVE.

teaching and the strength of his personality, he became an inspiration to artists and craftsmen alike. St Ives remained his home and his workplace for his lifetime and he was deeply involved in the artistic developments in the town in the years following the Second World War. He was made a Companion of Honour in 1973 and died at the height of his international fame at the age of ninety-two.

Another artist-craftsman who came to the area in 1920 was Alex Walker (1889–1964), a designer of fine silks, who set up a printing works in Newlyn. He was a Yorkshireman, and came from a family of mill owners and worked in his father's mill before setting up his own small silk mill. In response to an advertisement he engaged a young artist, Kathleen Earle, as a designer. She had trained at the Forbes' School in Newlyn, and enthusiastically persuaded Alex Walker to visit the artists' community. He found it much to his liking, returning many times and making many friends – particularly Ernest Procter, who encouraged him to sketch and draw.

In 1918 Alex Walker married Kathleen Earle. They moved to Newlyn, to Myrtle Cottage, where Dod Procter had lived, and in a group of derelict cottages opposite, known as 'Sambo's Row', they formed a silk-printing works, known as 'Cryséde', in 1920. Walker's interest in modern design had been developed by meetings in Paris with Raoul Dufy and Ossip Zadkine and he began to produce his own original designs and to commission the work of others. In addition to printed fabrics, local workers made gowns, scarves and other articles of silk. The business prospered, at first by mail order and later through a number of retail shops that Walker opened in Cornwall.

In 1925 Walker exhibited his paintings in London, at the Independent Gallery. These strong, vivid patterns, with titles such as 'Passion Flower', 'Canterbury Bells' and theatrical subjects such as 'Russian Ballet' and 'Dancer' were the basis for the hand-block designs which were printed in Newlyn on Vigil

St Ives girls modelling 'Cryséde' silk dresses. c.1927.

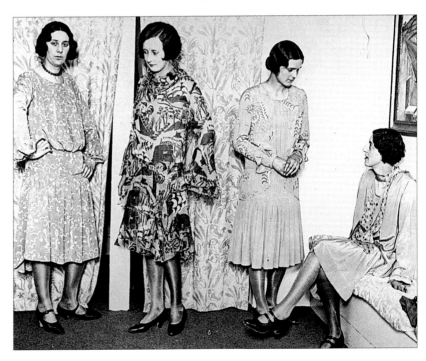

silk, which was made in Yorkshire. Other designs were inspired by the local landscape - 'Zennor', 'St Anthony', 'St Buryan'.

Soon after this successful exhibition, and with the business well established, Alex Walker invited Tom Heron, a manufacturer of blouses in Yorkshire and known as a patron of the avant-garde, to take on the direction of Crysède as manager. ('Crysède and the Designs of Alex Walker' by Hazel Berriman. *Arts and Crafts in Newlyn 1890–1930*. Newlyn Orion Gallery 1986). A decision was taken to enlarge the company and to seek larger premises which were created in 'The Island Works', a substantial factory converted from fish lofts on the Island in St Ives. Tom Heron's son, the artist, Patrick Heron, remembers his boyhood delight at the great

vats of brightly coloured dye prepared for printing on to the bleached silk. As the firm expanded so more retail premises were required, and the talented young architect-designer Wells Coates was given his first important commission – to design a number of shops and showrooms in modernist style for Crysède up and down the country. The quality of the printed designs benefitted from the use of such innovative artist-designers as Paul Nash and Cedric Morris. However the pressures of this considerable commercial undertaking affected Alex Walker and caused him to suffer a serious breakdown in health. He had a serious disagreement with Tom Heron and in 1930 the partnership was dissolved. Tom Heron later set up his own business, 'Cresta Silks', in Welwyn Garden City. Although Crysède continued in St Ives for a number of years it was a continuing struggle and it was finally closed in 1953. Alex Walker died in Falmouth in 1964.

During the 1920s the St Ives Arts Club changed from being a meeting place for professional painters, to include a more broadly based group including many writers and musicians. At the same time, readings and theatrical performances began to replace exhibitions and discussions on art. Other than the annual 'show days' exhibitions in the artists' studios, the only regular exhibitions in St Ives were still those held at Lanham's Gallery in the High Street, plus a few gift shops that showed paintings, usually of an inferior kind. But with increasing numbers of visitors coming to the town, artists felt the need for larger premises in which to show their work. In a move to consolidate the St Ives Arts Club it was suggested that members should not sell work in any gallery in St Ives other than Lanham's. Instead of reinforcing the Club's position, this restrictive rule further alienated many exhibiting members, and there was a move to form a new society, independent of both the St Ives Arts Club, and the commercial purposes of Lanham's Gallery.

A newcomer to St Ives, Commander George Bradshaw, played a leading role in these affairs. Bradshaw came to St Ives in 1924, having shown his paintings in the Royal Academy for the first time the previous year. In St Ives he painted vigorous seascapes and ambitious reconstructions of his sea-faring adventures. (Whilst serving in the Navy he had won the DSO for destroying a

ALEX WALKER

Men Working in a Violet Field near Trembath.

watercolour, 628 x 740mm.

By permission of
Polly Walker.

German submarine off the Shetland Isles.). In January 1927, as secretary of Lanham's hanging committee, he called a meeting to discuss the possibility of forming a 'society to advance art in St Ives by mutual co-operation' and to 'find ways to raise it from its present unimportant position in the art world'.

A week later the inaugural meeting of the St Ives Society of Artists was held at Lanham's Gallery. Moffat Lindner, who was a much respected figure in St Ives and a staunch champion of the colony, was elected as chairman. Founder members included G. F. Bradshaw, Martin Cock, Lowell Dyer, Bernard Leach, John Park, Mrs Shearer Armstrong, F. Spenlove, W. H. Titcombe, W. H. Truman and a number who were not artists.

In May that year, the Society held a retrospective exhibition at Lanham's Gallery of pictures by forty-one artists who had lived or stayed in St Ives, including Millie Dow, Louis Grier, Frances Hodgkins, John Park, Julius Olsson, Borlase Smart, Marianne and Adrian Stokes, and W. H. Titcomb. The

Studios in St Ives for the Show Days, March 1929.

DRAWN BY
FRANCIS ROSKRUGE.

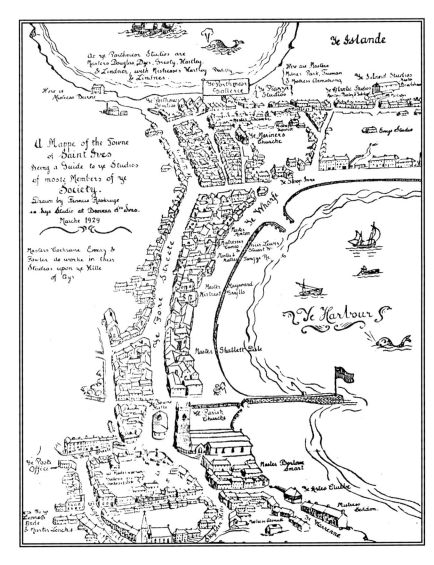

catalogue, which included a brief history of St Ives as an art colony, together with a map showing artists studios, was distributed to all the hotels. In January 1928 the new Society elected Moffat Lindner as its president. He had earlier been president of the Arts Club, and had helped it to survive during the difficult years of the War. The Society reinforced its membership by inviting a number of distinguished artists to become honorary members.* In the minute book a proposal was recorded 'that the St Ives and the Newlyn Societies of Artists be amalgamated into one Society to be known as the West Cornwall Society of Artists', but this well intentioned suggestion came to nothing. (From the minute book of the St Ives Society of Artists.).

A permanent gallery for the Society was created by converting Julius Olsson's old studio – two handsome rooms in the Porthmeor block overlooking the beach. With great celebration the first exhibition was opened by Olsson on 16 June 1928. In his address to a large audience of artists and art lovers. Olsson spoke warmly of the future of the Society. He remembered the twenty-five years that he had spent in the town and he felt sure that 'No Colony of Artists had such a reputation for work as St Ives and no Colony, not even Newlyn, turned out more work'. The exhibition was well supported by the older and established members and by newcomers alike. One of the most discussed exhibits was by the fifteen year old girl from Sennen, Joan Manning Saunders, who showed precocious talent with her painting 'The Pedlar'. Earlier in the year, her painting 'The Three Brothers' had been shown at the Royal Academy. The place of honour was occupied by Moffat Lindner's painting 'St Ives' Bay' described as a 'nocturne, Whistlerarian in treatment... a delightful harmony of blue and gold.' (Supplement to the *St Ives Times*, 22 June 1928.). Such large exhibitions soon became annual occasions. The new gallery was an immediate success and before long the Society had more that one hundred members, subscriptions were 10/6d per year for artist members, 5/- for associates, with lectures, criticisms, drawing classes and one-man shows during the winter months.

In March 1929, forty-one studios were open for the show-days, and the newly established Arts Ball took place, with decorations and fancy dress. Work for the Academy was taken to London in a specially hired railway carriage, at a charge of fifteen shillings per picture. The anonymous critic of the *St Ives Times* proudly announced:

> There is nothing eccentric about the art of the St Ives Colony. Cubism and such schools have not found their way down here yet. The art of St Ives is eminently sane and handsome... St Ives subjects are now views of popular beauty spots in and around St Ives, painted in quite strong colour and interspersed with evening views at dusk. Twilight studies and studies of the boats and harbour scenes. (*St Ives Times* 1929).

*These included Adrian Stokes, Arnesby Brown, Lamorna Birch, Julius Olsson and Stanhope Forbes, and later Algernon Talmage, Borlase Smart, Marcella Smith, Dorothea Sharp and Frances Hodgkins.

12

A MEETING IN ST IVES

Alfred Wallis' rag and bone cart outside his store in Quay Street, St Ives. On the door is painted 'A. Wallis Dealer in Marine Stores'.

PHOTOGRAPH BY PERMISSION OF ROGER SLACK.

This survey of painting in Cornwall ends in the quiet years between the two world wars. With the exception of Stanhope Forbes, those artists who had come to Newlyn as young men and women in the 1880s had dispersed. Many of the landscape and sea painters, who had achieved prominence in St Ives and Lamorna in the early years of the century, were now successful Academicians, mostly based in or near London. There were still many painters in St Ives, but their work lacked the impact of their predecessors. The town was a holiday paradise, but an artistic backwater.

In 1928, however, a meeting took place in St Ives which, although unremarked at the time, was a watershed in the history of modern art and of St Ives as an art colony. The young painters Ben Nicholson and Christopher Wood

ALFRED WALLIS

The Fishing Fleet.
oil on cardboard
PRIVATE COLLECTION.

ALFRED WALLIS

*St Ives Harbour and
Godrevy Lighthouse.*
painted on a pair of bellows
PRIVATE COLLECTION.

made a visit to St Ives in August that year. Ben Nicholson was still at the beginning of his career. He and his wife Winifred (née Roberts), also a painter, had come to Cornwall as guests of friends from the Hampstead Tennis Club, Marcus and Irene Brumwell. They stayed in a cottage at Pill Creek on the Truro River near Falmouth, alongside the Brumwell's summer home. In mid August they were joined by a friend, Christopher Wood, and on the second day of their stay the two young men were driven over to St Ives. They dismissed the car at the Malakoff, where they could look down upon the town and arranged to meet later on Porthmeor Beach. As Nicholson later recalled:

This was an exciting day, for not only was it the first time I saw St Ives, but on the way back from Porthmeor Beach we passed an open door in Back Road

ALFRED WALLIS

*The Hold House
port mear square island,
port mear Beach.*

painted on the back of an advertisement for an exhibition of the St Ives Society of Artists at the Porthmeor Gallery.

THE TATE GALLERY, LONDON.

211

West and through it saw some paintings of ships and houses on odd pieces of paper and cardboard nailed up all over the wall, with particularly large nails through the smallest ones. We knocked on the door and inside found Wallis, and the paintings we got from him then were the first he made. (Ben Nicholson 'Alfred Wallis' *Horizon*, January 1943).

The work that they saw was by Alfred Wallis (1855–1942), an untutored fisherman of an older generation. Born in the year of Sebastopol (he was two years older than Stanhope Forbes), he had only recently begun to paint. He had gone to sea at nine years of age, working as a cabin boy and cook, and at eighteen he was making trips from Penzance to the fishing grounds of St Johns, off Newfoundland. He had no real education; he taught himself to read and could write only with difficulty. At the age of twenty in Penzance, he married Susan Ward, who was twenty-one years older and had already borne seventeen children. She had two more by Wallis, but both died in infancy. Within this extended family, Wallis played a minor part. Inarticulate and undersized, he was more of a child than a parent, and Susan became the guiding spirit in the partnership. Nevertheless, he retained great affection for her during their long life together, and for her memory after her death.

Wallis gave help with the fishing, yet he was never able to afford a boat or even a share in a boat, and was given only the most menial jobs, usually on inshore boats from Mount's Bay. In 1890 he and Susan moved to St Ives, and Wallis became a marine scrap merchant, dealing in rope, iron and odds and ends. He became known as 'Old Iron' and could be seen in the streets calling for scrap metal. For a time he had a rag and bone store on the wharf with 'A. Wallis, Dealer in Marine Stores', crudely painted on the door. In 1912 he retired on his small savings, and he and Susan moved to the little terraced house at 3 Back Road West, where he lived for the rest of his life. Wallis continued to do odd jobs, and sold ice cream of his own manufacture to the holidaymakers. During the First World War he helped to build government huts on the 'Island'.

Susan died in 1922, and it was at about this time that Wallis began to paint, as he said 'for company'. He had probably started to draw long before. Jacob Ward, a relative, remembered that he sketched a lot when he had the marine stores, that is before 1912. Mr Edwards, a watchmaker in Fore Street, remembered Wallis' first paintings. 'Aw I dunno how to pass away time' said Wallis. 'I think I'll do a bit of paintin'. He returned next day with two or three paintings of boats done in house paint. 'What do'e think on they' he asked Mr Edwards, who examined them and showed them to Mr Armour, the antique dealer, before pronouncing, 'Well h'all I can say, me lad, is you done a mighty fine job on'en'. With this encouragement, according to Mr Edwards, Wallis 'Wen' on paintin'. (Recorded reminiscences of Alfred Wallis made by Dr Roger Slack from local inhabitants and relatives of Wallis.).

As a painter, Wallis was entirely self-taught. He wrote to his friend Jim Ede, Assistant Keeper at the Tate Gallery, who collected his paintings, 'so you cannot like me to those that have been taught both in school and paint. I have to learn myself, I never go out to paint, was never show them.' However, Wallis' pictures show a clear sense of design and a fresh vision the product of a natural talent, each the imagined memory of a specific incident. He painted boats he remembered from times past, sailing from St Ives harbour across a storm-tossed sea. He gave great care and attention to the details of rigging and set of sails. As he wrote: 'What i do mosley is what use To Bee out of my own memery what we may never see again as Things are altered all To gether There is nothing what Ever do not look like what it was sence i Can Rember.' (Letter to Jim Ede, 6 April 1935.).

Wallis had his own systems of drawing and perspective. The largest objects in the painting would be those which were most important – his house in Back Road West; Norway Square beside which it stood; the encircling harbour of St Ives, and the characteristic shapes of Smeaton's Pier and Godrevy Lighthouse. He used simple systems of composition, placing the flattened shapes of houses and boats as in an ancient map or a child's drawing. He preferred old or torn pieces of cardboard given to him by Baughan the grocer, which he would cut into irregular shapes to accommodate his design. He used few colours, usually from leftover tins of boat paint given to him by fishermen – deep greens, blues and blacks, and always the whitened transparency of the sea moving and tossing in his visionary world.

After Susan's death Wallis lived alone, a solitary, friendless man. He believed himself to be persecuted by his large family, and became a figure of fun for the small boys of the town. He was ignored by the resident artists of St Ives, yet felt himself to be an artist, doing as they did, portraying the familiar world in which he lived, and displaying his work to the public in the doorway of his cottage. He painted feverishly on every surface – the table on which he worked, jugs, bellows and even the cups and furniture. Increasingly he looked to the consolations of religion, which he found in the family Bible that he kept on his painting table.

Ben Nicholson and Christopher Wood saw in Wallis' work something for which they had been searching: a direct creative energy and the ability to speak clearly by the simplest means. In the first decades of the twentieth century, artists had persistently tried to see with the 'innocent eye' of the child or the 'primitive', a search for a more direct form of expression, a clearer emotional statement. The 'discovery' of Wallis was part of this discovery of innocence. In the sincerity of his untutored vision there lay one of the essential mainsprings – that of primitivism – which, with abstraction, formed the basis of the modern movement.

The clear vision and vitality of this anguished man, beset by personal difficulties, contained a poetry which appealed strongly to Nicholson. Nicholson observed that, 'Using the materials nearest to hand is the motive and method of the first creative artist. Certainly his vision is a remarkable thing, with an intensity and depth of experience which makes it more than childlike'. In Wallis' painting he found verification of a direction towards which he was already travelling. 'One only finds the influences one was looking for and I was certainly looking for that one'. (Ben Nicholson 'Alfred Wallis', *Horizon*, No.37 1943). Nicholson was to weld the directness of Wallis within his own forms of geometrical abstraction. In the tragically shortened life of Christopher Wood, the simplicity of Wallis strengthened his own poetic vision.

Christopher Wood (1901–1930) was the son of a Liverpool doctor. In his youth long periods of illness interrupted his education, but he entered Liverpool University to study architecture. He also became a member of the Sandon Studios Society, which saw itself as being in opposition to the University School of Art, and encouraged a less restrictive attitude. Here he met Augustus John who recognised his talent and persuaded him to paint. On John's suggestion Wood came to London where he met other artists and was introduced to the wealthy collector Alphonse Kahn, who invited him to Paris.

Christopher Wood.
TATE GALLERY ARCHIVES.

CHRISTOPHER WOOD (right)

Porthmeor Beach.

oil on board, 480 x 550mm.

KETTLES YARD GALLERY,
CAMBRIDGE.
The figure in the painting is said to be Alfred Wallis.

Still very young and highly impressionable, Wood was plunged into fashionable Parisian society and the company of avant-garde artists. He formed a close friendship with a Chilean diplomat, Antonio de Gandarillas, who assisted him financially and brought him into the international circle of artists and musicians surrounding Jean Cocteau, which included Georges Auric, Christian Bérard and visiting British artists such as Cedric Morris and Arthur Lett-Haines. Wood began a much interrupted art training and attended classes at the Académie Julian and at the Grande Chaumière but much of his time was spent travelling in the Mediterranean, visiting Greece, Italy and North Africa.

These were heady years, spent largely out of England and in the company of the internationally famous. Wood had evident talent and he drew on many sources. For a short time he designed clothes for Molyneaux and he was friendly with a number of minor painters in the School of Paris who looked to Modernism. The artists he most admired were Picasso and Cocteau and his meetings with them were the most memorable. On Picasso's recommendation, he produced designs for a production of *Romeo and Juliet* by Diaghilev, for which Constant Lambert had written the score. These were not used however, for Diaghilev favoured others by Max Ernst and Joan Miró. A further influence upon Wood at this time was Frank Dobson, whom he met in London. Among his many attempts to find a true direction for his work are a number of portraits which show Dobson's classical influence.

Christopher Wood's mother's family, the Arthurs, had lived in Cornwall, serving the Navy and the Church for several generations, and he had known Cornwall from boyhood. In 1926 he made a brief painting visit to St Ives and expressed his delight at the Cornish countryside writing of 'valleys with sides which fold like the pillows and counterpanes of my grandmother.' (Letter to Jeanne Bourgoint quoted in 'Christopher Wood The Last Years 1928–1930' Newlyn Orion Gallery, 1989. Catalogue introduction by Hilary Gresty).

Later in 1926, Wood met Ben and Winifred Nicholson for the first time in London. They seemed to offer him the stability his restless life required. Where he invited chaos, they sought order, and to his pagan hedonism they offered an austerity in accordance with their Christian Science beliefs. At Nicholson's instigation, Wood became a member of the Seven and Five Society, an exhibiting group of painters and sculptors which had been formed in 1920, of which Ivon Hitchens was the only founder member still active.[*] Nicholson had joined in 1924 and was already a leading member, and the Society was in the process of reorganising itself under his direction. In the 1920s and 1930s the exhibitions of the 'Seven and Five' became a focus for experimental, avant-garde painting in Britain, characterised by a free-formed Fauvism glowing with the subdued colours of the English landscape. The

WINIFRED NICHOLSON

Fishing Boat, Feock. 1928.

THE MONTPELIER STUDIO, LONDON.

CHRISTOPHER WOOD *(opposite)*. *PZ 134*, 1930.

oil on canvas, 510 x 710mm.

TOWNER ART GALLERY, EASTBOURNE.

[*]At no time were there seven painters and five sculptors, as the name indicates. From its formation membership was unlimited, and during the sixteen years of its existence included 56 members, mostly painters.

members at this time included Winifred Nicholson, Cedric Morris, David Jones, Frances Hodgkins, and John Piper; in 1928 and 1929 Barbara Hepworth and Henry Moore joined the Society.

Despite his profligate lifestyle Wood was deeply committed to his painting. In the spring of 1927 he wrote to Ben Nicholson:

> My life is in a whirlwind, so many ideas crush my brain, but I seem never to be able to concentrate on one that a thousand others disturb it. I begin so many things and finish so few at present; I won't worry and just go on in my own way, sometimes working all day long, and not producing anything at the end of it. You must know that I have never worked so hard before, and I am really having a life and death struggle with it, never as I knew before. Perhaps it means I am trying new and difficult things, and perhaps making progress. I don't think somehow that good or great things are ever done easily. ('Christopher Wood' Exhibition arranged by the Arts Council of Great Britain, 1979).

Christopher Wood's work was now taking on a more coherent form, and these 'great and good things' were seen later that year at his first exhibition in London, at the Beaux Arts Gallery, which he shared with Ben Nicholson and the potter William Staite Murray. Jean Cocteau wrote the catalogue introduction giving a simplistic view of Wood's precocious talent: 'in Christopher Wood there is no malice' he wrote 'there is something straightforward and naive – the freshness of a puppy who has not yet had distemper'. In spite of the success of this exhibition Wood's personal life remained complex and confused. A brief elopement to Paris with Meraud Guinness was brought to an end by the legal action of her parents, and he was increasingly influenced by his homosexuality. He became dependent upon the Nicholsons, and he spent the spring of 1928 with them at Bankshead, Winifred's home in Cumberland.

Towards the end of September the Nicholsons moved to a house in St Ives where they stayed for about three weeks. Wood remained at St Ives for about three months from September to November, living in Meadow Cottage behind Mr Baughan's shop, close to Wallis' little house in Back Road West. Wood wrote to Winifred Nicholson:

> Admiral Wallis I often see. I took him some baccy and a few papers last evening. He showed the lovely boats Ben sent him. I think he appreciated them as he had noticed the same constructions in his own pictures. He said when he came to my house 'They looked as well as anything, draw 'em off'... I do two a day cheap and nasty, at least I can't tell what they are 'til you and Ben have seen them. More and more influence de Wallis, not a bad master though. (Tate Gallery Archives).

Wood's many drawings of this time are clear, linear studies of the people of St Ives, the harbour and boats for example 'Fishermen and Boats' (1928), and 'Cornish Fishermen, the Quay, St Ives' (1928). As he became familiar with his theme, his work took on the simplicity of Wallis, and he even painted on pieces of board, using household paints and enamels. Wood's paintings were increasingly textured. He had earlier mixed sand with the primer of the canvas (a device used by Braque and other artists). In St Ives both Wood and Nicholson began to apply a thick white gesso ground, with the trade name of 'Coverine', which when rubbed down gave a distressed surface to the board and retained the transparency of thinly applied colour.

Christopher Wood also spent some weeks in Mousehole, near Newlyn. The paintings he did of this tiny port, its sandy bay within encircling harbour walls, are amongst his best. With a new assurance he paints the textured surfaces of the granite cottages, the grid of small fields that back the town and the silhouetted shapes of the dark-jerseyed fishermen.

The conviction that his work had gained in Cornwall was apparent in his exhibition of twenty-three paintings at Arthur Tooth's gallery in London in April 1929, and its reception was highly favourable. But although Cornwall held a magic for Wood and he had worked well there, he was restless and missed the company of others: 'I seem to live on the very edge of the world, but what an edge it is. I love this place and could stay here for ever if I had those around me for whom I care,' he wrote. In July he went to Brittany where he worked furiously for three months. He found many similarities between Brittany and Cornwall, as had other artists before, him and wrote to Winifred Nicholson: 'I may be motoring around Brittany to a little port near Brest which is called Douarnenez, rather St Ivesish I should think, but with real sailing boats. St Malo is very interesting but too big for me to understand quickly. I want to see the French crab boats we saw at Falmouth and St Ives so much three years ago. I looked everywhere for them and found none and was very disappointed for I came here for that reason'. (Tate Gallery Archives).

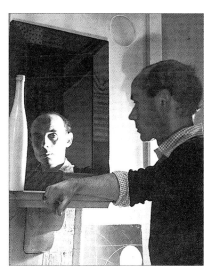

Ben Nicholson.

Photograph by
Humphrey Spencer c.1933.

NATIONAL PORTRAIT GALLERY, LONDON

As Wood entered the last stages of his personal tragedy, new and surreal elements appeared in his work. He had been invited to do the designs for a ballet by Boris Kochno, choreographed by George Ballanchine, for the 1930 C. B. Cochrane Review, to be called 'Luna Park' or 'The Freaks'. The setting was to be a circus, from which the freaks, liberated from their deformities, seized others to drag them into their mysterious world. The theme absorbed him and the paintings he produced at this time were also peopled with acrobats, freaks and circus animals. Their claustrophic atmosphere marks the black depression into which he frequently plunged, and in their strength of colour and intensity of feeling they contain a mark of finality. This bizarre subject coincided with Wood's growing addiction to opium, which had reached a critical point, as he had been deprived of pure opium by his increased separation from Gandarillas. (Conversation with Sir Francis Rose and Gerald Reitlinger quoted in 'Christopher Wood', exhibition of 1989 *op.cit.*).

In March 1930 Wood was in London for the opening of Cochrane's Review, and came briefly to Mousehole. In April he shared an exhibition with Ben Nicholson at the Georges Bernheim gallery in Paris, and then departed to Brittany. He painted little after this and in August returned to England in a state of tormented delirium. After a brief and troubled meeting with his mother and sister on Salisbury station, he left them and either fell or threw himself under the London train. He was twenty-nine.

At the time of their visit to St Ives, Christopher Wood and Ben Nicholson were close friends and had already achieved a fruitful collaboration as artists. Although essentially different in character, they had much in common. In his more austere way, Ben Nicholson had also spent many years of questioning and stubborn refusal to accept ideas that he thought outdated. His instinct was to withdraw from the sophisticated, highly cultivated world into which he was born, and to discover and develop his own talents. Later, he admitted that he

BEN NICHOLSON

*Drawing made on first
visit to St Ives.*

PRIVATE COLLECTION.

owed a lot to the poetic ideas of his father and the marvellously subtle sense of tone and colour, which is a continuing characteristic of Ben Nicholson's work, came from the same source.

Ben Nicholson (1894–1982) was the son of William Nicholson – a painter of portraits and still lifes, a friend of Whistler, sophisticated, dandyish and totally immersed in his painting. Ben's mother, Mabel Constance Pryde, who was also a painter, came from an aristocratic Scottish background. She was down to earth, rooted in firm common sense and the stablising influence on her family, and a circle of friends which included Max Beerbohm, Constance Collier and Marie Tempest. Ben Nicholson recalled that his mother, 'distressed by high flown talk would find herself wanting to scrub the kitchen table'. William (later Sir William) Nicholson and his brother-in-law James Pryde formed an artistic partnership, the 'Beggarstaff Brothers' and designed some of the best prints and posters in England up to that time.

Nicholson was not academic. At his school, Gresham's, he got into the cricket eleven as a new boy, a fact that meant more to him than his poor classroom performance. He went to the Slade School in 1910–11, but this had little to offer him, and he spent much time in the billiard room at the Gower Hotel with Paul Nash, a fellow student. Nicholson's remark about their friendship is illuminating: 'I was in the painting world trying to get out of it, he was out trying to get in.' (Letter to John Summerson, 6 May 1944). Nicholson did some work from the antique, drawing with a hard profile from early Italian examples. From 1911 to 1918 he lived mostly out of England, studying languages in France and Italy, with an extended visit to Madeira for health reasons (he was asthmatic). He was in London in the early years of the First World War and then spent some time in Pasadena, California, again for

BEN NICHOLSON

Porthmeor Beach,
1928–30.

CITY OF BRISTOL
MUSEUM AND ART GALLERY.

reasons of health. He returned to England in 1918 on hearing of the death of his mother. Soon after this he met and married Winifred Dacre, who was also a highly talented painter.

For some years, Ben and Winifred Nicholson continued to travel, spending the winters in Castagnole on the Italian border of Switzerland and the summers at Winifred's family home in Bankshead, Cumberland, where they both found subjects in the hills and farms. Ben produced little work in these early years, however, and the painting of a striped jug, which figures prominently in his father's well known painting of 'A Hundred Jugs' (1916), was one of the few products of his time at the Slade School.

In the early 1920s, Ben Nicholson made paintings of northern Italy, which have a Cézannesque spareness of line. In his still life paintings of this time there are strong references to Braque, Picasso and the Cubists. He used great economy of means, with little colour rubbed lightly on to a prepared ground. In 1922 he had his first one-man exhibition at the Adelphi Gallery, London, followed a year later by a joint exhibition with Winifred Nicholson at the Patterson Gallery, also in London. In 1924 he joined the Seven and Five Society, he became a prominent exhibitor and its president two years later. In these years Nicholson was rapidly coming to terms with the more advanced artists of his generation. He recalled the revelation of a Cubist painting by Picasso, seen in Paris in 1920, which seemed to him then completely abstract. He remembered it because of its colour 'an absolutely miraculous green deep,

BEN NICHOLSON

St Ives Bay, Sea with Boats, 1931.

oil and pencil on canvas, 415 x 560mm.

Manchester City Art Gallery.

potent and absolutely real – in fact none of the actual events in one's life have been more real than that – and it still remains the standard by which I judge any reality in my work.' (Letter to John Summerson 3 January 1948, published in 'Ben Nicholson', *Studio International*, 1969).

For Winifred Nicholson the early 1920s were years of great excitement and invention, 'Fizzing like a soda water bottle'. It was a new beginning; from the destruction of war had come the means to make a new future, in which art, in all its modern manifestations, appeared as the greatest component for good. She wrote of these sunny years:

> *We lived in white houses with large new windows, we ate simple food – the fruits of the earth. We wore sandles and ran barefoot along the boulevards, we talked in the cafes of the new vision, the new scale of music, the new architecture – and unnecessary things were to be done away with and all was to be functional. How young we were!* (Winifred Nicholson, catalogue to her exhibition at the Crane Kalman Gallery, London, 1975).

In Paris Winifred and Ben met the artists, their contemporaries 'great giants of innovation', in their studios. They entered wholeheartedly into this fascinating world of international art, where: 'almost everyone one met was expressing genius, inventiveness, dedication to that vision and sharing it with their friends.' (Winifred Nicholson *op.cit.*) They visited Brancusi at the Impasse Ronsard 'where you struck a great Chinese gong that carried you away to Tibet even before you entered the magic studio'. They climbed the many flights of steps to the spareness of Mondrian's studio, and met Picasso 'his eyes like black raisins... with the movements of a panther'.

In this early partnership Winifred Nicholson was a very active participant. With free expressive colour she captured her pleasure in the simplest of everyday delights – a vase of flowers seen against a window, with the landscape of Cumbria behind – and her work has a directness and innocence that she shares with Ben Nicholson and Christopher Wood. Together they were entering the world of modernism in which abstract art had a special meaning, an experience of near religious importance.

Following Ben Nicholson's first visit to St Ives he painted a number of landscapes and sea paintings of Porthmeor Beach. In the sea paintings 'Wallis-like' sailing boats bob on a rippling ocean, sometimes seen through an open window – a device shared with Christopher Wood and Winifred Nicholson. They are highly painted on a scrubbed ground, and have a sense of freedom and enjoyment. In his paintings of Pill Creek, done at the same time, the massing of dark trees and the pattern of water in the Cornish creeks have a new authority. A number of the Cornish paintings were shown at the exhibition that Nicholson shared with Christopher Wood at the Bernheim Gallery, Paris in 1930, where Nicholson was recognised as a new and significant talent, ready to enter the ranks of the avant-garde.

Ben Nicholson's work, and his life, were about to enter another period of important change. In the following year he had his first major exhibition in London, at the Bloomsbury Gallery. The young sculptor Barbara Hepworth, who saw the exhibition, found a very special meaning in his paintings, and soon she and Nicholson had formed a close friendship. In 1934 they were married.

In their work over the next years, Ben Nicholson and Barbara Hepworth pursued independent yet parallel paths in a development that led towards total abstraction. Soon they had become leaders among that small group of artists, architects and designers who had been strongly affected by the progressive movements emanating from the continental centres of Europe. Living in Hampstead, in the Mall Studios, they were a central part of a community that included such artists as Henry Moore, Cecil Stevenson, Paul Nash and later the European *émigrés* Walter Gropius, Naum Gabo, Marcel Breuer, and in the year before the outbreak of war, Piet Mondrian. Writers associated with them included Geoffrey Grigson, Roland Penrose, the critic Adrian Stokes and the spokesman of the group Herbert Read, who coined for them the title 'A nest of gentle artists'. At a time when all aspects of modern art were under continuous attack this embattled group defended the position of the modern movement. They hammered out their philosophy in a series of exhibitions and publications, which included the group 'Unit One', formed in June 1933 under the joint leadership of Paul Nash and Ben Nicholson, and the publication *Circle* an international survey of constructive art, which brought together the views of English and European avant-garde artists and architects.

In August 1939, with war imminent, Hepworth and Nicholson left their London studio and brought their young family to St Ives, at the invitation of their friend, the writer Adrian Stokes, who had recently bought a house in Carbis Bay. During the enclosed years of war they worked quietly in Cornwall, mainly from landscape sources. Nicholson's searching drawings explore the light and colour, the variations of coast and sea, tin mine, tor, cottage and harbour. Hepworth, severely restricted by the needs of a young family, explored in small scale works the movement of sea, currents and tides and the flight of birds – avenues for abstraction which took on a new reality in the Cornish landscape. The support of a few others in St Ives, notably Adrian Stokes, Bernard Leach and Naum Gabo, helped them to keep faith in their work. In the post-war years the significance of this exploration began to be understood, when it was presented on a world stage. It was seen that each had developed as a major artist and both were affected by the granite landscape of west Cornwall.

After the war, younger artists were soon drawn to St Ives by the presence of Nicholson and Hepworth and by the natural qualities of the town – the pattern of its streets, its sparkling light and colour – and its long association with generations of artists. The so-called 'middle generation' of the 1950s impatient to recover time lost from the rigours of war, included Peter Lanyon, Terry Frost, Patrick Heron, Bryan Wynter, Alan Davie and Roger Hilton. When, in their turn, their work was presented in the London galleries, St Ives became known as a centre of international abstraction. Even in the late 1950s when American abstract expressionism all but overwhelmed the international art scene, painting in St Ives retained its own particular character and individuality, and the town was again recognised as the most prominent centre for avant-garde painting in Britain.

Painting in Cornwall has added immeasurably to the progress of British art over the last century. Its artists have responded to the life of its people, and the light and colour of the coastline. They have been continuously refreshed by the life-enhancing qualities of its granite landscape, its coast and sea. For more than a century, a spiritual message has constantly come from the west, and the freedom and invention of artists in Cornwall has made its own powerful contribution to art in Britain.

(The detail of this progress from the 1930s to the 1970s requires its own full analysis. See *Painting the Warmth of the Sun – St Ives Artists 1939 to 1975* by Tom Cross, published by Westcountry Books).

INDEX